Names and Naming in *Beowulf*

Names and Naming in *Beowulf*

Studies in Heroic Narrative Tradition

Philip A. Shaw

BLOOMSBURY ACADEMIC
LONDON • NEW YORK • OXFORD • NEW DELHI • SYDNEY

BLOOMSBURY ACADEMIC
Bloomsbury Publishing Plc
50 Bedford Square, London, WC1B 3DP, UK
1385 Broadway, New York, NY 10018, USA
29 Earlsfort Terrace, Dublin 2, Ireland

BLOOMSBURY, BLOOMSBURY ACADEMIC and the Diana logo are trademarks
of Bloomsbury Publishing Plc

First published in Great Britain 2020
This paperback edition published 2022

Copyright © Philip A. Shaw, 2020

Philip A. Shaw has asserted his right under the Copyright, Designs
and Patents Act, 1988, to be identified as Author of this work.

Cover design by: Tjaša Krivec
Cover image: Français 185, fol. 126, Saint Léonard devant Clovis (© Bibliothèque nationale de France)

All rights reserved. No part of this publication may be reproduced or transmitted in any form or by any means, electronic or mechanical, including photocopying, recording, or any information storage or retrieval system, without prior permission in writing from the publishers.

Bloomsbury Publishing Plc does not have any control over, or responsibility for, any third-party websites referred to or in this book. All internet addresses given in this book were correct at the time of going to press. The author and publisher regret any inconvenience caused if addresses have changed or sites have ceased to exist, but can accept no responsibility for any such changes.

Every effort has been made to trace copyright holders and to obtain their permissions for the use of copyright material. The publisher apologizes for any errors or omissions and would be grateful if notified of any corrections that should be incorporated in future reprints or editions of this book.

A catalogue record for this book is available from the British Library.

Library of Congress Cataloging-in-Publication Data

Names: Shaw, Philip A., author.
Title: Names and naming in Beowulf : studies in heroic narrative tradition / Philip A. Shaw.
Description: London ; New York : Bloomsbury Academic, 2020. | Includes bibliographical references and index. |
Identifiers: LCCN 2020020652 (print) | LCCN 2020020653 (ebook) | ISBN 9781350145764 (hardback) | ISBN 9781350145788 (ebook) | ISBN 9781350145771 (epub)
Subjects: LCSH: Beowulf. | Names, Personal, in literature. | Epic poetry, English (Old)--History and criticism. | Onomastics in literature.
Classification: LCC PR1587.N36 S53 2020 (print) | LCC PR1587.N36 (ebook) | DDC 829/.3--dc23
LC record available at https://lccn.loc.gov/2020020652
LC ebook record available at https://lccn.loc.gov/2020020653

ISBN: HB: 978-1-3501-4576-4
PB: 978-1-3502-1167-4
ePDF: 978-1-3501-4578-8
eBook: 978-1-3501-4577-1

Typeset by RefineCatch Limited, Bungay, Suffolk

To find out more about our authors and books visit www.bloomsbury.com
and sign up for our newsletters.

For Gabriel

Contents

List of figures — viii
List of maps — ix
Acknowledgements — x
List of abbreviations — xi

Introduction — 1

1 The Geats, Brondings and Wylfings — 15

2 The Scyldings, Heathobards and Helmings — 53

3 The Scilfings — 103

4 The Finnsburh episode and the non-Scylding Danes — 115

5 Weland and the Wælsings — 133

6 The continental characters — 141

7 A glove in hood's clothing: Hondscio and the narrative tradition of *Beowulf* — 151

   Conclusion — 173

Notes — 183
Bibliography — 185
Indices — 199

Figures

0.1	Cotton Augustus ii.55 (S 1259)	12
1.1	Detail of fol. 82r of Munich, Bayerisches Hauptstaatsarchiv, HL Freising 3a, the Cozroh Codex	33
2.1	Detail of a charter of 848 AD recorded in Munich, Bayerisches Hauptstaatsarchiv, HL Freising 3a	61
2.2	Note of the lands in Offlow Hundred, Staffordshire	68
2.3	The will of Wulfric	69
2.4	London, British Library, Stowe Charters 37, face	70
2.5	Lease of land at Chisledon, Wiltshire, from the New Minster, Winchester, to Alfred, minister of King Æthelstan	73
2.6	Partial family tree of the royal house of Kent	99
5.1	Detail of the Reichenau confraternity book	139
7.1	Detail of Rochester manuscript, Cathedral Library, A. 3. 5. (*Textus Roffensis*), fol. 119v	159
7.2	Aerial view of Heidelberg and its suburbs with highlight indicating approximate centre of Handschuhsheim	163
8.1	The characters of Beowulf shown in tribal groupings and family relations, visually coded for the probable origins of their names	175

Maps

7.1 Map depicting places in the Fulda charter of 788 AD   160
7.2 Continental place-names formed with *Handschuh* 'glove' as a first element   162
7.3 Map of Handschuheim near Strasbourg and its immediate surroundings   164
7.4 Map of Henschleben and its immediate surroundings   165
7.5 Map of Stoke (previously *Andscohesham*) and its surroundings   166

Acknowledgements

During the long gestation of this book, I have incurred debts of gratitude too numerous to mention, and I must therefore apologise to everyone who has helped me with this work and whom I have either been unable or have forgotten to mention in what follows. I am grateful to the staff of numerous libraries and archives, including the David Wilson Library, the Hallward Library, the Bodleian, the Taylorian, the British Library, the Institute for Name Studies at the University of Nottingham, the Bayerisches Hauptstaatsarchiv, Burton-on-Trent Museum, Winchester College, Zürich Zentralbibliothek and Rochester Cathedral. I also wish to record my gratitude to the Leverhulme Trust for funding 'The Impact of Diasporas on the Making of Britain: Evidence, memories, inventions', which allowed me to undertake much of the initial research for this book. The University of Leicester also granted me a semester of research leave during which I was able to pursue this work. I have discussed this project a good deal with friends and colleagues including David Clark, Jayne Carroll, Julie Coleman, Paul Cavill, Luke John Murphy, Helen Ayers, John Baker and Christina Lee, and I am also grateful to Carole Hough and Richard North for very stimulating discussions of this material. The views I have arrived at here may not always be in harmony with their views on *Beowulf* or on onomastics, and any errors are, of course, entirely my own.

Abbreviations

ASPR	The Anglo-Saxon Poetic Records
CIL	Corpus Inscriptionum Latinarum
EEMF	Early English Manuscripts in Facsimile
EETS	Early English Text Society
EPNS	English Place-Name Society
ERGA	Ergänzungsbände zum Reallexikon der Germanischen Altertumskunde
ÍF	Íslenzk Fornrit
MGH	Monumenta Germaniae Historica
S	entries in the Electronic Sawyer are signalled by S followed by their number in the database
SPSMA	Skaldic Poetry of the Scandinavian Middle Ages
SrG	Scriptores rerum Germanicarum in usum scholarum separatim editi
SrM	Scriptores rerum Merovingicarum
SS	Scriptores (in Folio)

All references to the texts of *Beowulf* and *The Fight at Finnsburh* in the course of this study are to Fulk, Bjork and Niles (2008) by line number, unless otherwise stated. All translations are the author's own, unless otherwise stated.

Introduction

Not another book about *Beowulf*. While the protagonists of *Withnail and I* had 'gone on holiday by mistake', the present author wrote this book about *Beowulf* by mistake. What had been intended as a chapter about the personal names of the characters in the poem took on a life of its own and became the book the reader now holds in his, her, its or their *folmum*. The central purpose of this book is to present a new account of the personal names that appear in the poem, arguing that these provide important evidence for the origins of *Beowulf*. This is not a discussion about when *Beowulf* was composed, although this is a relevant question that will be touched upon in this introduction. Rather, this book considers the nature and transmission of the narrative materials that fed into the composition of *Beowulf*. These narrative materials, it is argued, were derived in substantial part from Continental Germanic sources. More than this, the book suggests an area on the Continent that may have provided the central narrative of Beowulf himself, and shows that some of the personal names in the poem may have been transmitted from Continental Germanic sources in written form. None of this demonstrates, of course, that elements of the poem did not also derive directly from Scandinavian traditions or from the imagination of the English poet, but the evidence presented in the course of this book helps to elucidate where these are possible lines of development, and where the poet must have depended on continental materials.

Although the individual arguments around each personal name that are presented here are sometimes complex, the overarching argument of this work is simple; while we have been accustomed to think about *Beowulf* mainly in terms of its English and Scandinavian contexts and sources, we should, in fact, see it as depending heavily upon heroic narrative traditions circulating on the Continent. This may be a surprising conclusion to many readers, but it also fits with the (admittedly limited) evidence we have for heroic narrative in continental contexts and with our picture of the tastes of ecclesiastics from the Continent working in early medieval England. The implications of this argument are very significant. The quite extensive and relatively early vernacular literary production of early medieval England can give the impression that England was alive with oral narrative traditions of heroic figures from the legendary past and that this contrasted with a relative lack of interest in such traditions on the Continent. When we note, however, that *Beowulf* owes much to narrative traditions brought from the Continent to England probably no earlier than the seventh or eighth centuries, and brought at least in part in written form, not orally, we must realign our perception of English heroic narrative, seeing it not as a peculiarly English phenomenon, but rather as part of a wider pool of heroic narrative tradition that may, in fact, have been larger and more vibrant on the Continent, although the vagaries of preservation have obscured much of the tradition.

For reasons of space, this book cannot hope to address all of the published material on *Beowulf* that might be brought to bear on this discussion, nor can it provide a comprehensive account of the numerous issues in source criticism and onomastic methodologies involved in undertaking a study of this kind. We must content ourselves, therefore, with a brief discussion of naming practices in Old English and other Germanic dialects and some short remarks on the dating of *Beowulf*, before plunging into the detailed discussion of the names of each of the different dynastic or tribal groupings in the poem. Within these, the reader will find discussions of specific problems with the source material at hand, but there is inevitably a great deal more that could be said. The author has done his best to compress a large and complex body of evidence into the confines of this slim volume. If this inevitably involves some omissions, it is to be hoped that this demonstrates the enormous importance of paying attention to the personal names of *Beowulf* and the clues that they can provide for disentangling the complex – and often shadowy – web of traditional heroic narratives that lie behind the poem.

Old English personal names and evidence for personal naming patterns

The Old English personal naming system was inherited from the Proto-Germanic naming system, so the name elements in use in Old English were mostly inherited from the Proto-Germanic stock of name elements. However, some name elements from that stock do not appear in the extant corpus of Old English personal names. That could, in some cases, simply be due to chance lack of attestation, but it seems highly probable that this was, in many cases, because those elements were either not brought to England by the Germanic-speaking groups who gave rise to Old English, or they were brought to England but fell out of use before our records of Old English personal names begin. For instance, the element that appears in Continental Germanic contexts in forms such as *Fraui-*, *Frowi-* and *Fro-* (Förstemann 1900: s.v. *FRAVI*) and in Scandinavia as *Frøy-* (see, for instance, Peterson 2007: s.v. *Frøy-*), is not clearly attested in early medieval England, suggesting that it was not used in Old English personal naming practices (see further pp. 79–80). At the same time, it was also possible for Old English speakers to develop new personal name elements, as in the case of *Peoht-/Peht-* (from the ethnonym *Pict*), which is attested nowhere else in the Germanic languages. Such innovations do not seem to have been common in English practice, however, whereas Viking Age Scandinavia seems to have been somewhat more innovative in creating new name elements (see Shaw 2011a), and some Continental Germanic dialects show signs of not inconsiderable innovation developed in contact situations with Romance speakers (see Arcamone 1997: 174). It is possible, therefore, to identify some personal name elements as specific to either the Scandinavian languages, the Continental Germanic languages, Old English or to a combination of two of these.

This point is of fundamental importance for this book, as the analysis presented here focuses on the evidence for where individual names in *Beowulf* were coined in the Germanic-speaking world. The nature of the evidence for geographical distribution of individual name elements in the Germanic languages is not entirely unproblematic. There are more copious records for some areas and periods than for others, and since absence of evidence does not constitute evidence of absence, we can never state with absolute certainty that a given name element did not exist in one or another part of the Germanic-speaking world; it is always possible that an element did exist but that no records of its use survive. Nevertheless, when we consider a fairly sizeable body of names together, as in this book, which considers all the personal names of human figures in *Beowulf*, we can be reasonably sure that the overall pattern of geographical distribution we encounter reflects genuine differences across the Germanic-speaking world. While any individual name element could be absent in an area due to a chance lack of records, it becomes much harder to argue that several different name elements that are absent in one area reflect only chance non-survivals, rather than evidence that at least some of those name elements appear in the poem due to influence from another area where they are attested.

The forms in which names appear may also indicate their broad geographical point of origin in the Germanic-speaking world, since personal names often reflect the wider linguistic developments in the languages in which they were used. Thus, the Proto-Germanic diphthong */au/ occurs in a name element used across the Germanic languages, Proto-Germanic */auða-/. In Old Norse, this element changed little in pronunciation, yielding names in *Auð-*, whereas in Old English, the consonant became /d/ and the diphthong developed to /æɑ/, which is usually spelt <ea>, yielding names in *Ead-*. On the Continent, this diphthong was still represented by spellings such as <au> early on, but later the diphthong monophthongised, producing spellings such as *Oth-* for this element. A speaker of one Germanic dialect, when faced with a name form from another dialect in which such changes were apparent, might recognise that this was a name formed using elements with which they were familiar in their own language, and silently replace one or both of the foreign elements with the cognate element(s) from their own language. For example, the name of the late seventh-century Frankish mayor of the palace Ebroin is rendered by Eddius Stephanus in his *Vita Sancti Wilfridi* by the Anglicised form *Eferwine* (Colgrave 1927: 52 (chapter 27)); in this case, the Frankish form *Ebr-* has been identified with Old English *eofor* and re-spelt accordingly, while the second element is given in its usual Old English form -*wine*. Such adjustment of names according to an author's or a scribe's own dialect can potentially obscure borrowing of names between dialects.

At the same time, when an author or a scribe does not adjust a name from another dialect in this way, it can sometimes be easy to identify the origins of such names due to these differences in the ways in which the pronunciation of individual elements developed in the different Germanic languages. For example, Bede seems generally to have been careful to try and preserve the spellings of names he found in his sources, and accordingly, we find the Frankish bishop Liudhard referred to in book 1, chapter 25 of Bede's *Historia Ecclesiastica* using the form *Liudhardo* (Plummer 1896: 1.45; Colgrave and Mynors 1969: 74) rather than an English **Leodheard*. The spelling *Liud-* for the first element here is characteristically Continental Germanic, so that even if we were unaware of Liudhard's origins, the form of his name would help us to identify him as being from the Continent rather than being an Englishman.

There are, thus, a number of considerations when examining any given personal name that may allow us to identify the name as deriving from a particular part of the Germanic-speaking world. At the same time, the origins of names can also be obscured. Many names consist of elements that were in use across the Germanic-speaking world and cannot, therefore, be assigned to a particular region unless there are distinctive spellings in different regions. However, these spellings may not be preserved when the name is written down by a speaker from another region. When considering the evidence for the use of a name in a particular region, moreover, we need to be aware of possible problems with different types of evidence. For early medieval England, a very large number of personal names is recorded in the *Domesday Book*, and in a not insignificant number of cases, names are recorded in this source that do not appear in any earlier English sources. It is possible that some of these names represent native Old English personal names that, through the vagaries of recording of names and survival of written sources, do not appear in earlier attestations, but the *Domesday Book* also records landowners of continental extraction, and the spread of Scandinavian personal names into English naming practices as a result of the Viking settlement in England may also be apparent in this corpus of names. A degree of caution is therefore required in assigning origins to names in the *Domesday Book*; we cannot simply assume that any name appearing in this source existed as an Old English name, and in the discussion that follows, we will tend not to rely solely on evidence from this source for the existence of an Old English name. Looking to another significant large source for early medieval England, the *Durham Liber Vitae* (a manuscript begun in ninth-century Northumbria as a record of members of, and donors to, an ecclesiastical community) records many names in its earliest stratum, and thus is very valuable as evidence for Old English naming practices around the ninth century. This text does, however, also record the names of non-English individuals, thus we find a significant body of personal names from the Continent and from Scandinavia recorded here. Careful work on the identification of names as belonging to one or other of these regions has been undertaken in Rollason and Rollason (2007), and we will refer to this as necessary in discussing the origins of individual names. This is also a broader issue with texts of this type, which record individuals enjoying some spiritual connection with a monastic house; turning to a continental example, the confraternity book of Reichenau records a significant body of Scandinavian personal names, not just Continental Germanic personal names (Jónsson and Jørgensen 1923; Melefors 2002: 965).

As well as treating particular texts with care, we must also be aware that certain groups of people can distort our picture of the dialect geography of personal names. The earliest generations of the royal house of Kent, for example, bear markedly Continental Germanic personal names, apparently reflecting a family fashion perhaps related to close political connections with their neighbours across the Channel (see further pp. 98–100 below). If we unthinkingly treated the names borne by members of this family as evidence for Old English naming practices, we might mistakenly identify as Old English some Continental Germanic personal names. Similarly, moneyers in early medieval England often bear Continental Germanic personal names (see Clark 1992: 465; Smart 1986), and we cannot, therefore, treat their names as evidence for English naming practices unless other evidence also points towards use of the names in question in England. In the discussion that follows, difficulties of this sort will be noted where relevant. The main body of this book undertakes an analysis of each of the personal names in *Beowulf*, considering the evidence the names provide for their region of origin within the Germanic-speaking world. Before proceeding with these analyses, however, it is worth considering briefly some previous work on the personal names of *Beowulf* and on its dating.

Personal names in *Beowulf*

The study of the personal names of figures in *Beowulf* has a long history, in which, alongside various treatments of individual names which will be discussed as necessary below, the work of Björkman (1920b) and Wessén (1927) stand out as important early works that remain essential references. Björkman (1920b) individually examines the majority of the personal names and tribal names in the poem, discussing the etymology of the names, the likelihood that they represent genuine Scandinavian names, and their potential relatedness to the names of the figures who correspond to the characters in *Beowulf*. Wessén discusses a more limited subset of the names in the poem, arguing that some names in the poem are Scandinavian names from Scandinavian sources, albeit in Anglicised forms, while others are the invention of the English poet (Wessén 1927: 53). The most recent treatment of the names in *Beowulf* as a body is provided by Peterson (2004) in her *Lexikon över urnordiska personnamn*. Peterson attempts to identify names in the poem that can be securely identified as Proto-Norse names, as distinct from names of other origin. This is a difficult exercise, and one from which a number of uncertain cases naturally arise. A less comprehensive, but still wide ranging and stimulating discussion is provided by Hammer (2005), who considers some of the personal names in *Beowulf* in relation to naming practices in Bavaria, seeing these names as evidence for the transmission of Danish narratives into that region, perhaps through the activities of early English missionaries to the Danes.

In some ways, the preoccupation with identifying the Scandinavian stratum in the personal names of *Beowulf* – a preoccupation shared by these four important treatments of the material – may distort our understanding of the names in the poem as a body of names interrelated through the narrative materials that underlie the poem. This book attempts to re-focus debate on the personal names in *Beowulf*, considering afresh the geography of the names and the implications that their probable geographical origins may have for our understanding of the poem and its sources. In doing so, we must naturally consider how *Beowulf* came to be produced, and we will consider in due course some of the key work in this area. In considering previous work on the personal names of the poem, however, we must consider not only the treatments of the names in terms of their place of origin and etymology, but also the debate around the potential meaningfulness of the names and the interaction of any meanings they might possess with the characterisation of their bearers.

There is a long history to the idea that the *Beowulf* poet created deliberately meaningful names for characters, reflecting their roles in the poem, or utilised pre-existing names of characters according to a reading of them as meaningful. For example, Müllenhoff (1889: 50–51) treats the names *Ecgwela* and *Heremod* as meaningful names, the latter reflecting Heremod's fearsome character; Panzer (1910–1912: 1.272) sees the name *Breca* as relating to a character in analogous folktales who is often identified as a stone cutter, here possibly originally termed a *stanbreca* 'stone breaker'; Malone (1941: 257) argues that the names *Hygd* and *Thryth* (but note that this may well be a misunderstanding of a noun, rather than a personal name; see below, p. 141) were treated by the *Beowulf* poet as meaningful names and their characters were developed by the poet according to those meanings; Rosier (1963) and Harris (1982: 415–17) both treat the name *Hondscio* — on the basis of its evident relationship with the Continental Germanic term for 'glove' — as relating to the imagery of hands in Beowulf's fight with Grendel. This view of the *Beowulf* poet as artful onomastician has been remarkably persistent. A few examples from recent work demonstrate the continuing impact of this idea. Owen-Crocker (2007: 276) claims that 'the poet regularly assigns names which may characterise by association', picking out *Unferð*, *Wiglaf*, *Freawaru*, *Breca*, *Beanstan*, *Froda*, *Halga* and *Hildeburh* as possible examples of such names. Others focus on identifying specific names as belonging to this type; Pakis (2008) identifies the name *Æschere* as a kenning denoting 'cremation, funeral pyre', while Breen (2009) adduces the possible compound *ðeowwealh* in Ine's law-code in support of the oft-repeated suggestion that the name *Wealhþeow* means 'foreign slave'. Owen-Crocker (2000: 160) advances the idea that the name *Hama* was treated by the poet as related to the word *hama* ('[snake] skin') and combined with

Hondscio, which she treats as meaning 'mitten', to create a punning reference to Grendel's dragon-skin glove.

There have also long been countervailing trends in scholarship on the personal names of *Beowulf*. Gordon (1935), for example, argued cogently for the view that the name *Wealhþeow* is a regular variation name, rather than one deliberately coined to characterise the queen (although he does take the view that variation names might have originated as meaningful compounds). Fulk (1987) showed the implausibility of regarding *Unferð* as a name coined by the poet as a characterising name, and also noted difficulties with a number of other, similar interpretations of personal names in the poem. More recently, Jurasinski (2007) provided an excellent overview of the debate around the meaningfulness or otherwise of *Wealhþeow*. He showed that the name is likely to have been a traditional variation name (i.e., a name formed by combining a pair of elements from a stock of name elements that could be combined in a very large number of variations, without any necessity that the name as a whole formed a meaningful compound) rather than a meaningful, characterising name. This position has also been espoused by Neidorf (2018a) and a rejection of the idea of characterising names in favour of transmission of ordinary names belonging to heroic figures well known in the context of the text's composition (if not necessarily so later in its transmission) implicitly underlies the cogent treatment of the personal names in *Beowulf* presented by Shippey (2014).

It is worth remarking that even recent contributions to this debate often fail to consider the alternative position presented by Robinson (1968: 50–57); the *Beowulf* poet might, Robinson argues, have depicted characters who were inherited from traditional narrative along with their names in such a way as to accord with his or her understanding of the meanings of their names' elements. This possibility would allow for the idea that names could be interpreted as meaningful by the poet without having to suppose that the poet invented names. Robinson presents substantial, clear evidence for the interpretation of pre-existing names in this way elsewhere in Old English literature, and this suggests that we should not lightly dismiss the possibility that traditional names, formed according to regular onomastic principles and thus not usually meaningful, could be interpreted as meaningful for literary purposes. One might also remark, however, that many of the examples outside *Beowulf* that Robinson presents are very clear cut, with authors making their interpretative work obvious to their audience, whereas the putative interpretative work in *Beowulf* is made far less obvious. Robinson (1968: 52–57) focuses particularly on the name *Hygelac* arguing, not entirely implausibly, for the possibility that an English poet could have interpreted this name with a sense such as 'instability of mind' (57). Yet the possibility of such an interpretation does not prove that the poet did, in fact, make this interpretation; it is not obvious to the present author that the *Beowulf* poet seeks to present Hygelac as frivolous or foolish, as this might suggest, and there is certainly no explicit reference to his name as bearing this sort of significance. For the purposes of this book, however, it does not matter whether or not the *Beowulf* poet interpreted traditional names as Robinson suggests, but simply whether personal names in the poem were names derived from the ordinary onomasticon or invented by the poet without necessarily adhering to pre-existing naming practices.

Examples of arguments and claims for the meaningfulness or otherwise of personal names in *Beowulf* could readily be multiplied, but since discussions of individual names will be noted below where appropriate, we need not dwell here on the volume of debate on this topic. It is, however, worth noting the renewed interest in the personal names of *Beowulf* in recent years, and it is to be hoped that this book provides a timely contribution to an important issue in scholarship on the poem. It will be observed in the discussion that follows, moreover, that the author's close examination of the personal names of the poem one by one has convinced him – as he hopes it will convince the reader – that the overwhelming majority of personal names in the poem are drawn from the ordinary onomasticons of the Germanic languages. With some important exceptions, such as Fulk (1987), much of the scholarship on the personal names of *Beowulf* has had a tendency to focus on the Old Norse and Old English onomasticons as comparanda for the personal names of the poem. This book, therefore, attempts to look across the full range of Germanic onomasticons and, in doing so, demonstrates the importance of Continental Germanic naming practices in understanding the personal names in the poem.

The production of *Beowulf*

The dating of *Beowulf*, the methods and circumstances of its composition, and the degree to which it drew on pre-existing traditions present complex problems, of which only the most cursory sketch can be provided here. The available facts are well known, simple and few, and it is their paucity that allows for the range of opinion on these matters. The poem refers to Hygelac's ill-fated continental raid, which is also mentioned by Gregory of Tours in his *Decem Libri Historiarum* (book 3, chapter 3; Krusch and Levison 1951: 99). Despite some dissent

(Christensen 2005), this identification remains widely accepted (see, for instance, Harris 2001: 486–87; Bazelmans 2009: 329; Biggs 2014: 140–42). The raid took place in the first half of the sixth century, perhaps around the year 520 AD (Biggs 2014: 141), thus providing a *terminus post quem* for the poem. The unique manuscript of the poem has been dated on palaeographical grounds to no later than the first quarter of the eleventh century (Lapidge 2000: 7–8). At some point between Hygelac's raid and the production of the manuscript, this poem was composed. This is not the place to rehearse in detail the debates that have taken place, and continue to take place, about the dating of the poem. However, work by Lapidge (2000) and Neidorf (2018b) on the manuscript transmission of the poem seems, to the present author, to offer some very strong evidence for dating the production of the poem in more or less its extant form to the period before the mid-ninth century.

Since the manuscript contains errors that demonstrate that it is a copy of an earlier example, we may be sure that the poem had some history of manuscript transmission. Lapidge (2000) argues from supposed scribal errors reflecting misreading of earlier letter forms (a type of error that Lapidge terms 'literal confusion') for the use at some point in the transmission of the text of an exemplar from before around 750 AD. However, Stanley (2002) criticises Lapidge's dating arguments, arguing that the sorts of literal confusion he adduces as evidence are capable of being produced in later Old English writing practices as well. This counter-argument is itself challenged by Clark (2009), who rightly contests Stanley's attempt to use the Old English gloss to the Arundel Psalter to demonstrate that a similar pattern of apparent literal confusions might be found in a text first written at a much later date. While Clark is perfectly correct about the Arundel Psalter gloss, his treatment of Lapidge's supposed literal errors is weakened by his failure to distinguish the direction of error. In writing <u> when <a> is intended, a scribe makes an error in one direction, but in writing <a> when <u> is intended, the error is in the opposite direction. Neither Lapidge nor Clark appear to consider this an important issue, although Stanley (2006: 66) notes in passing that a later scribe, unfamiliar with the open-topped <a> and therefore liable to misread it as <u>, would be unlikely to make a mistake in the opposite direction and misread <u> as <a>. This is, however, a point of considerable importance. If some of the literal confusions hypothesised by Lapidge are likely to have operated only (or mainly) in one direction, then this may affect the strength of his case, in which he treats errors in both directions as significant.

The issue of direction of literal confusion is addressed by Neidorf; in discussing the use in the manuscript of <d> where <ð> should be expected and

<ð> where <d> should be expected, Neidorf (2018b: 232–33) seeks to explain <ð> for <d> as the result of hypercorrection by a scribe or scribes who were accustomed to replacing <d> representing the dental fricative in an archaic exemplar by <ð>. Had the scribe(s) been working from an exemplar in which <d> consistently represented the dental fricative, then scribal efforts to update these spellings to <ð> would be expected to produce a text in which the dental fricative is usually represented by <ð> and occasionally by <d>, where an instance was missed by the scribe(s). That <ð> is also used to represent the plosive /d/ in the *Beowulf* manuscript could suggest the possibility that <d> and <ð> were simply confused at times by the scribe(s) because of their visual similarity to one another. Neidorf, however, argues that this is not the result of mere scribal inattention, but of erroneous scribal adjustment of <d> representing the plosive /d/ to <ð> because the scribe(s) frequently had to change <d> representing the dental fricative to <ð>. This argument is not without merit, but there are two issues in relation to Neidorf's position that deserve consideration.

The first issue is whether a hypothesis of hypercorrection is actually necessary in order to make sense of the evidence in the extant manuscript. This depends upon the question of whether visual confusion of <d> and <ð> is a likely difficulty for the scribe(s) to face. Anyone accustomed to reading Old English literary texts in their manuscripts is likely to have come across the letter forms in tenth- and eleventh-century manuscripts, in which <ð> is usually very readily distinguished from <d>. In hands of this period, <d> usually has only a very short ascender, whereas <ð> has a substantially longer ascender with a crossstroke cutting through it at around the mid-point. These letter forms are not easily confused with one another. In considering the possibility of an archetype of *Beowulf* dating from the ninth century or earlier, however, we must consider very different letter forms. In some ninth-century hands, <d> and <ð> appear quite similar, with essentially the same size and placement of ascender, and only the additional bar on the <ð> distinguishing it from <d>. Consider, for example, the forms of <d> and <ð> in the name *Guðmund* in London, British Library, Cotton Augustus ii.55 (see Figure 0.1; this name appears near the right-hand end of the penultimate line). This is an early ninth-century single-sheet charter (S 1259) that is either the original or a near contemporary copy of it. Clearly, some scribes in the early ninth century wrote a hand in which <d> and <ð> might quite easily be misread one for the other. This does not, of course, demonstrate that Neidorf's hypothesis of scribal hypercorrection is incorrect, but it raises the possibility that a scribe at some point in the chain of transmission of *Beowulf* could have been working with an exemplar in which <d> and <ð>

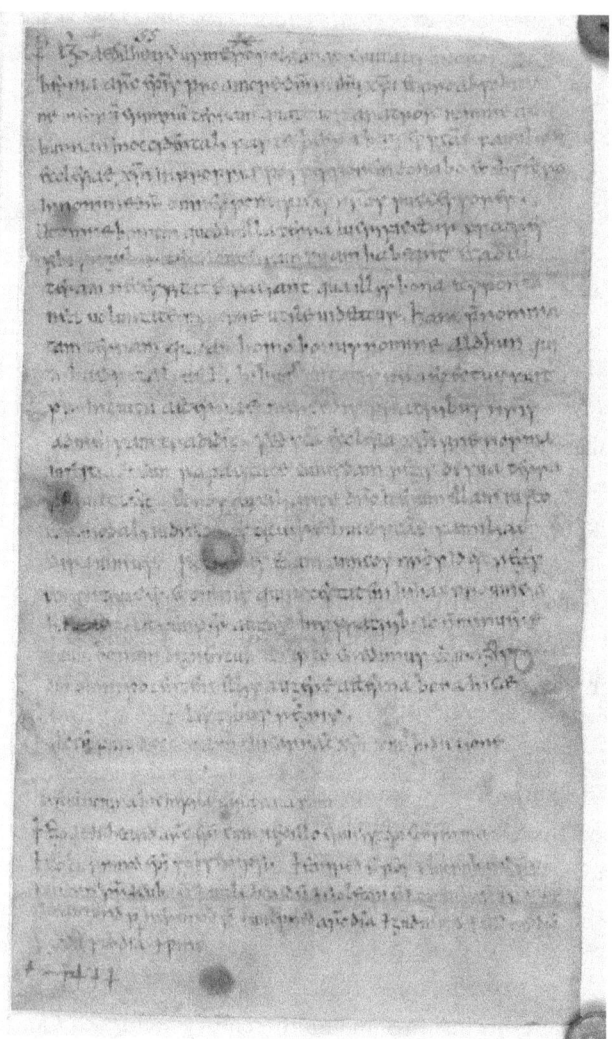

Figure 0.1 Cotton Augustus ii.55 (S 1259), London, British Library, (© The British Library Board).

looked quite similar and could easily have been confused. A scribe working with such an exemplar might readily have produced the mixture of confusion of <d> for <ð> and <ð> for <d> that we see in the extant text of the poem without having made any attempt at correction, and therefore without having hypercorrected.

The second issue with Neidorf's argument is that he misreads the significance of confusion of <ð> and <d> as dating evidence. Citing, among others, the present author's work, he claims that 'well before the end of the eighth century **ð** had completely displaced **d** as the letter for representing the dental fricative, while **d** came exclusively to represent the alveolar stop' (Neidorf 2018b: 231). Neidorf here misrepresents Shaw (2013a), who, in fact, demonstrates that a shift of this sort had occurred in Kentish and Mercian orthographic practice by the end of the eighth century, but that at least one conservative individual – Archbishop Æthelheard of Canterbury – continued to use <d> for the dental fricative into the early ninth century. Neidorf thus ignores the complexity of the situation. Our evidence is regionally distributed, with a lack of clear data for the situation obtaining in Northumbria, East Anglia or the West Saxon orbit. Even in Mercian and Kentish centres, we should not be surprised to find some (probably older) individuals who continued to use <d> for the dental fricative into the early ninth century. Even if we accept Neidorf's reading of the confusion of <d> and <ð> in the *Beowulf* manuscript as being the result of scribal engagement with an archetype in which <d> was used to represent the dental fricative, an archetype of this sort could certainly have been produced as late as the early ninth century, and possibly even somewhat later than this.

In the discussion that follows, a dating of *Beowulf* to between around 700 and 850 AD is taken as a plausible starting point. This is, however, a date for the first writing of the Old English poem which, with some changes in transmission, is represented in the extant *Beowulf* manuscript. The Old English poem, of course, is certainly not simply the imaginative creation *ex nihilo* of a single individual who put it into writing at some point during this period. How exactly the poem as we have it came to be written down is unclear, although we can be reasonably certain that at least some of the narrative material was traditional. In other words, narratives such as the death of Hygelac or Sigemund's dragon slaying must have been passed around in oral form – and quite possibly in written form as well – prior to the original writing of *Beowulf*. A key difficulty lies in determining how much of the narrative material of the poem is traditional. Some of it clearly is, but this does not mean that all of it is. Frank (1991: 97–98) views Beowulf, for example, as a character invented by the *Beowulf* poet and set against a backdrop of traditional narratives, a position that Neidorf (2013a: 554–55) rejects, preferring to see Beowulf as a traditional figure. The study of the personal names in the poem is key to understanding the traditionality or otherwise of some significant figures and, more broadly, therefore, to understanding the traditions from which the poem springs.

1

The Geats, Brondings and Wylfings

The named Geats in *Beowulf* represent a substantial proportion of the characters in the poem whose names are given. Since they are also the tribal group of the hero, it is helpful to begin with this group of characters, although, as we shall see, Beowulf himself does not appear to be tightly integrated into the royal house of the Geats as depicted in the poem. Beowulf's name, and those of his family members, mark him out as distinct from the main body of the Hreðling dynasty, and it is with this dynasty that we begin our exploration of the names of Geats in the poem.

The royal house of Hreðel

The central figures of the Hreðling dynasty are Hreðel, his son Hygelac and grandson Heardred. These figures constitute the main line of succession to the throne of Geatland, while Hreðel's other sons Herebeald and Hæðcyn exist within a self-contained episode in which the latter accidentally kills the former – an episode that appears to be closely related to the narrative of Hǫðr's accidental killing of Baldr in Scandinavian mythological narratives. On these grounds alone, we might suspect that these two figures represent an addition to the dynastic genealogy from another tradition and, as we shall see, the probable origins of the names of these two characters also bear out this interpretation. Female figures also provide links for the insertion of additional figures into the dynastic tradition (a point noted by Shippey 2014: 65). Hreðel has an unnamed daughter, whose marriage with Beowulf's father Ecgþeow links Beowulf and his relatives Ecgþeow, Wihstan, Wiglaf and Ælfhere to the Hreðlings. Similarly, Hygelac's unnamed daughter provides the means of linking Wonred and his sons Wulf and Eofor into the Hreðling dynasty. In the cases of Beowulf and of Wulf and Eofor, it seems likely that these figures developed separately from the main dynastic tradition of the Hreðlings, and may well have been attached to the

Hreðlings at some point in the development of *Beowulf* itself. The only named female figure among the Hreðlings, moreover, is Hygelac's wife Hygd, who, together with her father Hæreð, could represent another addition to the central tradition. This leaves the figures Swerting and Hereric, who are loosely specified relatives of the central Hreðling figures Hygelac and his son Heardred. Given that the poet tells us almost nothing about these figures, we could be forgiven for thinking that they are peripheral figures but, in fact, the probable origins of their names are consistent with these names having formed part of the core Hreðling dynasty. As we shall see, the names of figures in the Hreðling dynasty are not uniformly of Scandinavian origin; the core dynastic figures as outlined here bear names that could be of Scandinavian origin (although Continental Germanic origin is not out of the question) whereas the peripheral groups show signs of deriving from either Continental Germanic or Old English tradition. In order to demonstrate this clearly, we will consider each group in turn, looking first at the core Hreðling dynasty, before turning to the peripheral groups.

The dynastic core of the Hreðlings

The head of the dynasty of the Hreðlings, Hreðel, bears a name that Peterson (2004: 39) interprets as plausibly Proto-Scandinavian, arguing that it is formed from the element **Hrōþi-*, which is attested in her runic and her place-name material, and the diminutive suffix **-ilaz*. If we treat *Hreðel* as a West Saxon form, then this is entirely etymologically plausible, as the result of i-mutation of /o/ in West Saxon is represented as <e>. We should note, however, that the form of this name varies in the text of *Beowulf*; while it usually appears in forms where the stem vowel is represented by <e> (lines 374, 1847, 2191, 2358, 2430, 2474 and 2992), it does occur on two occasions with <æ> for the stem vowel; at line 454 we encounter the form *Hrædlan* and at 1485 *Hrædles*. Although these forms with <æ> are very much in the minority, they are significant variants; they do not represent obvious errors, but rather suggest an earlier spelling of the name that has apparently been updated in most of the references to Hreðel in the text. These two forms appear to reflect the use of <d> to represent the dental fricative in early Old English, suggesting that they may be spellings preserved from a form of the text dating no later than the eighth century or perhaps the early ninth century (see Lapidge 2000: 29–34 and Shaw 2013a). It seems possible, then, that forms such as *Hreðel*, with the stem vowel represented by <e>, represent the result of updating of the text during the course of its transmission, while the forms with <æ> representing the stem vowel give us an insight into the original form of the name.

If the original form of this name had the stem vowel /æ/, this would suggest that this is not, in fact, a name formed with the first element *Hrōþi-. This vowel would suggest instead that this name is formed either with an element related to Old English *hræð* 'quick' that appears in Continental Germanic names as *Hrad-/Hrat-* (Förstemann 1900: s.v. HRADA), or with an element that appears in Scandinavian names as *Hreið-* (Lind 1905–1915: s.v. *Hreiðarr*, *Hreiðmarr*, *Hreiðúlfr*, *Hreiðunna* and *Hreiðunnr*) and in Continental Germanic names as *Hraid-/Hrait-/Raid-* and similar (Förstemann 1900: s.v. HRAID). The only possible bearers of a name containing one or other of these elements in early medieval England are an eighth-century Abbot of Abingdon (*PASE*: *Ræthhun 2*) and a Bishop of Leicester (*PASE*: *Ræthhun 1*), who may well be the same person. Given the frequent omission of initial <h> in representations of his/their name, moreover, it seems quite likely that he/they was/were of Continental Germanic origin, and that this simply provides additional evidence for the Continental Germanic name element *Hrad-/Hrat-*. As Shaw (2011b: 84–86) points out, then, it is possible that the name *Hreðel* in *Beowulf* derives either from this specifically Continental Germanic element *Hrad-/Hrat-*, or from the Scandinavian and Continental Germanic element *Hreið-/Hraid-*, although derivation from *Hrad-/Hrat-* might account more straightforwardly for the alternation between <æ> and <e> spellings that we observe in the text of *Beowulf*. Given that this alternation can be satisfactorily accounted for by updating of the text in the course of transmission, however, it seems unwise to prefer one possible derivation over the other, and we must content ourselves with the observation that *Hreðel* could represent a Scandinavian or a Continental Germanic name.

Hreðel's son Hygelac bears a name that is, if anything, even less regionally distinctive, although here we have also to consider the possibility of another textual witness to this figure. Peterson (2004: 39) includes the name *Hygelac* among those she considers plausibly Proto-Scandinavian in *Beowulf*, noting the presence of the second element of the name in her corpus of personal names from early Scandinavian runic inscriptions. Both elements occur (although not in combination) in the Viking Age runic material from Scandinavia assembled in Peterson (2007: s.v. *Hugaldr, Hugbiǫrn, -læikr/-lakr*). It is possible, then, that this combination of elements could have been used as a name in pre-Viking Age Scandinavia, although it seems not to have been a common name if it was in use. On the Continent, in contrast, this combination of name elements is attested, although the name is not especially common (Förstemann 1900: s.v. *HUGU*). In England, *PASE* identifies two individuals under the name form *Hyglac* (*PASE: Hyglac 1–2*) and this name appears four times in ninth-century contexts in the *Durham Liber Vitae* (Rollason and Rollason 2007: 2.132). This would appear, then, to be a rare name that might occur in most, if not all, areas of the Germanic-speaking world, and it would therefore provide no evidence for the geographical development of the narrative materials of *Beowulf*.

It is also, however, worth addressing the evidence for the Scandinavian king who bears this name in the work of Gregory of Tours, in the *Liber Historiae Francorum* and in the *Liber Monstrorum*. If, as is often accepted, there was an actual Scandinavian king in the early sixth century who bore this name, then this would provide compelling evidence that Hygelac and his disastrous raid formed the basis of a narrative tradition, although we might still question whether this narrative tradition was created originally in Scandinavia, among the losing party or their neighbours, or in Frankia or its environs, among the victors. The identification of Hygelac with the figure mentioned by Gregory, in the *Liber Historiae Francorum* and in the *Liber Monstrorum* has, however, been questioned by Christensen (2005), who argues that the name forms given in these sources cannot safely be identified with the name *Hygelac* in *Beowulf*. While this questioning of a long-held assumption is salutary, the fact that the name *Hygelac* need not be identical with the name(s) recorded in the other sources does not demonstrate that the figure Hygelac in *Beowulf* was not based on the Scandinavian king with a similar name who is evidenced in these other sources. To insist on a precise equivalence between the names is perhaps to expect too much consistency in a popular narrative tradition that probably circulated orally, especially when we consider the chronological and geographical distance that separates Gregory from the *Beowulf* poet. We might be cautiously positive, then, about this identification and the possibility that the Hygelac of *Beowulf* was ultimately based on an historical figure whose fatal last venture was memorialised, perhaps in Scandinavian tradition, but certainly in Continental Germanic tradition.

The name of Hygelac's son Heardred is also not especially regionally distinctive. Peterson (2004: 38) treats this name as one of the Proto-Scandinavian personal names in *Beowulf*, although she also notes an Old English and a Continental Germanic form of the name. *PASE* records three bearers of this name, all of them in the later eighth century (*PASE*: s.v. *Heardred 1–3*). Insley,

Rollason and McClure (Rollason and Rollason 2007: 2.125) also treat the name form *Heared*, which appears in S 1431b, as an instance of *Heardred*, although they do not explain why they prefer this interpretation to the possibility that this is a form of *Heahred*. In the *Durham Liber Vitae*, the name *Heardred* appears several times in early ninth-century contexts (see Rollason and Rollason 2007: 2.124 for a list of instances). Förstemann (1900: s.v. *HARDU*) lists a considerable number of instances of this name from Continental Germanic contexts. In fact, this name is considerably better attested in England and on the Continent than it is in Scandinavia; Peterson apparently includes this name as Proto-Scandinavian on the basis that the two elements used in forming the name appear in other combinations in her early Scandinavian runic material. This certainly makes it possible that this particular combination was used in Scandinavia, but the strongest evidence for the use of this combination of elements as a name is in England and on the Continent.

Slightly less central to the Hreðling dynasty are Hereric and Swerting, each of whom appears only once in references to Heardred and Hygelac, respectively, as their *nefa* ('nephew', although other relationships such as grandson may also be possible; ll. 1962 and 2206). Peterson (2004: 38) identifies the name *Hereric* as plausibly Proto-Scandinavian, with evidence for the first element to be found in her corpus of early Scandinavian runic inscriptions, and evidence for the second element in her place-name material. In the Viking Age runic inscriptions from Scandinavia both elements are well attested, although this specific combination of elements is not found (Peterson 2007: s.v. *Hær-, -rīkr*). *PASE* identifies three bearers of this name (*Hereric 1–3*), and the individual elements *Here-* and *-ric* are common in Old English naming practices. On the Continent, this name is quite common, and is also found in Gothic naming practices (Förstemann 1900: s.v. *HARJA*). We can be quite confident, therefore, that this name occurred throughout the Germanic-speaking world, and therefore sheds no light on the development of the narrative materials of *Beowulf*.

The name *Swerting* at first glance presents the strongest evidence among the central figures of the Hreðling dynasty for a Scandinavian origin. This name is one of those considered by Peterson (2004: 40) to be plausibly Proto-Scandinavian, although the base element of the name is not attested elsewhere in her early data. This name is, however, attested in Viking Age runic inscriptions from Scandinavia (Peterson 2007: s.v. *Sværtingr*) and the element *Svart-* is also attested in the names of the first Scandinavian settlers in Iceland in the name *Svartkell* (Benediktsson 1968: 1.56). This is certainly a name that formed part of

Scandinavian naming traditions, although it does not seem to have been especially common. At the same time, the base element of this name is certainly attested, although not very often, on the Continent (Förstemann 1900: s.v. *SVARTA*), as is the suffix *-ing* (Förstemann 1900: s.v. *-ing*). The combination of this element with this suffix, however, does not appear to be attested on the Continent. There is, then, slightly better evidence for this as a Scandinavian name, but we cannot rule out the existence of this name on the Continent. It does not appear to have existed as an Old English name, and the base element seems not to have been used in forming Old English names. Insley and Rollason identify the two instances of this name in twelfth-century contexts in the *Durham Liber Vitae* as the Scandinavian name *Svertingr* and note that the name is 'quite well attested [. . .] in Domesday Book, as the name of moneyers and in other documents' in England (Rollason and Rollason 2007: 2.236). This would suggest that Swerting most probably originated in Scandinavian tradition, and this might be taken to indicate that we should prefer a Scandinavian origin for the rest of the dynastic core of the Hreðlings. However, we should note that a figure called *Swerting* clearly existed in English genealogical tradition by the early ninth century, on the evidence of the *Historia Brittonum*; this text included this name in a genealogy of the kings of Deira that in other respects closely resembles the corresponding genealogy in the Anglian collection (Dumville 1975: 1.241). There is no reason to suppose that this was an innovation on the part of the author of the *Historia Brittonum*; it is far more likely that this is a name that existed in the common ancestor of the Anglian collection and the source of the *Historia Brittonum*. Dumville (1976: 45–50) dates the origins of the Anglian collection to the second half of the eighth century, which could be consistent either with a transfer of Swerting from the narrative traditions reflected in *Beowulf* into the genealogical tradition, or *vice versa*. Whether this reflects Scandinavian influence in one or other tradition, or Continental Germanic influence, is harder to decide. This leaves us with the possibility that the dynastic core of the Hreðlings developed either in Scandinavia or on the Continent.

The likelihood is, then, that the figure named *Swerting* in *Beowulf* derived originally from a Scandinavian tradition, although we cannot absolutely rule out his development in a continental context. Taken together, the dynastic core of the Hreðlings have names that suggest the origins of this dynasty either in Scandinavian or Continental Germanic tradition. The name *Swerting* might sway us somewhat in favour of seeing this group of figures as originating in Scandinavia.

Hreðel's mythological sons: The problem of Herebeald and Hæðcyn

That Hreðel's sons Herebeald and Hæðcyn represent an intrusion of another narrative tradition into the Hreðling dynasty has long been suspected; it has been suggested that the narrative in *Beowulf* in which Hæðcyn accidentally shoots his brother Herebeald is a reflex of the myth of Hǫðr killing Baldr (see Björkman 1920a: 33-34 and Fulk, Bjork and Niles 2008: xlvii-xlviii for summaries of the various positions taken on this matter; see also O'Donoghue 2003). The names of both brothers contain elements that appear to correspond to the mythological names: *-beald* corresponding to *Baldr* and *Hæð-* to *Hǫðr*. O'Donoghue (2003: 84), for instance, describes the elements *beald* and *hæð* as 'exact cognates' of *Baldr* and *Hǫðr*, respectively. While this is clearly true in the case of *Baldr*, the name *Hǫðr* would appear to be cognate with the element that usually appears in Old English personal names as *Heaðu-* (see Orel 2003: s.v. **xaþuz*). Kitson (2002: 113-14) makes a cogent case for a derivation of *Hæðcyn* from a Scandinavian form with this same first element, but his case treats the form in *Beowulf* as an Anglicisation of a Scandinavian form in which the vowel that appears at the end of the Old English first element *Heaðu-* had already been lost. In other words, his argument takes the view that the first element of the name was not identified by the *Beowulf* poet as cognate with Old English *Heaðu-*, but rather was transcribed based on the way it sounded in Old Norse. This contradicts O'Donoghue's claim of direct cognacy, but it does not constitute an argument against the identification of *Hæðcyn* as a reflex of *Hǫðr*.

The case for a relationship between Hæðcyn and Hǫðr seems to the present author to be fairly strong. It should be noted, however, that the various Scandinavian sources for the figures Baldr and Hǫðr never give their names in forms consisting of two elements, as is the case in *Beowulf*. In the *Prose Edda* and in eddaic poetry, for instance, these two figures are always *Baldr* and *Hǫðr* (see, e.g., Faulkes 1988: 45-8; Faulkes 1998: 1.17-19; Kristjánsson and Ólason 2014: 1.299 *et passim*). In Saxo Grammaticus's *Gesta Danorum*, they appear as *Balderus* and *Hotherus* (Friis-Jensen and Fisher 2015: 1.142-61). Despite their agreement on the names, the Scandinavian sources treat the narrative in widely varying ways, differing on elements such as the divinity or humanity of these figures, their family relationship (or lack thereof) and the contexts (feasting or battle) and mechanisms (missile or sword) of Baldr's death. It is striking, therefore, that these sources all agree so closely on the names, while evidencing so much variation in the other narrative elements. If the narrative of Herebeald's death at the hands of Hæðcyn in *Beowulf* is based on Scandinavian tradition, therefore, it has been transformed in a very dramatic way, with conscious re-working of the names of these two figures.

The question that then arises is when and where this re-shaping might have taken place. As Kitson (2002: 113) remarks, the second element *-cyn* of *Hæðcyn* is not used in Old English personal names. Kitson (2002: 113) points to this second element as indicative of Scandinavian origin, but a few instances occur on the Continent of a cognate second element that could have been identified by an Old English speaker with *cyn* (Förstemann 1900: s.v. *CONJA*). The second element could thus reflect a re-shaping of the name *Hǫðr* either in Scandinavia or on the Continent. The first element *Hæð-* bears a general resemblance to the well-attested element *Heaðu-*, but, *pace* Kitson (2002: 113), it is probably not a variant form of this element. *PASE* records one instance of the name form *Hæðred* in the witness list of a tenth-century charter (*PASE*: s.v. *Hæthred 1*; S 425). In a ninth-century section of the *Durham Liber Vitae* we also find the form *Haeðberct*, and Insley, Rollason and McClure treat this form and the form *Hæðred* as evidence for an Old English form of the well-attested Continental Germanic name element derived from *haidu* 'beauty' (Rollason and Rollason 2007: 2.123). It is thus possible to account for the first element *Hæð-* as an Old English element, but the second element indicates that the name as a whole must represent an Anglicisation of a foreign name. As noted above, Kitson (2002: 113–14) explains the unusual first element in *Hæðcyn* as the result of transcription of an Old Norse form. This is linguistically plausible, but it implies that the mythological name *Hǫðr* was adjusted to an early form of *Hákon* in Scandinavia (for the view that *Hæðcyn* represents an Anglicisation of *Hákon*, see also Melefors 1993: 66 and Peterson 2004: 36). As we have seen, there is no evidence for a version of the Baldr/Hǫðr narrative in Scandinavia in which this has occurred, despite the survival of several witnesses to this narrative, including some in which the characters are euhemerised and presented as human beings.

We cannot discount the possibility that the name *Hæðcyn* is the result of a Scandinavian re-working of Hǫðr as a human figure with a name consisting of two ordinary naming elements. The evidence for this figure in Scandinavia, however, seems to speak against this view, and, as we shall see, the re-working of the name *Baldr* as *Herebeald* in *Beowulf* also seems unlikely to have taken place in a Scandinavian milieu. The alternative, given the geographical restriction of the second element of this name, is that it resulted from re-working of *Hǫðr* by a Continental Germanic speaker. If we posit that the name *Hǫðr* was received by a speaker of a Continental Germanic dialect in its Proto-Scandinavian form

*Haþuz, then it is, of course, possible that they would have identified it with the cognate name element in their own tongue and re-worked it as a personal name with the first element *Heaðu-/Hathu-*. In this case we might expect the character in *Beowulf* to be called *Heaðucyn*, unless we envisage a development whereby a Continental Germanic speaker identified *Haþuz with *Hathu-* and produced a name form such as the attested form *Hadacuan* (Bruckner and Marichal 1956: 62–63 (no. 139)), which was then interpreted by an English-speaking individual as relating to *Hæð-* because the Continental Germanic forms lack the diphthong resulting from back mutation in *Heaðu-*. Another possibility would be that our putative speaker of Old English or a Continental Germanic dialect would have sought to re-work this name by removing the ending and adding a second element, in which case they might have removed *-u(z)* and treated *Haþ-* as the first element in the new name; this might then have been represented as *Hæð-* by an Old English speaker.

The possibilities presented here do not admit of certainty. We cannot rule out Kitson's interpretation of *Hæðcyn* as deriving directly from an early Scandinavian form of *Hákon* with the Proto-Scandinavian *haþuz as its first element. At the same time, this interpretation is somewhat problematic if we accept that the figure called *Hæðcyn* in *Beowulf* derives ultimately from the mythological figure called *Hǫðr*. This seems a plausible route of derivation to the present author, and such a derivation seems likely to have involved a re-working of the name outside Scandinavia. Turning from Hæðcyn to his victim, Herebeald, the case against a Scandinavian origin for these two figures is strengthened; the name *Herebeald* does not feature among the plausibly Proto-Scandinavian personal names in *Beowulf* identified by Peterson (2004), and this name is also not recorded in Viking Age Scandinavia (Benediktsson 1968; Peterson 2007). In England, however, there is some evidence for the use of this name. *PASE* records four supposed individuals bearing this name. *Herebeald 1–3* are all applied to ninth-century moneyers associated with the Canterbury mint, raising questions as to whether these are not all the same individual. *Herebald 1* is an early eighth-century abbot of Tynemouth mentioned in book 5, chapter 6 of Bede's *Historia Ecclesiastica* (Plummer 1896: 1.289; Colgrave and Mynors 1969: 464). The Canterbury moneyer or moneyers could conceivably be an individual or individuals from the Continent, given the not uncommon occurrence of certainly Continental Germanic names among moneyers working in England in the late Old English period (Clark 1992: 465; Smart 1986). The abbot of Tynemouth, however, is not said by Bede to be of continental extraction, and it therefore seems likely that this represents an instance of the use of this name as a native Old English name. Since both elements of this name are common in Old English naming practices, moreover, it would not be surprising to find that this name was in use. It is worth noting, however, that it seems to have been a very rare name in early medieval England. On the Continent, in contrast, this name is extremely common; in the Continental Germanic materials assembled by Förstemann (1900: s.v. *HARJA*), this name occurs numerous times. This might, then, suggest that the figure called *Herebeald* derived from English or continental narrative materials, with continental materials representing the more likely of the two possibilities.

In considering the origins of this name, however, we must also consider its possible relationship with the name of the Scandinavian deity Baldr. If, as seems likely, *Herebeald* represents a re-working of the Scandinavian mythological name *Baldr*, then this has implications for our reading of the origins of this name in *Beowulf*. If an Old English poet were trying to generate a name with *h*-alliteration (which is metrically required at line 2463a) and formed with two naming elements, from the single-element name *Baldr*, then one might expect the poet to have used a somewhat more common Old English name fulfilling these criteria, such as *Hygebald*, borne by perhaps three different individuals (*PASE*: s.v. *Hygebald 1–3*). The frequency of use of *Hygebald* is not, however, very much higher than that of *Herebeald*, so we should be cautious about placing too much weight on this. As we have seen, however, this name is very common on the Continent (Förstemann 1900: s.v. *HARJA*), and it would therefore have been a very natural choice for a Continental Germanic-speaking individual as a way of re-working *Baldr* into a name consisting of two elements and alliterating with the name of his brother.

On balance, then, the likelihood is that the narrative of Herebeald and Hæðcyn that appears in *Beowulf* was the result of re-working of a Scandinavian narrative on the Continent, although we cannot rule out a similar re-working in an English milieu. It is interesting, moreover, to note that this re-working has focused on creating alliteration based on the name *Hǫðr* rather than on *Baldr*. Considering the Scandinavian narrative, and especially its mythological versions, one might perhaps have expected Baldr to be the more salient of the two brothers and therefore to have provided the focus for alliteration. This would not have presented problems in terms of the availability of a second element cognate with the name *Hǫðr* (Förstemann 1900: s.v. *HATHU*; *PASE*: s.v. *Beorhthæth, Beornhæth, Pæogthath, Wulfhath*). The fact that *h*-alliteration is created in re-working *Baldr* as *Herebeald* may, then, suggest that a key motivation for this alliteration was the fact that *h*-alliteration characterises the names of the other members of the Geatish royal house, such as *Hreðel* and *Hygelac*. The possibility of integrating Baldr and Hǫðr into the Geatish genealogy is created by the fact that *Hǫðr* has *h*-alliteration; the re-working of *Baldr* therefore cements this possibility by providing both brothers with the necessary alliteration. While this could have been the work of the *Beowulf* poet, for the reasons discussed above it seems somewhat more likely that the re-working of these names took place on the Continent. This may, therefore, suggest that they were inserted into the Geatish royal house in a continental context.

The evidence here is suggestive rather than certain, but it raises the possibility that *Beowulf* derives, in part, from a Continental Germanic source that already included the narrative of Herebeald and Hæðcyn as a digression attached to a narrative around the Geatish dynasty. This would seem to imply two separate processes of transmission of material from Scandinavia to the Continent. The core of the Hreðling dynasty shows signs of deriving its personal names straightforwardly from Scandinavia, whereas the narrative of Herebeald and Hæðcyn involves elaboration of the Scandinavian names in a probably Continental Germanic milieu. While we could suppose that all of these figures were transmitted from Scandinavia as a single unit, this would involve selective adjustment of just the names of Herebeald and Hæðcyn, and it would also involve positing a Scandinavian narrative in which Baldr and Hǫðr had already been incorporated into the Hreðling dynasty. While later Scandinavian authors such as Saxo Grammaticus and Snorri Sturluson took a euhemeristic approach to pre-Christian Scandinavian deities that could have accommodated such a narrative development, it would be odd to find a (necessarily pagan) Scandinavian narrative pre-dating *Beowulf* that inserted two divine figures into a human royal house. The euhemeristic incorporation of Scandinavian deities into the legendary tradition of the Hreðlings reflects a Christian worldview that we might more plausibly locate on the Continent or in England in the period immediately leading up to the composition of *Beowulf*. Of these two possibilities, moreover, the Continent is the more likely, given the probable origins of the names of the two brothers.

Wives and daughters of the Hreðlings

The complexity of the development of the Hreðling dynasty, as depicted in *Beowulf*, is compounded when we turn to the women of the family. The core of the dynasty appears to have consisted in the first instance of male figures, and the unnamed daughters of Hreðel and of Hygelac seem to feature simply to provide links that anchor Beowulf and his family, and Wonred and his sons, to the core of the dynasty. We might reasonably suspect, then, that these peripheral families did not originally form part of the dynasty, but have been set against its backdrop at some point in the transmission of the core dynasty from Scandinavia. Similarly, Hygelac's wife Hygd and her father Hæreð may not have formed part of the dynastic tradition from the outset. As we shall see, moreover, the probable origins of the names of figures in these sections of the family tree point towards their having originated outside Scandinavia, contributing to the emerging picture of a set of narratives accreting around the Hreðlings in an extra-Scandinavian context.

Beowulf's family

Beowulf is linked to the Hreðlings via his father Ecgþeow, the husband of Hreðel's unnamed daughter. This father and son pairing have names that are suggestive of Continental Germanic origins for these figures. If we begin with the father, we find that the first element *Ecg-* that occurs quite frequently in Old English personal names (see, for example, *PASE*: s.v. *Ecgbald, Ecgbeorht, Ecgburg, Ecgfrith, Ecgheard, Ecglaf, Ecgmund, Ecgwine* and *Ecgwulf*) clearly derives from Proto-Germanic **aʒjō* 'blade' (see, e.g., Felder 2003: 48). This element is not, however, certainly attested in Scandinavian personal naming practices. Peterson (2007: s.v. *Ā-* and *Ag-*) notes the possibility that some of her Viking Age names from runic inscriptions contain reflexes of Proto-Germanic **aʒjō* in forms realised as *a-, ag-, ak-, uk-*, possibly *auk-*, and *ah-* in the runic inscriptions. Yet, as Peterson (2007: s.v. *Ā-*) notes, the realisation *a-* could also derive from **ana-* or **anu-*. This leaves only the names *Agmundr, Agni* and *Agviðr* in forms with the other realisations, and Peterson indicates, quite correctly, that these forms could still derive from two possible Proto-Germanic roots: **aʒjō* 'blade' or **aʒez* 'fear'. If we consider evidence outside the runic corpus, however, we find that the form for the reflex of **aʒjō* that we should expect in Old Norse, namely *Egg-*, does not occur as a personal name element, unless we include the name *Eggþér*, which occurs as the name of a mythological figure in *Vǫluspá* (Dronke 1969–2011: 2.18 (stanza 41); Kristjánsson and Ólason 2014: 1.301 (stanza 41)) and in the forms *Egtherum* and *Egtherus*, as the name of a king of Bjarmaland and a Finnish raider respectively, in Saxo Grammaticus's *Gesta Danorum* (Friis-Jensen and Fisher 2015: 1.342, 1.460). These instances do not provide straightforward evidence for the currency of this name element in ordinary Scandinavian naming practices; rather, they seem to show that this complete name existed as a name applied to outsider figures, whether giants or non-Germanic neighbours, in Scandinavian narrative tradition (the possible implications of this in relation to *Beowulf* will be considered below). It is therefore simpler to suppose that the runic forms that Peterson identifies are not derived from Proto-Germanic **aʒjō* 'blade', and that there is, in fact, no compelling evidence that there was a Scandinavian personal name element derived from this form.

Since Proto-Germanic **aʒjō* 'blade' does not appear to have formed part of Scandinavian personal naming practices, we should probably consider *Ecgþeow* a name created outside Scandinavia. When we consider the second element *-þeow*, moreover, we see that this name is unlikely to have originated in England. *PASE* records only one individual whose name contains *-þeow*, the legendary ancestor of Mercian kings called *Angelþeow* (*PASE*: s.v. *Angeltheow*). This individual's name occurs in the *Anglo-Saxon Chronicle* (Bately 1986: 38; Taylor 1983: 20, 27; O'Brien O'Keeffe 2001: 37, 48) and in Æthelweard's *Chronicon* (Campbell 1962: 25), but, as discussed in relation to the name *Ongenþeow* (see below), the form of his name in different witnesses to the Mercian dynastic tradition varies very widely. The key point here is that this individual appears to form part of the pre-migration ancestry of Mercian kings, a position that seems to be confirmed by the genealogical information concerning the continental Offa given at *Beowulf* lines 1957–62, which places figures from this part of the genealogy in the pre-migration past of the poem, although Angelþeow himself may be lacking from the genealogy in *Beowulf* (but see discussion in relation to the name *Eomer* at pp. 145–6). This name can be seen, therefore, as a name inherited as part of a legendary dynastic tradition that may well have been created outside England. There is, then, no compelling evidence for the use of this name element in Old English naming practices, and we can therefore be fairly confident that the name *Ecgþeow* originated in a continental milieu.

The character named *Ecgþeow* is Beowulf's father, but he does not exist in the poem solely as part of descriptions of Beowulf as his son. We learn a little of Ecgþeow at lines 262–5, where we discover that he lived into old age. More importantly, however, at lines 373–5 we discover that his wife (and presumably, therefore, Beowulf's mother) was the daughter of Hreðel, king of the Geats, and at lines 459–72 Hroðgar tells Beowulf that his father was involved in a feud with the Wylfings, killing an individual called *Heaðolaf* and seeking sanctuary with the Danes before Hroðgar settled the feud for him. These narrative fragments appear to do two key things; on the one hand, they provide Beowulf with a dynastic relationship with the Geatish royal family and, on the other hand, they also provide him with a relationship of duty to the Danish royal house through the oaths that Ecgþeow swore to Hroðgar (l. 472). As we shall see, the name *Beowulf* itself seems likely to have been a Continental Germanic name originally, so we can see the brief details of Ecgþeow's life as serving to cement Beowulf – a figure who seems highly unlikely to have come from Scandinavian tradition – into the two Scandinavian legendary dynasties that are central to the legendary backdrop against which Beowulf's exploits are set. Ecgþeow, in other words, shows every sign of having developed on the Continent, as part of the development of the narrative of Beowulf the monster-slayer in that milieu.

It is also interesting to consider in this context the Scandinavian instances of the cognate name *Eggþér*. The application of this name to enemies from non-Germanic neighbouring tribes by Saxo Grammaticus (Friis-Jensen and Fisher 2015: 1.342, 1.460) is in some ways reminiscent of the scant biographical detail that *Beowulf* provides about Ecgþeow. Although Ecgþeow clearly belongs to the Germanic-speaking world of the western Baltic, the key event in his life that impinges on the narrative of *Beowulf* is his feud with the Wylfings. One of the most salient elements of his depiction is, therefore, his combat with a neighbouring tribe, and in particular with the individual named *Heaðolaf*. The figures called *Egtherum* and *Egtherus* by Saxo are represented solely as combatants engaged in warfare that culminates in single combat with a champion or king. While the tribal relationships involved are clearly different, as are the outcomes of these combats, the basic representation as a figure engaged in single combat that forms part of a wider enmity with a neighbouring tribe is broadly similar. Dronke (1969–2011: 2.143) seeks to relate Saxo's figures to the figure named *Eggþér* in *Vǫluspá*, suggesting that 'some legend of him may have caused Saxo to use him as a Finnish/Lappish enemy of the Swedes'. The appeal here to an unknown legend linking the figure in *Vǫluspá* with the figures in the *Gesta Danorum* seems to ignore the potential that *Beowulf* offers for understanding the nature of these Scandinavian figures. Taken together, Ecgþeow in *Beowulf* and the two figures in the *Gesta Danorum* could plausibly reflect a narrative tradition around a human heroic figure with this name who engages in single combat. At first sight, the figured called *Eggþér* in *Vǫluspá* appears the odd one out; Dronke (1969–2011: 2.143) interprets him as a 'pastoral giant', a characterisation that seems rather at odds with the martial figures depicted by Saxo and the *Beowulf* poet. The broader context of Eggþér in *Vǫluspá*, however, belies the pastoral impression that might be created by the reference to him as a 'herdsman'. The poem describes Eggþér as a 'herdsman of the giantess', whose musical activities on a grave mound are accompanied by a red cockerel who perhaps reappears (with somewhat drabber plumage) in the next stanza at the halls of Hel (Dronke 1969–2011: 2.18 (stanzas 41–42); Kristjánsson and Ólason 2014: 1.301–2 (stanzas 41–42)). The association of Eggþér with death here is clear, and in context it seems that we should treat the phrase 'gýgiar hirðir' ('the ogress's herdsman'; text and translation from Dronke 1969–2011: 2.18) not as a literal statement of pastoral activity, but rather as a metaphor for someone who leads individuals to Hel. If the original figure underlying all these depictions were a hero associated with fatal single combat, then a re-imagining of this figure in a mythical context could plausibly have produced such a depiction. Perhaps we should not insist, however, on seeing all of these figures as so closely related; the similarities between Beowulf's father and the figures recorded by Saxo are sufficient to suggest a heroic single combatant, whose name may then simply have been preserved in Scandinavian tradition and re-used in Vǫluspá without regard to the narrative that originally surrounded this figure.

While there is evidence, then, for a Scandinavian cognate of the name Ecgþeow, this evidence probably post-dates the initial composition of Beowulf, and may reflect the transmission of a figure with this name, known for a heroic single combat, into Scandinavia from elsewhere. Set within the wider evidence for personal naming practices in different parts of the Germanic-speaking world, this name can most readily be explained as originating in a Continental Germanic milieu. The first element of the name Ecgþeow does not appear to have been productive in Scandinavian personal naming, while the second element does not appear to have been productive in Old English personal naming; both elements, however, are not uncommon in Continental Germanic personal names (see Förstemann 1900: s.v. AG, THIVA). On balance, then, it seems that Ecgþeow should be seen as originating in continental heroic tradition, from where he passed into Beowulf.

Turning to his son, the name Beowulf presents interesting problems. There are few recorded instances of its use as a given name for historically attested individuals, and this has no doubt contributed to the popularity of the interpretation of the name as a poetic invention, a kenning 'bee-wolf' meaning 'bear' (for a summary of the development and popularity of this view, see Fulk 2007: 116–17; recent adherents of this idea include McKinnell 2005: 131 and Owen-Crocker 2007: 270, while Abram 2017: 411 offers an alternative interpretation of the name as meaningful in relation to a putative connection between Beowulf and the character Sigmundr in Vǫlsunga saga). Some scholars (Wormald 2006; Neidorf 2013a) have also regarded the attestation of the name in the *Durham Liber Vitae* as evidence simply of the adoption of the name from the heroic narrative. This position can be reconciled with the view that it is an ordinary but rare name, but it is more readily sustained if one believes the name to be an invention. If the name were an ordinary but rare name, it would be essentially impossible to decide whether any given attestation of the name for a historically attested individual was the result their being named after the heroic figure or simply one of the rare uses of a rare name. Short of finding an instance of the name *Beowulf* that pre-dates the events depicted in the poem, we cannot be certain whether the heroic figure Beowulf was the first bearer of this name. Even if we were to find an earlier attestation, moreover, it would still be possible to argue that Beowulf himself derived from an earlier story and was transplanted into the historical setting of the Scylding dynasty and their Geatish and Swedish neighbours. This would, however, seem like special pleading, and we might be inclined to accept the more obvious inference that *Beowulf* was not a name invented for the hero. It should also be noted that we cannot prove that the name was invented, although we may be able to prove the converse.

Arguing against those who would regard the name *Beowulf* as an invention, Fulk (2007) seeks to show that *Beowulf* is an ordinary name of the variation type. Fulk's arguments are worth considering in detail, as they have an important bearing on the question of the etymology of the name *Beowulf*. Fulk demonstrates that it is philologically possible that the name *Beowulf* has as a first element **Beow-*, deriving from a divine name that is only attested in Old Norse, in the form *Byggvir*. Fulk offers this etymology as an alternative to the etymology that treats the first element of *Beowulf* as cognate with Old English *beo* 'bee'. This etymology has a long pedigree, as Fulk (2007: 116–17) notes. Fulk admits that he cannot disprove this etymology (2007: 135), but he prefers one deriving the name element from a divine name, as this allows him to view the name as 'not artful but ordinary, a name such as any figure in heroic legend might bear [. . .] a name of the theophoric type [i.e. a name containing an element derived from the name of a deity]' (2007: 118). This interpretation is motivated by Fulk's general dissatisfaction with treatments of personal names in *Beowulf* as artful coinages designed to reflect on the characters of their bearers or on wider themes in the poem, as well as his specific distrust of the notion that *Beowulf* might be a kenning 'bee-wolf' (meaning 'bear'), which thus connects the hero with folk tales of the bear's son type and with the Scandinavian hero Bǫðvarr Bjarki (Fulk 2007: 112–18). The present author shares Fulk's disquiet at both the general proposition that the anthroponymy of the poem is artful, and at the specific idea that Beowulf himself must be regarded as bear-like. That he is to be connected with Bǫðvarr Bjarki, however, appears quite possible, and this identification need not rest on any bear-like qualities he may or may not possess. This is a question that is considered in some detail below, in relation to the name *Hondscio*.

There are reasons to doubt some of the arguments put forward by Fulk. While his philological reasoning is undoubtedly sound, it merely demonstrates that *beo* is not the only possible etymon for the first element of the name *Beowulf*. The fact that his proposed etymology produces a theophoric name is at best inconclusive; the etymology involving the word *beo* 'bee' produces a theriophoric name (i.e., a name in which one of the elements is derived from a word for an animal) a name type that is also not uncommon in the Germanic languages. Of course, the best-known names of this sort make reference to large and/or fierce animals (e.g., consider names such as *Wulfstan*, referencing the wolf, *Eofor*, referencing the wild boar, and *Arngrímr*, referencing the eagle). Theriophoric names less often involve creepy-crawlies (names such as *Wyrmhere*, of course, can relate as easily to the senses of *wyrm* 'snake' and 'dragon' as to the sense 'worm'). This fact leads Neidorf (2013a: 563) to suggest that it is presposterous to view *Beowulf* as having the first element *beo*:

> A name with 'bee' as its prototheme has no parallel formation and would probably have seemed ludicrous to an Anglo-Saxon with a basic understanding of the propriety and logic of the conceptual categories constituting the onomasticon. Animals do comprise a group of name-themes, such as *wulf*, *hrafn*, and *eofor*, but these are animals with martial associations, appropriate for an onomasticon with prominent themes like *heard*, 'courageous'—they are never insects.

Neidorf is simply incorrect in his assertion that the animals that are referenced in theriophoric name elements were never insects. At least one theriophoric name element involving a creepy-crawly appears to be attested in several Continental Germanic names containing the element *lop* 'louse', including names such as *Lobaheri*, *Lobahilt* and *Lopolf* (Förstemann 1900: s.v. *LOBA*). The discussion of the putative name *Beow* (see pp. 62–3), moreover, also suggests that the formation of names from terms denoting insects was a definite possibility. There is, therefore, no particular reason to reject *beo* as a name element on the grounds that it derives from a noun meaning 'bee'; this would simply be a rare theriophoric name element, as opposed to a rare theophoric name element. While Neidorf might be inclined to reject bees as unsuited to the warrior ethos that produces such theriophoric names as *Wulfberht* or *Hrafnkell*, it is far from clear that the English (or, indeed, their Germanic-speaking neighbours) would have regarded bees in the same way. Consider, for example, the Old English metrical bee-charm that requires the charmer to address the swarm as *sigewif* 'victory women' (Cambridge, Corpus Christi College, MS 41, p. 182; edited by Grendon 1909: 168 and Dobbie 1942: 125). Jordanes also uses bees as a metaphor (albeit possibly one with classical roots) for warlike migrant peoples in his *Getica* (see Rix 2015: 37–38). Cultures that can regard bees in this light need not have seen a name element deriving from a word meaning 'bee' as inappropriate for the naming of a hero such as Beowulf. We should beware of hasty judgements as to what would or would not seem 'ludicrous to an Anglo-Saxon'.

Another problem that presents itself with Fulk's interpretation is its reliance on a belief in the existence in early Germanic-speaking societies of a deity whose only attested reflex is the figure called *Byggvir*, who appears only in *Lokasenna* and its prose introduction (Dronke 1969–2011: 2.342–43 (stanzas 43–46); Kristjánsson and Ólason 2014: 1.416–17 (stanzas 43–46); see also Sayers 2016: 26). While one cannot rule out the possibility that *Byggvir* is the reflex of a Common Germanic deity, a great deal of weight must be placed on the testimony of *Lokasenna* in reconstructing such a deity, and although Dronke (1989: 97–107) argues cogently for the origins of this poem in the pre-Christian period, this does not demonstrate that Byggvir existed outside Scandinavia or before the Viking Age (the fascinating treatment of this figure by Sayers (2016: esp. 23–26) sets him in a potentially much wider context of northern European tradition, but without demonstrating that a figure of this sort was known by this particular name outside Scandinavia). Fulk's objections to *beo* as the etymon of the first element of the name *Beowulf* do not seem to the present author to be sufficiently strong that they compel us to adopt a belief in a pre-Viking Age ancestor of the *Poetic Edda*'s Byggvir. On the whole, the balance of probability seems to incline somewhat more towards the interpretation of *Beowulf* as consisting of *beo* 'bee' and *wulf* 'wolf'. This does not for a moment, of course, imply that the name is a kenning meaning 'bear'; it is perfectly satisfactory to interpret it simply as an ordinary variation name.

In seeking to understand the name *Beowulf*, of course, we must also consider its attestations outside the poem. Wormald (2006: 79) makes slightly ambiguous reference to 'the notorious sole case of a **Beowulf**, a monk in the Lindisfarne *Liber Vitae*'. It is unclear whether this statement was intended to apply only to the Old English onomastic evidence, or if Wormald was unaware that this name is attested elsewhere in the Germanic-speaking world. The name is, to be sure, a rare one, but it is not attested only in *Beowulf* and the *Durham Liber Vitae*. It is attested in Scandinavia in the form *Bjólfr* as the name of a settler in *Landnámabók* (Fulk 2007: 125; Benediktsson 1968: 2.306). In England, besides the monk bearing this name who is recorded in the earliest stratum of the *Durham Liber Vitae*, there is another individual with this name (in the form *Beulf*[*us*]) recorded in the *Domesday Book* (*Domesday Book* xiv; Williams and Martin 1991: fol 82r). It is on the Continent, however, that we have the best evidence for this name. Fulk (2007: 125) notes 'Continental Germanic *Biulfus* and *Piholf*' but does not elaborate on who bore these forms of the name. The form *Biulfus* belongs to an archbishop of Strasbourg who flourished around the first half of the seventh century AD, to judge from his position in the later list of bishops which provides the only evidence for him (Strecker 1937: 510 and see 508–10 on the dating of the list and Bloch et al.: 1908–1928: 1.218 on the possible dating of Biulfus). The form *Piholf* is found as the name of a witness in the record of a donation of land at Palzing in Bavaria to the nearby Cathedral of Freising, which took place in 807 AD, and was copied into the Freising cartulary later in the first half of the ninth century (Munich, Bayerisches Hauptstaatsarchiv, HL Freising 3a, fols 82v–83r; see Figure 1.1 and also Wagner 1876: 40). To these we can also add the form *Biulfi*, the Latin genitive of *Biulfus*, in the place-name *Biulfi curte*, found in a record of a land grant in the *Liber Memorialis* of the Abbey of Remiremont

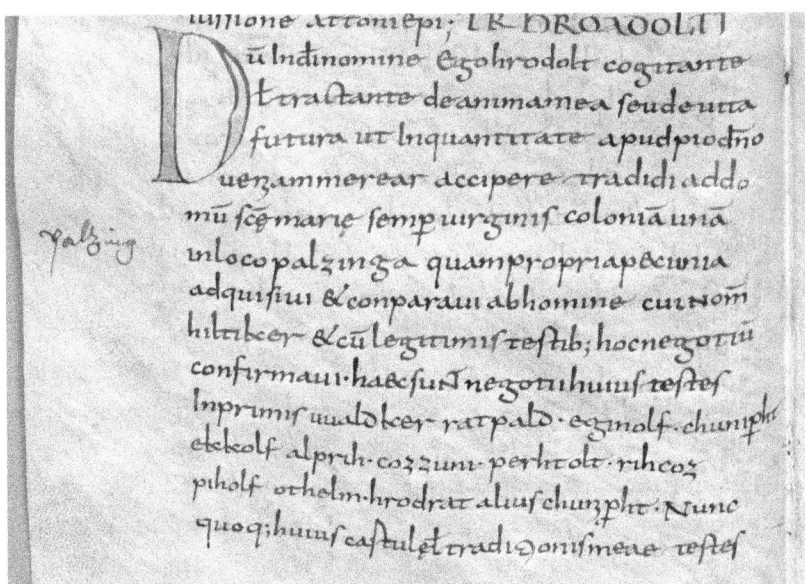

Figure 1.1 Detail of fol 82r of Munich, Bayerisches Hauptstaatsarchiv, HL Freising 3a, the Cozroh Codex, showing the name form *piholf* at the start of the penultimate line.

(Hlawitschka, Schmid and Tellenbach 1970: 1.40). Hlawitschka, Schmid and Tellenbach (1970: 1.282) identify this as a reference either to Biécourt, Vosges or to Biocourt, commune de Bleurville, Vosges. These places are fairly close to one another, and both lie around fifty miles from Strasbourg. It is tempting to suppose that one or both places may owe its name to Biulfus the Archbishop of Strasbourg or that this name was particularly in vogue in the region around Strasbourg. There is insufficient evidence, however, to support either of these propositions, and the evidence of the same name in use in Bavaria in the early ninth century (though the witness who bore the name is most likely to have been born before 800 AD) suggests that we should be cautious in attempting to identify any particular centre of distribution for this name.

The name *Beowulf* is not, then, as little attested as is sometimes suggested. It is certainly not a common name, but neither is it unique nor unprecedented. The fact that the name is better attested on the Continent than in Scandinavia or England does not necessarily suggest that it originated as a Continental Germanic name. Fulk (2007: 125) points out that the Old Norse and Continental Germanic forms of the name could represent loans from England. All else being equal, this is true; the very slight majority of forms in Continental Germanic offers no evidence of the direction of influence. It is worth noting, however, that in Archbishop Biulfus we have evidence of a bearer of the name who cannot have been given his name much after the beginning of the seventh century at the very latest. The place-name *Biulfi curte* may well also be a relatively early place-name, although, as Godiveau (1988: 10) points out, it can be difficult to determine how early place-names in -*court* are (see also discussion in de Planhol and Claval 1994: 63–64). Since the central datable moment in *Beowulf* is Hygelac's raid, which took place perhaps around 520 AD (see discussion of the name *Hygelac* at pp. 17–18), we have evidence here of use of the name *Beowulf* in quite close chronological proximity to the setting of the poem itself. Of course, the importance of this is dependent on whether or not we understand Beowulf to have been an historical figure. If he was, and if he succeeded Hygelac as king of the Geats, then narratives about him could have begun to circulate in the early sixth century, during his lifetime, but a narrative in which he died cannot have come into existence until somewhat later, perhaps the 630s at the earliest (but considerably later if we take literally the poet's claim that Beowulf ruled for 50 years). This is not to suggest that we should believe that Beowulf was a historical figure who lived in the early sixth century; it seems to the present author that this is one of those things we simply do not know – and perhaps never will. We can, of course, imagine other quite compelling scenarios, such as the insertion of an older, folkloric monster-fighter into the historical setting of the Scylding dynasty. The Continental Germanic cognates of *Beowulf* do not demonstrate conclusively whether the name was in use before the heroic narrative arose.

A more fruitful line of inquiry lies in the use of the name element *beo* in names other than *Beowulf*. If the name element could be shown to be used in other two-element names formed on the variation principle, this would provide good evidence that it was an ordinary, if rare, part of the onomasticon. Unfortunately, no clear evidence for this exists, but it is suggestive that single-element names formed with this element appear on the Continent. Förstemann (1900: s.v. *BIH*) seeks to ascribe forms such as *Bio* and *Bia* to a root related to Old High German *pihal* 'axe', suggesting that a derivation from *bia* 'bee' is unlikely. However, Kaufmann (1968: 60) accepts – rightly, in the current author's view – that this is a plausible derivation for such name forms. This does not certainly demonstrate that *beo* was used as a variation element, as these names could conceivably be hypocoristic forms (shortened forms, often used familiarly) of *Beowulf* itself. However, other theriophoric name elements such as *wulf* and *hrafn* are often used as the basis of single-element names (see, for instance, the numerous examples listed by Förstemann 1900: s.v. *HRABAN* and *VULFA*) and it seems unlikely that these are all to be interpreted as hypocorisms. On balance, it seems likely that on the Continent at least, *beo* existed as an ordinary name-forming element. In Scandinavia and England, by contrast, the first element *Beo-* appears to occur only in the name *Beowulf*. This tends to suggest that the name *Beowulf* was an ordinary Continental Germanic name, as it is in the Continental Germanic-speaking area that we find evidence for the use of *beo* as an independent name element. We might hypothesise, then, that *Beowulf* was imported into England and Scandinavia with the Beowulf narrative and thus in these areas we find no trace of other names formed with the element *beo*.

Both Beowulf and his father have names that point towards an origin in Continental Germanic narrative tradition. As we have seen, Ecgþeow ties Beowulf into the Hreðling dynasty through his marriage with Hreðel's daughter, but also links him with the Scyldings through Hroðgar's settlement of his feud with the Wylfings. This suggests that, just as Herebeald and Hæðcyn represent a Continental Germanic addition to the Hreðling dynasty (albeit one apparently deriving ultimately from Scandinavian myth), so Beowulf and his father can be seen as a Continental Germanic addition. This suggests that the central narrative of *Beowulf* may well have arisen in the first place in a Continental Germanic milieu or, if it came from elsewhere, the names of the central character and his father were created in such a milieu.

It is puzzling, then, that the rest of Beowulf's family do not have names that point towards a Continental Germanic origin. Beowulf is aided in his final battle against the dragon by his kinsman Wiglaf, who is the son of a figure called Wihstan and related in some way to another individual called Ælfhere. The latter name provides us with no indications as to the area of origin of this part of Beowulf's family tree; the name *Ælfhere* consists of two name-forming elements that are very common in the early Germanic languages, the reflexes of Proto-Germanic */albaz/ 'elf' and */xarjaz/ 'army'. Names formed with these elements are attested across the Germanic languages, and this particular combination is well attested in Old English, Old Norse and in Continental Germanic dialects. For Old English, *PASE* lists 24 bearers of this name, which, even allowing for the possibility that some of these are actually the same person, is a significant number. For Old Norse, the second element derived from Proto-Germanic */xarjaz/ is difficult to distinguish from the elements derived from */warjaz/ and */ʒaizaz/ (Peterson 2007: s.v. *-arr*), except in the earliest runic inscriptions, where the form **swabaharjaz** on the Rö stone demonstrates the existence of this name element in Scandinavia (Peterson 2004: 16). Bearing in mind the difficulty in identifying this name element unequivocally in the Scandinavian material, it may occur in a number of early Scandinavian place-names in *-lev* (Peterson 2004: 22) and also in the Viking Age Scandinavian runic corpus (Peterson 2007: s.v. *Alfarr*). On the Continent, this name is also quite well attested (Förstemann 1900: s.v. *ALFI*). This name does not, therefore, shed any light on the origins of the narrative tradition concerning Wiglaf and his relatives, since it could have been coined in any part of the Germanic-speaking world.

The names *Wiglaf* and *Wihstan*, however, are perhaps more revealing. While we cannot locate the origins of these names with absolute certainty, they seem potentially to be indicative of English origins for this part of Beowulf's family tree. *Wiglaf* features among those names in *Beowulf* that Peterson (2004: 40) considers to be plausibly Proto-Scandinavian; the first element is attested in her early place-name material, but the second element is otherwise attested in her corpora only in *Beowulf*. Nevertheless, the individual elements used in forming this name are not uncommon in names found on Viking Age runic inscriptions in Scandinavia (Peterson 2007: s.v. *-læifr/-lafr, Vīg-*) although this specific combination is not attested. It is not improbable, therefore, that this name did exist in Scandinavian naming traditions, although it was evidently rare. The evidence is also limited on the Continent, although here this combination of name elements is attested, albeit only once, as the name of a witness to a ninth-century land donation (Wigand 1843: 45, no. 228; Förstemann 1900: s.v. *VIGA*).

It is interesting, then, that *PASE* notes six individual bearers of the name *Wiglaf* (*PASE: Wiglaf 1–5, 7*), along with a general entry for bearers of this name in the *Domesday Book* (*PASE: Wiglaf 6*). This name also occurs once in an early ninth-century context in the *Durham Liber Vitae* (Rollason and Rollason 2007: 2.158). Although this is not a very large number of bearers, it nevertheless presents a striking contrast with the situation elsewhere in the Germanic-speaking world, especially when we consider that the evidence from early medieval England makes up only a small proportion of the overall body of evidence for Germanic personal names. This contrast tends to suggest that this name was a more significant feature of Old English naming traditions than of those elsewhere in the Germanic-speaking world. We might, then, tentatively suppose that the figure Wiglaf may have been named by an Old English speaker, as part of the creation of the Old English poem, although we must allow that his name could have formed part of Scandinavian or continental narrative materials.

The situation is not dissimilar with the name *Wihstan*. Peterson (2004: 40) lists this as a plausibly Proto-Scandinavian name in *Beowulf*, noting the presence of the second element of the name in her early place-name data. This second element, however, is common in England as well as Scandinavia; *PASE* notes, for example, 127 bearers of the name *Ælfstan*, 126 individuals called *Æthelstan*, 95 called *Leofstan* and 125 named *Wulfstan*. Even allowing for some double counting and false positives in these figures, this was clearly a hugely popular name element in England. On the Continent, the popularity of this element seems considerably lower, but it is nevertheless solidly attested (Förstemann 1900: s.v. *STAINA*). The second element *-stan*, therefore, offers no particular insight into the origins of the name.

The first element of this name is more problematic. The forms *Weohstanes* (ll. 2613 (apparently in error for *Weohstan*; see Fulk, Bjork and Niles 2008: 89) and 2862), *Weoxstanes* (l. 2602) and *Wihstanes* (ll. 2752, 2907, 3076, 3110 and 3120) that appear in *Beowulf* (and the form *Vésteinn* in *Kálfsvísa* (Faulkes 1998: 1.89 (l. 16)), if we accept that this refers to the same figure, as Fulk, Bjork and Niles (2008: lxiii fn. 3) suggest; see also Shippey 2014: 68) show evidence of derivation from Proto-Germanic **wīxaz* 'holy', with the /x/ causing breaking of the root vowel that distinguishes it very clearly from the more common Old English name element *Wig-*, which derives from Proto-Germanic **wīʒaz* 'war-like'. In Scandinavian and Continental Germanic names, however, the elements deriving from Proto-Germanic **wīʒaz* and **wīxaz* are not always readily distinguishable from their written forms (Peterson 2007: s.v. *Vī-*, *Vīg-*; Förstemann 1900: s.v. *VIGA, VIHA*). It is therefore difficult to arrive at very firm conclusions on the frequency of this name element in Scandinavia and on the Continent. In relation to the specific name under discussion, however, we might note that, while a name that could be cognate with Old English *Wihstan* occurs in a few Viking Age runic inscriptions in Scandinavia (Peterson 2007: s.v. *Vīstæinn*), no such name occurs in the continental data assembled by Förstemann (1900: s.v. *VIGA, VIHA*).

In England, however, three individuals have been identified by *PASE* as bearers of this name. One was an ealdorman who died around the beginning of the ninth century (*PASE: Wiohstan 2*), while the other two are mentioned in charters, one dated to the late eighth century (S 1184; *PASE: Wiohstan 1*) and one to the first quarter of the tenth century (S 1206; *PASE: Wiohstan 3*). This might suggest that, like his son Wiglaf, Wihstan is likely to be a narrative detail created by an Old English speaker. Of course, we cannot rule out Scandinavian or continental development of this figure, but the balance of probability weighs somewhat in favour of an English origin. Perhaps, then, a Continental Germanic narrative around Beowulf as a giant slayer was augmented by the addition of the dragon fight in England, and Wiglaf and his immediate relatives were added in this context, to provide Beowulf with a second in this final fight. It is by no means impossible, however, that these figures also formed part of the Continental Germanic development of the narrative of Beowulf's heroic deeds. We also cannot entirely rule out a Scandinavian origin for these figures, although this would involve a very complicated scenario in which Scandinavian narrative material, perhaps unconnected with Beowulf or connected with a differently named but otherwise similar Scandinavian heroic figure, was transferred to Beowulf in England or on the Continent. There is no simple answer here, but the likely possibilities are either that these figures developed on the Continent along with Beowulf and Ecgþeow, but with names that were rare on the Continent, or that they developed separately from Beowulf and Ecgþeow in England, where these names appear to be somewhat more common.

Hygelac's wife and daughter

As with Beowulf and his father Ecgþeow, Hygelac's in-laws Wonred, Wulf and Eofor through his unnamed daughter have names that point towards Continental Germanic origins. While the names *Wulf* and *Eofor* could point to other areas of origin, the name *Wonred* is best explained as a Continental Germanic personal name. The name of the father *Wonred* can therefore be seen as anchoring his sons to an origin in a Continental Germanic milieu. The situation is possibly similar with Hygelac's wife Hygd and her father Hæreð although, in this case, the evidence is less certain; the name *Hygd* is problematic and, while the only plausible etymology that the present author has been able to identify is a Continental Germanic etymology, this must remain a tentative interpretation of the name's origins. The name *Hæreð* would also be consistent with Continental Germanic origins, but we cannot rule out Scandinavian origins for this name. Perhaps, then, Hygd and Hæreð formed part of the Scandinavian core of the Hreðling dynasty, but it is also possible that they belong among the Continental Germanic additions to this dynasty.

The name *Wonred* is another that has attracted interpretation as a name deliberately coined by the *Beowulf* poet in order to characterise the individual so named (Weyhe 1908: 36; Bloomfield 1949: 414). Such interpretations have perhaps been prompted in part by the lack of a name element *won-* in other Old English names. According to Björkman (1920b: 119), neither England nor Scandinavia furnishes examples of names formed with this element; he, therefore, prefers to interpret the name as an Anglicisation of the Scandinavian name *Vandráðr*. The latter name is, in his view, cognate with Old High German *Wanrat*, a name which, at first glance, appears to be more readily explained as a cognate of (or perhaps the source of) the name *Wonred* in *Beowulf*. Björkman suggests two mechanisms for the loss of /d/ in the Old English name *Wonred*, one phonological and one lexical. On the one hand, this may represent a simplification of the consonant cluster /ndr/, parallel to the simplification of /ndl/ in the ethnonym *Wenlum* in *Widsith* (Malone 1962: 24 (l. 59)), which can be compared with the form *Wendla* for this ethnonym in *Beowulf* (l. 348). On the other hand, the Angliciser could have been influenced by Old English compound words containing the adjective *wan* 'lacking', such as *wansped* 'poverty'. Both these mechanisms seem possible, but it is not clear that recourse to either is necessary.

It is clear from the evidence presented by Förstemann (1900: s.v. *VAN*) that the Continental Germanic onomasticon contained an element that is often represented as *wan* and that appears as a first element in a range of two-element names including not only *Wanrat*, but also *Wanbald*, *Wanibert*, *Wanburg*, *Wanfrid*, *Wanhard*, *Wanheri*, *Wanmund* and *Wanulf*. Förstemann (1900: s.v. *VAN*) notes but rejects the possibility that the name element *wan* derives from the adjective meaning 'lacking', which exists in Old High German and Old Saxon as well as Old English, and he is also sceptical about any possible connection with the divine ethnonym *Vanir*. This scepticism seems justified; the adjective meaning 'lacking' is semantically unlikely, since Germanic name elements generally encode positive values, while the Vanir are not attested outside Old Norse mythography, raising serious questions as to the likelihood that their name furnished part of the Continental Germanic onomasticon. Förstemann's preferred interpretation of the name element *wan* is that it is related to Old High German *wān*, Old Norse *ván*, Gothic *wens* 'hope, expectation' (1900: s.v. *VAN*). These forms are cognate with Old English *wēn* (see Orel 2003: s.v. **wēniz*), which might perhaps be the first element in the name *Uuenoðus*, which was borne by a minister of Æthelræd recorded in the charters S 1038 and S 862 (*PASE*: s.v. *Wenoth 1*). This name form is, however, anomalous in these late tenth- and eleventh-century charters in using the digraph <uu> to represent /w/, since wynn is otherwise the norm in these charters and in other material of this period. This suggests, perhaps, that this is a Continental Germanic name in which a Continental Germanic spelling has been preserved (see Shaw 2013a: 132–33 for another instance of preservation of an individual's idiosyncratic spelling of their name). It is possible, then, that the Continental Germanic name element *wan* had a very rare English cognate *wen*, but the evidence for this is weak at best. What is very clear, moreover, is that this name element not only existed but was also quite common on the Continent.

In view of the existence of Continental Germanic *wan*, it seems unnecessary to explain the name form *Wonred* as an Anglicised form of *Vandráðr*. The lack of medial /d/ in the form *Wonred* needs no explanation if we suppose that *Wonred* represents Continental Germanic *Wanrad*. Since the expected English cognate of *Wanrad* would be **Wenred*, the form in *Beowulf* is most readily explained as an Anglicised form of the Continental Germanic name. Unlike the proposed Anglicisation of *Vandráðr*, however, this Anglicisation requires no special explanation of the form that it produces. The Continental Germanic second element -*rad* has a regular cognate -*ræd* or -*red* in Old English, and the use of <o> rather than <a> in the first element is unremarkable, reflecting the common variation between <o> and <a> spellings before nasal consonants in Old English. It is, of course, also possible that the name was originally spelt *Wenred*, and that a scribe misread the first <e> as <o> somewhere in the transmission of the text. It is difficult to find evidence of scribal misreading of <e> as <o> in the transmission of *Beowulf*, although a number of literal confusions occur (see Lapidge 2000). The one case of which the present author is aware is the form *sceaðona* in line 274, which might have been expected to read *sceaðena*, in line with the weak genitive plural noun ending elsewhere in the poem. Editors have not, however, been in any rush to emend the form (see Fulk, Bjork and Niles

2008: 11). On balance, the single hypothesis that *Wonred* represents an Anglicised form of the attested Continental Germanic name *Wanrad* seems preferable to the twin hypotheses that *Wonred* is a scribal error for *Wenred and that this form is therefore evidence of an otherwise unattested native English name.

None of this proves beyond doubt that Björkman's interpretation of *Wonred* was wrong, or that *Wonred* could not represent a native English name. Both these interpretations, however, require more complex hypotheses to sustain them. The balance of probabilities seems, therefore, to weigh somewhat in favour of the view, argued above, that *Wonred* is a straightforwardly Anglicised form of the Continental Germanic name *Wanrad*, which can be added to the list of personal names in *Beowulf* that are more readily explained as imports from the Continental Germanic onomasticon than as Scandinavian imports or native formations.

Wonred's sons, in contrast, have names that could be of Scandinavian or Continental Germanic origin. Peterson (2004: 37) lists *Eofor* among her corpus of early Scandinavian personal names. She presumably does so because later Scandinavian sources record the name *Jǫfurr* (Peterson 2007: s.v. *Jǫfurr*). The situation is, however, complex; the Old English word *eofor* and its Old High German cognate *ebur* straightforwardly derive from Proto-Germanic *eburaz, whereas the Old Norse word *jǫfurr*, used poetically with the sense 'prince', appears to be the result of analogy with forms elsewhere in the paradigm (Peterson 2007: s.v. *Iōr-*). As Peterson (2007: s.v. *Iōr-*) points out, there is evidence in Scandinavian personal naming of a personal name element derived from the etymologically expected form *jórr. This raises questions about when the analogical form developed and when it began to be used as a personal naming element. If it were already in existence before the creation of *Beowulf*, then we could reckon with Old English *Eofor* as an Anglicisation of *Jǫfurr*. However, if only *jórr was in use at this date, then this possibility seems considerably less likely. Neither the etymologically expected form nor the analogical form appears in the pre-Viking Age data in Peterson (2004), with the exception of the name *Eofor* in *Beowulf* itself. The Viking Age runic material gathered in Peterson (2007) affords instances of both, but this is of little help in determining the chronology of the analogical development in Scandinavia, which could have taken place a good deal earlier. We can, therefore, argue that *Eofor* could arise from an Anglicisation of a Scandinavian name, but we cannot be sure that this was its origin.

It is also possible that *Eofor* derived from a Continental Germanic source, since the use of this element as a simplex name is not uncommon on the

Continent (Förstemann 1900: s.v. *EBUR*). In England, however, the simplex name form does not appear to be attested, to judge from its absence from the *PASE* dataset. On the other hand, *PASE* does record the names *Eoferheard*, *Eofermund* and *Eoferwulf*. These names, however, all belong to moneyers from the tenth century or later, and we might therefore reasonably suspect that these were individuals from the Continent, given the unusual concentration of Continental Germanic names among moneyers in England in the late Old English period (see Clark 1992: 465; Smart 1986). We can be reasonably confident, then, that *Eofor* was not in common use as a name in early medieval England, and we should see the occurrence of this name in *Beowulf* as reflecting either a Scandinavian tradition (directly or via the Continent) or a continental tradition.

The name of Eofor's brother *Wulf* is more straightforward. It could certainly be a Scandinavian name; it is very common in Scandinavian naming traditions and it is no surprise that Peterson (2004: 40) lists this among the names in *Beowulf* that she identifies as Proto-Scandinavian, although this name does not occur in her runic or place-name datasets. Nevertheless, the name is extremely common in Viking Age runic inscriptions from Scandinavia (Peterson 2007: s.v. *Ulfr*) and no fewer than five of the first generation of settlers of Iceland recorded in *Landnámabók* bore this name (Benediktsson 1968: 1.77, 1.161, 2.244, 2.276, 2.319). This Scandinavian name also appears several times in the *Durham Liber Vitae* (Rollason and Rollason 2007: 2.242), although the cognate Old English *Wulf* does not appear. *PASE* has two entries for this name, one for someone named *Wlf* in the Lincolnshire Domesday survey (*PASE*: s.v. *Wulf 2*) and one for an individual called *Wulf* whose mid-eleventh-century will, catalogued as S 1532, appears in English and Latin versions in a seventeenth-century manuscript, and in a Latin-only version in a thirteenth-century manuscript (London, British Library, Cotton Nero D. i, folio 151v). The *Domesday Book* instance could well represent the Scandinavian *Úlfr*, leaving just one potential instance noted by *PASE* of a native Old English name *Wulf*. Given the date of the will and the lack of other instances as an Old English name, however, it seems quite possible that *Wulf* in this instance represents an Anglicisation of Scandinavian *Úlfr*, rather than evidence for a native Old English name. We might also consider the possibility of an Old English name *Wulf* in the Exeter Book poem *Wulf and Eadwacer*, although it has been suggested that this represents a Scandinavian name (Frank 2007: 29) or is not a name at all (Orton 1985: 225–28). There is, then, no clear evidence for a native Old English name *Wulf*. On the Continent, in contrast, this name is clearly attested, although it is not as common as in the Scandinavian evidence (Förstemann 1900: s.v. *VULFA*).

This name is certainly plausible as a name derived from Scandinavian tradition, but it is also possible that a figure with this name could have been created in a Continental Germanic context. The recognition and Anglicisation of the name to *Wulf* would be a simpler matter if the *Beowulf* poet was working from a continental exemplar or tradition, where the Scandinavian loss of initial /w/ would not obscure the relationship of the name with the Old English word *wulf*. On the other hand, S 1532 would appear to provide evidence for Anglicisation of what was probably the Scandinavian name, and the potential difficulties created by loss of /w/ should not be overstated. We can, therefore, treat this name as being of Scandinavian or continental origin, consistent either with the transmission of narrative material directly from Scandinavia to England, or from or via the Continent.

Owen-Crocker's (2007) interpretation of the names *Eofor* and *Wulf* as meaningful names, reflecting the ferocity of the characters who bear them, depends upon her belief that the *Beowulf* poet habitually coined meaningful names or developed the characteristics of figures in the poem according to his or her perception of the meaning of their names. As the discussions in this book repeatedly demonstrate, the personal names in the poem almost all belong to the ordinary onomasticon – albeit not always the Old English onomasticon – and there is therefore no strong reason to seek to interpret them in this way. The specific claim about the names *Eofor* and *Wulf* is open to the obvious objection that many characters in the poem display considerable ferocity; it therefore seems odd that this pair should have been singled out for meaningful names reflecting this common characteristic of warriors in heroic poetry. It is perhaps more likely that the brothers both have names consisting of a single element derived from a word for an animal because one name suggested the other to the individual who created them, but this does not mean that we should understand the names as characterising names. Whether these names were created in Scandinavia or on the Continent cannot be ascertained from these two names alone, but given that the name of their father is best explained as a Continental Germanic name, the simplest reading here is that father and sons all represented a narrative tradition that developed on the Continent. We could suppose, instead, that Wulf and Eofor formed part of a Scandinavian narrative that was transmitted to the Continent and that they were there provided with a father. This is certainly not impossible, but clearly the hypothesis of a Continental Germanic origin for all three is simpler.

A similar situation obtains with Hygelac's wife Hygd and her father Hæreð. Peterson (2004) does not include *Hæreð* in her corpus of Proto-Scandinavian names from *Beowulf*, but in her later work on Viking Age names she does note some names in Scandinavian runic material that could be related to it; Peterson (2007: 305) treats the name **haruþs** on the Rök stone as belonging to a mythical individual, but Peterson (2007: s.v. *Hærrøðr*) notes a human name formed, in her view, from *Hær-* plus *-freðr* that could be Anglicised as *Hæreð*. However, the entry for 787 AD in manuscript D of the *Anglo-Saxon Chronicle* records the arrival of three ships of *Norðmenn* from *Hæreðaland* (Cubbin 1996: 16; in manuscript F the form is *Hereðaland*, see Baker 2000: 53), which is, in all probability, an Old English realisation of the name *Hordaland* (Old Norse *Hǫrðaland*; see Cleasby, Vigfússon and Craigie 1957: s.v. *Hörðar*) for a region in Norway. The root of this form corresponds exactly with the personal name form *Hæreð* in *Beowulf*, suggesting that we might wish to relate this personal name to the Old Norse ethnonym *Hǫrðar*. That a personal name derived from this ethnonym, albeit one that is rare, existed in Scandinavia seems clear from the two individuals called *Hǫrðr* in *Landnámabók*, one of whom was one of the earliest settlers of Iceland and the other belonged to the subsequent generation (Benediktsson 1968: 1.57, 1. 140). It would be possible, then, for the name of this figure to have originated in Scandinavia, although the evidence for the currency of this name in this region is extremely limited.

This name also appears to have existed as a rare name on the Continent, where it is attested as early as the sixth century AD in the writings of Agathias and Procopius, and in a number of instances in the eighth and ninth centuries (Förstemann 1900: s.v. HARUD; Keydell 1967: 36 (l. 17) [book 1, chapter 20]; Haury 1905–1913: 2.632 (l. 3) [*On the Wars*, book 8, chapter 26]). On the Continent, then, this name is somewhat better attested than in Scandinavia. In England, however, there is no clear evidence for a form of this name. *PASE* records the rare name *Herred* for four individuals, and notes another individual under the headform *Herrid*, which is probably simply a variant form of *Herred*. We should not, however, expect a form with a final /d/ or a double medial consonant in a putative Old English cognate of the Scandinavian and Continental Germanic name, so this is unlikely to represent a form of the same name. The deacon called *Heared* in the decree of a council of Clofesho in 803 AD (S 1431b) can also be discounted; it seems highly probable that his name is simply a form of *Heahred*, which is an attested Old English name (*PASE*: s.v. *Heahred 1–2*). This leaves only the name *Haret* recorded in the Suffolk *Domesday Book* (Rumble 1986: 66.6), which may well represent a form of this name, but at this date is likely to be a Continental Germanic import rather than a native English name. On balance, therefore, a Continental Germanic origin is most likely for the name *Hæreð* in *Beowulf*, although a Scandinavian origin is also possible.

When we turn to Hæreð's daughter Hygd, however, a Scandinavian origin seems less plausible. Peterson (2004) does not include this name among those in *Beowulf* that she identifies as plausibly Proto-Scandinavian. Björkman (1920b: 76) notes that this name is otherwise unattested and suggests that it was a *Phantasiename* created by the *Beowulf* poet to mirror the name of her husband Hygelac. There is, indeed, no evidence of such a name in *PASE* or in the *Durham Liber Vitae*, and Förstemann (1900) does not note any obviously related name forms. Nor does anything resembling this name feature in the Viking Age runic materials from Scandinavia assembled by Peterson (2007). Given that the personal names of *Beowulf* are otherwise overwhelmingly created using the normal principles of name formation in the Germanic languages, however, it seems worth exploring the possibility that this was not a *Phantasiename* as Björkman suggests, but rather another name formed using these principles.

The name *Hygd* appears to be formed on a root that occurs not uncommonly as the name element *Hyge-* in Old English personal names such as *Hygebald* and *Hygeberht* (*PASE*: s.v. *Hygebald*, *Hygeberht*; see also Rollason and Rollason 2007: 2.132 for the slightly wider range of names formed with this first element attested in the *Durham Liber Vitae*). This name element is also very common in Continental Germanic personal names (Förstemann 1900: s.v. *HUGU*) and also occurs occasionally in Viking Age personal names in Scandinavia (Peterson 2007: s.v. *Hugaldr*, *Hugbiǫrn*). The root of the name is thus unproblematically to be identified with a well-known name-forming element. This leaves the final *-d* to be interpreted. This is not entirely straightforward, but suffixes in *-d* were in use in Continental Germanic personal naming practices; Kaufmann (1968: 8–9) briefly discusses suffixes in *-d* used in forming personal names on the Continent, and Förstemann (1900: s.v. *-d*) notes various names formed using these suffixes, including several female names. Examination of *PASE* and the *Durham Liber Vitae* does not yield any clear examples of female names in early medieval England formed with such a suffix, nor do they appear to have been productive in Scandinavian personal naming.

One can, then, provide an interpretation of *Hygd* as deriving from a Continental Germanic personal name formed on the base element *Hugi-* with a *-d* suffix; such a name might appear in a continental context in a form such as **Hugida*. While this form is not, to the best of the present author's knowledge, attested, Förstemann (1900: s.v. *HUGU*) does note the form *Hugizo* in a tenth-century source. This name is formed with a different suffix in *-z*, but Kaufmann (1968: 9) notes an eleventh-century individual called *Hubertus* whose name appears to have motivated the hypocoristic forms *Hubezo* and *Hubetho*. This suggests that alternation between suffixes in -*z* and suffixes in a dental consonant could occur, and the attested form *Hugizo* might therefore have existed parallel to forms such as **Hugida* or **Hugitha*. The form *Hygd*, then, represents an Anglicisation of a form such as **Hugida* with i-mutation of the root vowel and the loss of the Continental Germanic feminine ending in *-a*. This Anglicisation might also have been influenced by the Old English word *hygd* ('mind, thought'; DOE: s.v. *hygd*). Given the very limited evidence available, this interpretation cannot be treated as certain, but it provides a plausible explanation for the name form *Hygd* that fits with the general pattern of derivation of personal names in *Beowulf* from the ordinary onomasticon. If we accept this interpretation, then it seems most likely that Hygd and her father Hæreð were added to the Hreðling dynasty in a Continental Germanic milieu, along with many of the other peripheral family groupings in the dynasty as it is represented in *Beowulf*.

Beowulf's backstory: The Brondings and the Wylfings

The picture that is emerging of the Hreðling dynasty and its satellites in *Beowulf* is a complex one, with some uncertainties about the boundaries of the core dynasty, which could represent a tradition deriving from Scandinavia. Nevertheless, there is some very suggestive evidence for the role of a Continental Germanic milieu or milieux in the development of the narrative of Beowulf and his family, and some of the other satellite families also appear to belong to such a context. If Beowulf and his family belong to a narrative developed (whatever its place of origin) in a continental context, then we should expect that the figures belonging to the tribal groupings of the Brondings and the Wylfings, who provide elements of the backstory of Beowulf and his father Ecgþeow, also developed in a continental context.

In the case of the Wylfings, however, the only Wylfing certainly identified by name in the poem is Heaðolaf (although it is not implausible that Wealhþeow also belongs to this tribal group; see p. 90 below). His name features in Peterson's (2004: 38) listing of plausibly Proto-Scandinavian names in *Beowulf*, combining a first element found in her runic corpus with a second element that, while it is not found in her runic or place-name corpora, is found several times in *Beowulf*, and is well attested in later Scandinavian sources. In the Viking Age runic material treated by Peterson (2007: s.v. *-læifr/-lafr*), for example, the second element *-læifr* or *-lafr*, which appears in Old English as *-laf*, occurs with around 16 different first elements, demonstrating its popularity within the variation system of naming. In *Landnámabók*, this element is similarly productive, occurring in the names *Friðleifr, Geirleifr, Guðleifr, Hjǫrleifr, Hrolleifr, Ísleifr, Oddleifr, Óleifr, Véleifr* and *Þorleifr* (Benediktsson 1968: 2.242, 2.244; 1.172, 2.256; 1.100, 1.105, 1.163; 1.41, 1.100, 1.150; 2.220, 2.389; 1.85, 2.226, 2.386; 1.172, 1.182, 2.243; 1.73, 1.136, 2.324, 2.340, 2.380; 1.72, 2.284; 1.54, 1.58, 1.63, 1.92, 1.95, 1.119, 1.127, 1.135, 1.178, 1.201, 2.254, 2.272 n. 3, 2.278, 2.281, 2.310, 2.313, 2.342, 2.355, 2.374, 2.383, 2.385). Peterson is surely correct, then, in suggesting that this name could be an early Scandinavian name.

At the same time, we should also note that in the Continental Germanic context this name would also be unremarkable; both elements used in forming this name are common on the Continent (Förstemann 1900: s.v. *HATHU, LAIFA*). It is worth remarking, however, that the one instance of a name combining these two elements noted by Förstemann (1900: s.v. *LAIFA*) is drawn from a list of personal names in Graff (1834–1842: 2, col. 50) that provides no indication of the sources for these name forms, and we should therefore treat this with caution. In England, we find names formed with *Heaðu*- and with -*laf* in the *Durham Liber Vitae* (Rollason and Rollason 2007: 2.124–25 and 2.134). *PASE* also records a number of names in *Heaðu*- (*Hathobald, Hathoberht, Hathored, Hathowald, Hathowulf, Hathufrith, Hathulac, Heathuwulf*) and in -*laf* (*Beorhtlaf, Beornlaf, Burlaf, Cenlaf, Ceollaf, Cunlaf, Cynelaf, Deorlaf, Dæglaf, Eadlaf, Ecglaf, Hunlaf, Ordlaf, Oslaf, Seaxlaf, Sælaf, Wiglaf, Wihtlaf, Wulflaf, Wærlaf*). There is, then, no reason to regard the name *Heaðolaf* as distinctive to any specific part of the Germanic-speaking world. This is not inconsistent, however, with the hypothesis of a Continental Germanic origin for Beowulf, his family, and the associated characters from other tribal groups, of course, since this name could have arisen in a Continental Germanic context.

When we turn to the Brondings, who are represented in *Beowulf* by Breca and his father Beanstan, we find a clearer case for Continental Germanic origins for these characters' names. The name *Breca* is neither attested in Old English nor Old Norse, but Förstemann (1900: s.v. *Brecho*) suggests that a personal name *Brecho* might form the first element of the place-name *Breckenheim*, first attested in a thirteenth-century copy of a mid-tenth-century land grant in the form *Brechenheim* (Sickel 1879–1884: 207). There is also some evidence for the existence of a variation element *brec*- in the form of the name *Brecosind* (Förstemann 1900: s.v. *Brecosind*). Björkman (1919: 170–74) suggests that the name is etymologically related to the Old English verb *brecan* 'to break' but rejects a number of earlier interpretations of the name and states that it remains difficult to interpret. Interestingly, he also (1919: 174 and see also 177) states that it 'offenbar kein nordischer Name ist' ('is obviously not a Scandinavian name'). The effort to identify an interpretation of the name is probably a misguided one; in the absence of evidence to the contrary, it seems safe to suppose that, like the vast majority of the personal names in *Beowulf*, *Breca* is an ordinary personal name. The fact that such names have etymologies does not imply that the names were understood as meaningful by their users. What is significant, however, is that this name appears to be very rare, and only attested on the Continent.

There is also some evidence for an Old English name *Brica*, in the form of the place-name *Brickendon* (in Hertfordshire). This is first attested in the form *Bricandun* in a late tenth-century charter (S 894), which is suspicious and recorded only in a fourteenth-century manuscript. This name would be cognate with the similarly rare Continental Germanic name *Bricho/Bricco* (Förstemann 1900: s.v. *Brecho, Bricco*). It is possible that we should see *Breca* as an alternative form of this name. If we do so, however, this does not substantially alter the picture; this remains a rare name, mainly attested on the Continent, and the form with <e> that we see in *Beowulf* is only attested on the Continent. The forms *Breca* in *Beowulf* and *Breoca* in *Widsith* (Malone 1962: 23 (l. 25)) are best explained by the hypothesis that this name was borrowed from the Continent. In the case of *Widsith*, the development of an <eo> spelling reflects a regular back mutation of Old English /e/ that might be expected in the Kentish dialect of Old English (Hogg and Fulk 2011: 1.154–56 §5.105).

We should also note that the character Breca in *Beowulf* forms part of a royal genealogy that alliterates on *B-*. His father is named *Beanstan*, and in both *Beowulf* and *Widsith*, he belongs to the tribe called the *Brondingas*, whose name might be taken to imply an ancestor with the name *Brand/Brond*. Björkman (1919: 174–77) notes some alternative possible etymologies, but the point here is not the actual origin of the tribal name, but rather that an Old English poet or audience might readily have treated the name *Brondingas* as implying a founding figure called *Brand/Brond*, in the same way that the Scyldings are provided with a founding figure called *Scyld*. The alliterating genealogy is reminiscent of the other royal genealogies in the poem, and this, together with the independent appearance of Breca in *Widsith*, tends to support a view of Breca and the Brondings as a legendary dynasty who were not invented by the *Beowulf* poet, but rather drawn from the pre-existing stock of legend. The evidence of the name *Breca*, moreover, suggests that this legendary dynasty may well have been created on the Continent rather than in England, and certainly not in Scandinavia.

The name of Breca's father *Beanstan* presents a more complicated picture. It appears to have a first element *bean* 'bean', but such a first element is not otherwise attested in any Germanic language. Given that the personal names in *Beowulf* are generally explicable as ordinary Germanic names, and given that *Beanstan* has an entirely unremarkable Germanic second element, it would seem that some explanation is required for this anomalous name. One possibility is that it represents a scribal error. *PASE* notes seven individuals called *Beornstan* known from early medieval England, and it is not impossible that *Beanstan* is a scribal error for this name. In 901 AD, King Edward granted Bishop Æthelwulf some land by the River Wylye in Wiltshire, and among the witnesses was a *dux* whose name appears as *Beorstan* (London, British Library, Additional 15350, fol. 88v). In five other charters (S 359, 365, 366, 369, 1443) of the years 900–903 AD, however, a witness called *Beornstan* appears, who is described as a *minister*. In addition to these five charters, there are four more purportedly of the same period which are either certainly later forgeries or suspicious; two of these (S 360, 370) also include *Beornstan minister* as a witness, while the other two (S 380, 1205) simply give the name *Beornstan*. The latter could perhaps be another individual called *Beornstan*, as a priest of this name also attests S 1443 alongside *Beornstan minister*. It seems plausible that *Beorstan dux* and *Beornstan minister* are the same individual, as *PASE* supposes, and *Beorstan* is to be explained as a scribal error for *Beornstan*. A similar error is evidenced, moreover, in the forms *Beorstanus* and *Byrstan* for the name of Bishop Beornstan of Winchester (931–934 AD) in S 407 and S 423 (dubious), respectively (*PASE*: s.v. *Beornstan* 5). Bishop Beornstan's name otherwise appears in forms which represent the final /n/ of the name element *Beorn-* as <n>.

The relative similarity of <r> and <n> in insular minuscule of this date could fairly easily cause a copyist to miss one of the two in a contiguous sequence through eye-skip, producing *Beorstan* or **Beonstan*. In earlier insular hands, moreover, <r> and <n> can be even more similar to one another, as Lapidge (2000: 21–23) notes in his discussion of the possible archetype of the *Beowulf* manuscript. The form **Beonstan*, produced through eye-skip, might well have been corrected by a later scribe to *Beanstan*. It is worth noting, however, that **Beonstan* never actually occurs. This could be because the sequence <beorstan> superficially matches the pattern of an Old English two-element name in combining elements derived from two nouns, *beor* 'beer' and *stan* 'stone', and might therefore be more likely to be created than **Beonstan*. Yet this does not seem particularly satisfactory; an Old English scribe writing or copying a charter witness list would be accustomed to copying Old English personal names and would therefore be unlikely to invent a new name element *beor*. A purely mechanical error, rather than a misreading as a different lexical item, seems more likely in this case, and it is possible that <r> rather than <n> was usually produced simply because scribes wrote the first letter <r> and then, in looking back at their exemplar, mistook the second letter <n> for <r> and moved straight on to the following letter (in this case, <s>).

If *Beanstan* in *Beowulf* represents a garbled form of the name *Beornstan*, then this obviously represents a fairly common name in early medieval England, as the discussion above demonstrates. On the Continent, this name does not appear to be attested, although both elements are attested, albeit the element that generally appears as *stain/stein* is rare as a second element (Förstemann 1900: s.v. *BERA/BERIN, STAINA*). This name also appears to be unattested in Scandinavia, although the second element *-steinn* is not uncommon in the Viking Age runic material assembled by Peterson (2007: s.v. *-stæinn*) and also appears to be attested in the early place-name material collected in Peterson (2004: 28). Although *-biǫrn* is common as a second element in later Scandinavian personal naming, Lind (1905–1915: s.v. *-biǫrn, Biǫrnkarl, Biǫrnmundr, Biǫrnúlfr*) notes only three names in which it appears as a first element, and there do not appear to be any instances in Peterson's (2007) Viking Age runic material. If we treat *Beanstan* as a garbled form of *Beornstan*, then, the likelihood is that it represents an addition to the narrative by an Old English speaker.

This is not, however, the only explanation open to us. We might also consider the possibility that *Beanstan* results from the Anglicisation of a Scandinavian or a Continental Germanic personal name. Although no obvious candidate presents itself for a Scandinavian personal name that might have been Anglicised as *Beanstan*, the problematic first element *Bean-* could potentially be explained with reference to Continental Germanic naming. Förstemann (1900) claims that there are Continental Germanic names with the first elements *Ben-*, *Bon-* and *Baina-*. The latter, which would derive from the Continental Germanic cognates of Old English *ban* 'bone', seems potentially problematic. As Förstemann himself notes, this element is quite rare, and some instances could conceivably derive from an element *Begin-*, a form of *Baga-* with lengthening of the stem (Förstemann 1900: s.v. *BAINA*). There is, however, perhaps only one attested instance of *Bag-* with this stem lengthening, in the name form *Paginolf* (Förstemann 1900: s.v. *BAG*). All in all, this does not seem a likely source for the form *Bean-* in *Beowulf*. The rare Continental Germanic element *Bon-* also seems unlikely to yield *Bean-* in Old English. On the other hand, Förstemann (1900: s.v. *BEN*) suggests that forms of *Ben-* with a geminate final consonant (i.e. *Benn-*) are alternative forms for *Bern-*, the Continental Germanic cognate of Old English *Beorn-*. We might suppose, then, that an Old English scribe was confronted at some point in the manuscript tradition of *Beowulf* with the sequence <benn>, deriving either from a Continental Germanic *Benn-* or *Bern-*, with confusion of <r> and <n> (as discussed above) having caused the <r> of *Bern-* to be miscopied as <n>. Confronted with this sequence <benn>, a scribe might then have misread the first <n> as <u>, due to the similarity of these two letters, each composed of two minims. The resulting sequence <beun> might then have been deliberately adjusted to the more familiar *bean* or the confusion of <u> and <a> in the course of the transmission of *Beowulf*, discussed by Lapidge (2000: 10–19), might have caused such a development. This is clearly a possible line of development for the form *Beanstan*, but it is complex, and perhaps somewhat more complex than the possible development from an Old English name form *Beornstan*, discussed above.

It is difficult, then, to arrive at an entirely satisfactory explanation for the name form *Beanstan* in *Beowulf*. There is no reason to identify this as a form of a Scandinavian name, but it could plausibly derive from an English or a Continental Germanic name, although in neither case is this a straightforward derivation. Perhaps, then, we must leave *Beanstan* as an open case, remarking simply that its origins are uncertain, but that it may well represent a part of the narrative tradition of *Beowulf* that came into existence outside Scandinavia. When set alongside the name of his son Breca, however, this name is probably consistent with a Continental Germanic origin for these two figures; this fits with the hypothesis that Beowulf, his relatives, and the characters from other tribes who interact with him and his relatives, all belong originally to a Continental Germanic narrative tradition.

In the background: Beowulf

The central figure for whom we have entitled the poem *Beowulf* is anything but central to the Hreðling dynasty. This is not a statement that will surprise any student of the poem. But what has not been appreciated heretofore is the extent to which Beowulf and the other figures who form the peripheral sections of the Hreðling family tree have personal names that originate in Continental Germanic dialects, rather than in Scandinavia or in England. The picture is further complicated, moreover, by the fact that Herebeald and Hæðcyn are best interpreted as a Continental Germanic re-working of the divine figures Baldr and Hǫðr from Scandinavian myth. The fact that Wihstan and his son Wiglaf are potentially of Old English origin also adds complexity to the picture. The core

Hreðling dynasty at least could have come from Scandinavia, while Herebeald and Hæðcyn clearly did, although the treatment of the core dynasty differs from that of the mythological interlopers. The question naturally arises whether we are looking here at a wholesale re-working of Scandinavian material on the Continent that involved the replacement of many Scandinavian personal names with Continental Germanic names. This is certainly not impossible, and the development of Herebeald and Hæðcyn seems to provide some evidence to support a hypothesis of this sort. It seems equally possible, however, that Herebeald and Hæðcyn represent an isolated insertion of additional material from Scandinavia, while Beowulf and much of the Hreðling periphery represent Continental Germanic narrative traditions that have been set against the background of the Hreðling dynasty – which could itself represent either a Scandinavian or a Continental Germanic tradition.

2

The Scyldings, Heathobards and Helmings

Just as the Hreðlings and their satellites form an important backdrop for Beowulf as hero and for that part of the poem set in Geatland, the Scyldings and their satellites provide the main setting for the earlier parts of the poem. In this chapter, we consider the Scylding family as well as the named figures at the Scylding court who have no clear family relationship with the Scyldings, such as Unferð and Æschere. We will also consider the royal house of the Heathobards, which is tied to the Scyldings through marriage, while the next chapter will turn to the royal house of the Scilfings, which is also linked through marriage to the Scyldings. As with the previous chapter, we will consider the core of the dynasty before turning to the peripheral groups.

The Scylding dynasty

The core of the Scylding dynasty is large, consisting of the main line of succession from Scyld Scefing through Beow to Healfdene, whose sons Heorogar, Hroðgar and Halga and grandsons Heoroweard, Hreðric, Hroðmund and Hroðulf correspond in some but not all cases to figures who are also attested in Scandinavian narrative tradition. Healfdene and his descendants have names that are consistent with Scandinavian origins, and this is consonant with the evidence for several of these figures in Scandinavian narrative traditions. When we consider Healfdene's ancestors, however, we find that their names do not point towards a Scandinavian origin, but rather they suggest elaboration of the ancestor figures of the royal line in Continental Germanic and English contexts.

Healfdene's Ancestors

The originating figure of the Scyldings should, if we simply follow the logic of the tribal name Scylding, be Scyld. In English royal genealogical traditions, however, Scyld has a father Sceaf, and this father appears to be reflected in the patronymic form *Scefing* in *Beowulf*. This could be taken to imply that the *Beowulf* poet knew of a father for Scyld called *Scef*, and we therefore begin our consideration of Healfdene's ancestors with this name. Peterson (2004) does not list *Scef* among those in *Beowulf* that she identifies as plausibly Proto-Scandinavian, nor does it appear in Viking Age runic materials (Peterson 2007) or in the names of the earliest settlers of Iceland in *Landnámabók* (Benediktsson 1968). It does appear in Snorri Sturluson's *Prose Edda*, but only as part of Snorri's account of the Skjǫldung dynasty (corresponding to the Scyldings of *Beowulf*), and is clearly based on English sources, since Snorri gives the name as *Seskef*, mistakenly including the Old English definite article *se* as part of the name (Faulkes 1988: 5; Bruce 2002: 58). There is, then, no reason to identify this name as Scandinavian in origin. There is also no sign of a similar name in the Continental Germanic materials assembled by Förstemann (1900).

There is little evidence that this name formed part of Old English naming traditions. *PASE* records no bearers of this name apart from the legendary ancestor figure who appears in *Beowulf* and in the West Saxon royal genealogy recorded in some manuscripts of the *Anglo-Saxon Chronicle* under the year 855 AD (see, e.g., Taylor 1983: 33; O'Brien O'Keeffe 2001: 57) and in Æthelweard's *Chronicon* (Campbell 1962: 33). However, there is one reference in the *Domesday Book* to an individual called *Sceua* (Munby 1982: §69.20) which could possibly represent a form of an Old English name *Scefa* or *Sceafa*, although von Feilitzen (1937: 356) decisively rejects such an identification, preferring to interpret this name as an Old Norse by-name *Skeifi*, related to the attested Scandinavian name *Skeifr*. Even if we did accept this identification, however, this would not demonstrate that this name formed part of Old English naming traditions; the possibility would remain open that the name attested in the *Domesday Book* derived from the ancestor figure, rather than existing prior to the creation of this figure. A similar consideration applies to the form *Sceafa* which appears in *Widsith* as the name of a legendary ruler of the Lombards (Malone 1962: 24 (l. 32)). Chambers (1912: 201) and Bruce (2002: 15–17) both treat this figure as another instance of the figure Sceaf of *Beowulf* and the English royal genealogical tradition (see also the discussion of different views on this question in Malone 1962: 193–94). This seems a plausible position to take, and we should therefore consider the development of this figure.

The instances and uses of the figure Sceaf in medieval literature have been explored at length by Bruce (2002). This discussion will, necessarily, be briefer but also different in focus, trying to elucidate how this figure came into being.

While Sceaf is mentioned not infrequently in medieval literature, it is worth noting that he appears only in texts from England and in a few Icelandic genealogies that clearly derive from English textual traditions (see the collection of texts in Bruce 2002: 89-157). The origins of this figure are to be sought, then, in English tradition, and the earliest references to this figure are those in *Beowulf* and *Widsith*. The reference in *Widsith* provides no information beyond the bare fact that someone called *Sceafa* ruled the Lombards, a fact that features nowhere else in the references to Sceaf assembled by Bruce (as Bruce 2002: 16 points out). Niles (1999: 191-92) has plausibly suggested that this represents an effort to claim the Lombards as one of the ancestral tribes of the English by ascribing them a ruler from the West Saxon royal genealogical tradition. The origins of Sceaf are to be sought, therefore, in *Beowulf* and the genealogical tradition.

The genealogical tradition probably post-dates *Beowulf*, with the addition of the figures Scyld and Sceaf to the West Saxon genealogy likely to have taken place around the time of Alfred the Great (in the *Anglo-Saxon Chronicle*, these figures first appear in the genealogy ascribed to Æthelwulf, Alfred's father, under the year 855; see Davis 1992: 29-30). *Beowulf*, then, probably represents a witness to the tradition from which this genealogy extracted the figures of Scyld and Sceaf. If we consider the genealogical tradition as deriving from *Beowulf* or something very like it, then the most striking point of difference between the genealogical tradition and its source is that the miraculous arrival by boat is ascribed in *Beowulf* to Scyld, but in the genealogical tradition to Sceaf. This is not immediately obvious in the *Anglo-Saxon Chronicle*, where Sceaf is not described as arriving mysteriously by boat as a child, although Davis (1992: 30) may well be right to see the birth of Sceaf in Noah's ark as an echo of this narrative that incorporates it into Christian tradition. The earliest clear reference to Sceaf's childhood arrival by boat comes in Æthelweard's *Chronicon*. Æthelweard, writing in the late tenth century, provides a version of the *Anglo-Saxon Chronicle* entry for 855 to which he adds a brief narrative of Sceaf's origins (text and translation from Bruce 2002: 91-92):

> Ipse Scef cum uno dromone aduectus est in insula oceani que dicitur Scani, armis circundatus, eratque ualde recens puer, et ab incolis illius terræ ignotus. Attamen ab eis suscipitur, et ut familiarem diligenti animo eum custodierunt, et post in regem eligunt; de cuius prosapia ordinem trahit Aðulf rex.

> And this Sceaf arrived with one light ship in the island of the ocean which is called Skaney, with arms all round him. He was a very young boy, and unknown to the people of that land, but he was received by them, and they guarded him

with diligent attention as one who belonged to them, and elected him king. From his family King Æthelwulf derived his descent.

Leaving aside for a moment the obvious difference that Æthelweard ascribes the infant voyage to Sceaf while the *Beowulf* poet ascribes it to Scyld, the narrative that Æthelweard provides here bears some similarity to, but is not entirely in step with, the narrative of Scyld's arrival in *Beowulf*. In the poem, we are told that Scyld was sent forth as a child over the sea (ll. 45–46) and that he was 'found destitute' by the Spear-Danes (l. 7a). The poem does not specify that the child was sent in a boat, although this would be an unsurprising inference for an audience to draw. The fact that the child was surrounded by weapons is also absent from *Beowulf* which, in contrast, suggests that he was destitute. An audience could be forgiven, however, for imagining that Scyld was found with treasures as a child. In describing the treasures assembled in Scyld's funerary ship, the *Beowulf* poet observes that 'nalæs hī hine læssan lācum tēodan, / þēodgestrēonum, þonne þā dydon / þē hine æt frumsceafte forð onsendon / ǣnne ofer ȳðe umborwesende' (Fulk, Bjork and Niles 2008: 4, ll. 43–46; 'not at all did they provide him [Scyld] with fewer gifts, treasures of a nation, than did those who sent him forth at the beginning, alone over the waves as a child'). An inattentive listener or reader might suppose, on coming across this statement, that Scyld arrived by sea in a boat surrounded by weapons, like that in which he is described departing this world. One can reach this conclusion, however, only if one has forgotten that nearly forty lines earlier, Scyld is described as arriving in a state of destitution. As Fulk, Bjork and Niles (2008: 116) rightly point out, this statement comparing the treasures of Scyld's arrival with those of his departure is clearly an instance of litotes, and the *Beowulf* poet does not intend for a moment to suggest that Scyld arrived surrounded by costly weapons. It is likely, then, that Æthelweard's narrative of Sceaf's arrival is based on *Beowulf*, or something very like it, but filtered through some misunderstanding of the narrative.

Much has been made of the potential agricultural associations of Sceaf (see, for instance, Tolley 1996; Bruce 2002: 24–29). It should be noted, however, that the earliest material relating to this figure contains no overt reference to agricultural concerns: in *Beowulf*, Sceaf is no more than a name that we might infer from the patronymic form *Scefing*; in Æthelweard's version of the child in the boat narrative, in which Sceaf features as the child, Sceaf is surrounded by weapons, not by symbols of agriculture; in the genealogical tradition, he features either as a name only, or as a son of Noah born in the ark; and in *Widsith* he is transferred to the Lombards as a king, with no mention of agricultural associations. In this material, then, it is only the possibility that Sceaf's name derives from the word *sceaf* 'sheaf [of grain]' that suggests agricultural associations. The agricultural resonances of this figure are not made explicit until the twelfth century, when William of Malmesbury provides another version of Sceaf's arrival (text and translation from Bruce 2002: 157):

> Iste, ut ferunt, in quandam insulam Germanniae Scandzam, de qua Jordanes historiographus Gothorum loquitur, appulsus naui sine remige puerulus, posito ad caput frumenti manipulo dormiens, ideoque Sceaf nuncupatus, ab hominibus regionis illius pro miraculo exceptus et sedulo nutritus, adulta aetate regnauit in oppido quod tunc Slaswic, nunc uero Haithebi appellatur.

> This Sceaf, they say, landed on an island in Germany called Scandza mentioned by Jordanes the historian of the Goths, as a small child in a ship without a crew, sleeping with a sheaf of wheat laid by his head, and hence was called Sheaf. The men of that country welcomed him as something miraculous and brought him up carefully, and on reaching manhood he ruled a town then called *Slaswic* but now Hedeby.

It is evident that William's version of the narrative is broadly similar to that of Æthelweard, but William has made an effort to identify the island on which Sceaf arrived based on his knowledge of Jordanes. At the same time, William provides apparently contradictory geographical information in ascribing the rulership of Hedeby on the Danish peninsula to Sceaf. For the purposes of this discussion, however, the key innovation in William's version is the sheaf of wheat at Sceaf's head. This may have featured in some lost source employed by William, but it seems simpler to suppose that William invented this detail based on his belief that the name *Sceaf* was derived from the Old English word *sceaf* 'sheaf'. William evidently knew Æthelweard's *Chronicon*, as he passes comment on it in his preface (Mynors, Thomson and Winterbottom 1998-1999: 1.14-15) and it therefore seems reasonable to suppose that his narrative derived from that source. William was also able to read Old English, as he based his life of St Wulfstan closely on an Old English version (Winterbottom and Thomson 2002: 10-11; see also p. xvi on how William may have handled this source) and elsewhere in his *Gesta Regum Anglorum* he evinces a specific interest in the meaning of another Old English personal name, glossing the name *Thunor* as 'thunder' (Mynors, Thomson and Winterbottom 1998-1999: 1.388-89). In view of his evident interest in Old English etymologies, it would not be surprising, therefore, if William readily identified the name *Sceaf* as deriving from the Old

English word *sceaf* 'sheaf' and developed the narrative in accordance with this identification.

There is, however, some reason to believe that William may have been following pre-existing traditions associating Sceaf with a sheaf of grain. The thirteenth-century *Abingdon Chronicle* describes a peculiar event in which the land holdings of the monastery of Abingdon were miraculously confirmed by a shield bearing a sheaf of grain and a taper that was set afloat on the Thames by the monks (see Tolley 1996: 11). While this could be dismissed as a later fabrication, perhaps influenced by William's work, Tolley (1996: 11) makes a strong argument for a lost source for this narrative from the late Old English period. If there were such a source, then it is possible that William had another source or sources besides Æthelweard's *Chronicon* that related to Sceaf's arrival, and that the sheaf at the child's head derived from this source (or sources). The possible relationship between the Abingdon narrative and the Scyld/Sceaf narrative is, however, tantalisingly difficult to characterise. The conjunction of a floating shield and a sheaf of grain seems as if it might in some way echo a narrative involving an arrival by boat combined with someone whose name relates to the word *scield* 'shield' and someone whose name relates to the word *sceaf* 'sheaf', but the similarities do not seem to compel certainty that there is a connection. If there is a connection, however, it would appear to suggest the same sort of coupling of Scyld and Sceaf that seems to exist in *Beowulf* and this would be at odds with the ascription of the miraculous arrival by boat to Sceaf in the works of Æthelweard and William.

The development of the narrative tradition of Sceaf's arrival is clearly complex and problematic. Whether the association of Sceaf with grain was created by William of Malmesbury or in the late Old English period, however, there is little, if any, clue in *Beowulf* to such a relationship. The fact that the mysterious arrival by boat is ascribed in the poem to Scyld rather than Sceaf, moreover, suggests that we might wish to reassess the origins of the figure Sceaf as he appears (albeit fleetingly) in *Beowulf*. If we discard the supposed connection with grain, we might reasonably ask whether the name Sceaf could be accounted for in other ways. We should consider, moreover, whether we are even dealing with a name here. Given Scyld's mysterious arrival by boat, it is very curious that the name of his father appears to be known. The arrival by boat might be expected to have obscured Scyld's antecedents, and we should therefore think about the possible interpretations of *Scefing* as an epithet rather than a patronymic. The idea that it might mean 'associated with a sheaf' has, of course, been suggested (Fulk, Bjork and Niles 2008: 111), but this brings us back to the tenuous association with grain. Given the evidence presented so far in this book, however, for the influence of Continental Germanic narrative materials in the development of *Beowulf*, an alternative possibility presents itself. The form *scefing* in the *Beowulf* manuscript clearly contains the Old English suffix *-ing*, but the initial element *scef-*, while it could be a rare spelling of Old English *sceaf* 'sheaf', is also remarkably similar to the Old High German word *skef* 'ship'. This appears in the spelling *skef* in Tatian's gospel harmony (see, for instance, St Gall, Stiftsbibliothek, Cod. Sang. 56, p. 120; Sievers 1960: 108–9) and in the spelling *schef* in the Old High German *Physiologus* (Steinmeyer 1916: 130). Given that Old English scribes rarely used the letter <k>, *scef* would represent the most obvious transliteration of Old High German *skef* for an Old English scribe who had failed to identify the word as cognate with Old English *scipu*. Since *-ing* is a patronymic form in Continental Germanic dialects as well as in Old English, this raises the possibility that a Continental Germanic nickname *Scefing* 'son of the ship' was brought into the English narrative tradition and there reinterpreted in relation to the Old English word *sceaf* 'sheaf'. Such a nickname would make perfect sense for a child who arrives mysteriously in a boat and would also remove the logical difficulty created by knowing the name of the father of a mysterious foundling. While it is difficult to arrive at any certainty on this point, it seems to the present author that we should seriously consider the possibility that this is the origin of the form *scefing* in *Beowulf*.

It seems possible, then, that the forms of the name *Scef* that appear to relate to the Old English word *sceaf* 'sheaf' are the result of folk etymologisation of an otherwise puzzling name form deriving from a Continental Germanic narrative involving the mysterious arrival by *skef* 'ship' of an infant who was therefore nicknamed 'the son of the ship'. This process might be thought to have involved some sort of transmission of written material whose Continental Germanic spelling is reflected in the form *Scef* in *Beowulf*. It is not impossible, however, that such a transmission could also have taken place through oral transmission, although this seems somewhat less likely to have created confusion of this sort. The difficulties presented by this supposed personal name, which does not appear to have existed as a personal name anywhere in the Germanic-speaking world apart from in the specific genealogical tradition concerning this figure, are dispelled by this interpretation of the supposed patronymic *Scefing* in *Beowulf*. The genealogical tradition can be seen as extrapolating a figure named *Sceaf* from this patronymic form, which itself makes a great deal more sense within the narrative of *Beowulf* as a nickname which reflects Scyld's mysterious origins. This can be seen as further evidence for the transmission of narrative materials for *Beowulf* from the Continent.

If the by-name *Scefing* relates to a Continental Germanic narrative of the foundling Scyld, then we should, of course, expect the name *Scyld* to be one that could have originated on the Continent. More than this, it seems unlikely that this name originated anywhere other than the Continent. This name is one of the key elements in the Scylding dynastic tradition, which is attested both in English royal genealogies and in Scandinavian narrative texts. Outside this tradition, there is little evidence for this name; Peterson (2004) does not list this among her plausibly Proto-Scandinavian names from *Beowulf*, nor does it appear in Viking Age runic material from Scandinavia (Peterson 2007) or among the earliest settlers of Iceland (Benediktsson 1968). It is also lacking from the *Durham Liber Vitae* and from the evidence for England assembled in *PASE* (leaving aside the instances in royal genealogies, which are noted here). Only on the Continent is there some slight evidence for this name. Förstemann (1900: s.v. *SCILDU*) notes a place-name, *Schiltasdorf*, that could contain this name, as well as a handful of Continental Germanic names in which *scilt* is employed as a variation element in two-element names (namely *Sciltolf*, *Gotascilt* and *Lantscild*) and a place-name *Sciltenkeim* which might contain a weak name *Scilto* derived from this element. It is particularly interesting to note, moreover, that the form *Sciltung* appears as the name of one of the hosts of Saxon hostages in a ninth-century list of hostages and their hosts in Alamannia (Boretius and Krause 1883–1897: 1.234; see also Rembold 2018: 58). This name appears to correspond precisely to the Old English form *Scylding*, used in reference to the Danes in *Beowulf* as the 'followers of Scyld'. We might, however, posit that the figure Scyld could have arisen as a misunderstanding of a Continental Germanic personal name *Sciltung* as a patronymic, from which *Scyld* was derived as a back formation.

We must also consider, however, the form *Sculd* found as the name of a witness in a mid-ninth-century charter related to Freising (see Figure 2.1). The long bar that passes through the <l> and the ascender of the <d> in this name form could be a mere otiose stroke, but before diagnosing it as otiose, we must consider the possibility that it is an abbreviation mark, comparable with the very clear abbreviation marks passing through the descender of the letter <p> in a number of names in *-perht* in this witness list. If it is an abbreviation mark, then it would seem plausible that this may, in fact, be another form of the name *Sciltung*, perhaps to be expanded as *Sculdung. The transmission of a form such as this to early medieval England would explain the Old English form *Scylding*, in which the Old English form *-ing* of the patronymic suffix could have caused i-mutation of the /u/ in the root element, with the resulting root vowel being

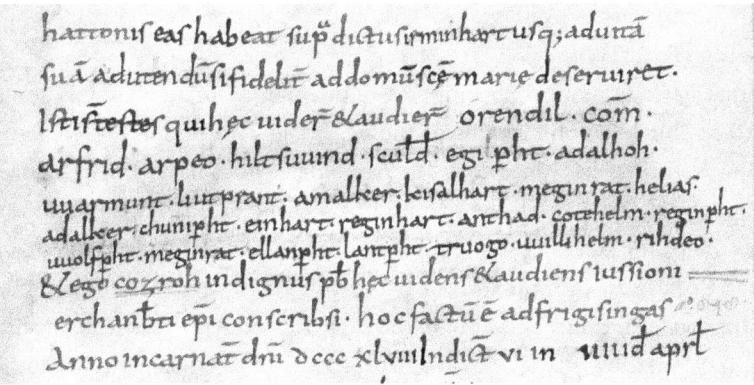

Figure 2.1 Detail of a charter of 848 AD recorded in Munich, Bayerisches Hauptstaatsarchiv, HL Freising 3a. [Available at: http://daten.digitale-sammlungen.de/bsb00003037/image_751 March 2019].

spelt <y>, as is usual in Old English orthographic practice. That *Sciltung* and *Sculd*[*ung*?] are name forms from Alamannia and Bavaria, contiguous areas in the south of what we would now call Germany, suggests that their relative rarity may be the result of their restriction to this region.

When we consider the other names formed with this element, moreover, we find that they, too, probably belong to this region. *Schiltasdorf* may well refer to Sillersdorf, just north west of Salzburg in Bavaria (Förstemann 1913–1916: s.v. *Schiltasdorf*), while *Sciltenkeim*, from which Förstemann (1900: s.v. *SCILDU*) infers a weak name form *Scilto*, is in all probability Schiltigheim near Strasbourg (see Förstemann 1913–1916: s.v. *Sciltenkeim*). The names *Sciltolf*, *Gotascilt* and *Lantscild* all occur in confraternity books. *Sciltolf* appears in a list of the brothers of the community of *Suraburc* (Surbourg) in Alsace (Piper 1884: 222 (col. 228, l. 32)); *Lantscild* features in a list relating to the monastery of Hornbach (Piper 1884: 102 (col. 342, l. 3)); and *Gotascilt* has been added to a page of the older St Gall confraternity book adjacent to a list of names relating to Strasbourg (although the form in the text is, in fact, *Gotasilt*, raising questions about the identity of the second element; see Piper 1884: 41 (col. 101, l. 6) and Schmid 1986: 121). It is not entirely clear how much weight we should place on this evidence, given that our records of Continental Germanic personal names may disproportionately represent this region. Nevertheless, whether we treat both *Sciltung* and *Sculd*[*ung*?] as cognate with *Scylding*, or treat the latter as *Sculd* and see it as cognate with the name *Scyld* itself, it seems clear that the origins of the figure called *Scyld* may be better sought on the Continent than in England or

Scandinavia, and possibly particularly in the southern region stretching from Alsace to Bavaria.

That *Scyld* is in all probability a Continental Germanic name is somewhat startling, but the complexities of the genealogical tradition are compounded when we turn to his son, Beow. The name *Beow* does not actually occur in the extant text of *Beowulf*. In the manuscript, we find at lines 18 and 53 the name *Beowulf* for the son of Scyld. It has long been recognised, however, that a figure called *Beaw* features as the son of a figure called *Sceldwa* or *Scealdwa* in the West Saxon royal genealogy as set out in the entry for 855 AD in some manuscripts of the *Anglo-Saxon Chronicle* (Taylor 1983: 33 s.a. 856 AD; Bately 1986: 46 s.a. 855 AD; Cubbin 1996: 23 s.a. 855 AD; O'Brien O'Keeffe 2001: 57 s.a. 856 AD). Given the similarity between the names of both father and son in these sources, it is generally held that the form *Beowulf* for this figure in the manuscript is the result of a confusion with the hero of the poem at some point in the poem's transmission (for a useful summary of the treatment of this evidence, see Fulk, Bjork and Niles 2008: xlviii-l). This seems a persuasive argument and, if it is correct, then Beow and his ancestors Sceaf and Scyld represent a dynastic tradition that was well known in early medieval England.

The name *Beow*, however, is anomalous among the personal names in *Beowulf* in that it is not clearly attested as a personal name applied to actual human beings. In a charter of 931 AD granting land at Ham in Wiltshire, the bounds include as a landmark *beowan hammes hecgan* (S 416). This could be taken to contain a personal name *Beowa*, but this would be a weakly inflected personal name, thus not identical with *Beow/Beaw*. We might also be wary of assuming that this landmark includes a personal name. We should also consider whether the name in *Beowulf* was, in fact, originally *Beow*. The Old English word *beow* means 'barley' and much has been made of the possibility that *Beow* and *Scef* (compare the Old English word *sceaf* 'sheaf') reflect some sort of concern with the production of cereal crops (see, for instance, Fulk 1989; Bruce 2002: 27-29). The name form *Beow* is, however, a conjecture based on the evidently mistaken form *Beowulf* in the *Beowulf* manuscript. In the *Anglo-Saxon Chronicle*, the son of *Sceldwa/Scealdwa* is consistently called *Beaw*. This corresponds exactly in form not with the word *beow* 'barley', but with the word *beaw* 'gad-fly' (*Dictionary of Old English*, s.v. *bēaw*). It is perfectly feasible that the copyist who changed the name in lines 18 and 53 to *Beowulf* did so because they encountered the form *Beaw* rather than *Beow* and believed it to be an error for *Beowulf*. We need not assume that in earlier versions of the poem this figure was called *Beow*.

This also raises the possibility that the name of this figure is an ordinary, albeit very rare, personal name. A runic inscription on a small, tweezer-like object discovered in 2009 near Baconsthorpe, Norfolk, is interpreted by Hines (2011: 290) as recording the name of the rune-carver as a form of *Beaw*. This interpretation has been challenged by Bammesberger (2012), who presents an alternative reading in which the personal name is disposed of entirely; this is an ingenious suggestion, but one that seems to involve unnecessary complexities. A more serious challenge to the existence of the name *Beaw* (outside the royal genealogies), however, is posed by Waxenberger's (2012: 183 and 191) reading of the Baconsthorpe inscription, which notes the difficulty of deciding whether the name being represented is *Beaw* or a variant form of *Beadu*. The latter would represent a name formed from a common personal name element and is thus a plausible reading. However, the inscription is simply difficult to read at the relevant point, and we thus cannot discount the possibility that it does contain a form of *beaw*, apparently used as the name of the carver.

There are numerous uncertainties here. An Old English name *Beaw*, deriving from a word meaning 'gad-fly', would be plausible in that it parallels other personal names deriving from names of insects, such as *Wicga* (PASE: s.v. *Wicgga 1–2*; Bosworth and Toller: s.v. *wicga*) and *Budda* (PASE: s.v. *Budda 1*; S 29; Parsons and Styles 2000: s.v. *budda*). However, we cannot be sure that it is attested outside the genealogical tradition, although it is not implausible that this name appears on the Baconsthorpe inscription. If this were an ordinary personal name, it would appear to be one that developed in England. Even if the name were created purely as part of the development of the genealogical tradition, it would appear to represent an English development, and this is also consonant with the absence of this name from Scandinavian materials that record a king named *Skjǫldr*, cognate with Old English *Scyld*. This would suggest, then, that the adoption of *Beaw* into the narrative tradition of *Beowulf* formed part of the English stage of development of the poem.

The stages of the Scylding genealogy above Healfdene are, then, somewhat complex. While Scyld Scefing appears to represent a Continental Germanic development, his son Beow is best explained as an English addition to the genealogy. In some ways this is an unsurprising pattern, reflecting the fact that the early stages of the English royal genealogies demonstrate the engagement of the early medieval English with their continental past. To find a figure whose name reflects Continental Germanic naming traditions, and whose son's name reflects Old English personal naming practices, is essentially consistent with a view of these genealogies as developing relatively early in the Old English period from traditions that belong to the period of the migrations. As we shall see, however, this early section of the genealogy contrasts sharply in this respect with the section that follows it in *Beowulf*, which seems to owe more to a Scandinavian narrative tradition. This is perhaps also unsurprising when we reflect that Scyld and Beow do not have the same descendants in the English royal genealogies that they have in *Beowulf*; it makes sense to see the presence of these figures in *Beowulf* as the result of their addition in England to the Scandinavian narrative traditions surrounding Healfdene and his descendants. The Skjǫldung dynasty of Scandinavian tradition, in other words, probably gained its name some time after the formation of this tradition in Scandinavia, as a result of influence from English narrative tradition in which Scyld had been grafted onto this dynasty.

Healfdene and his Descendants

While not all Healfdene's descendants have personal names that are unique to Scandinavia, some of them do have names that are unlikely to have originated elsewhere, and all of them have names that could have originated in Scandinavian tradition. To begin with Healfdene himself, his name is treated by Peterson (2004: 38) as one of the Proto-Scandinavian names in *Beowulf*. This is consistent with the fact that this name is not infrequently recorded in Viking Age Scandinavian runic inscriptions (Peterson 2007: s.v. *Halfdan*) and occurs also in *Landnámabók*, although notably here it occurs only as the name of three different kings (Benediktsson 1968: 1.136, 2.314, 2.370). This name does not appear to form part of native Old English onomastic traditions, although it does appear in a few early medieval English sources. The name was borne by two of the Viking kings who ruled part or, at times, the whole of Northumbria in the ninth and tenth centuries, and thus appears in sources such as the *Anglo-Saxon Chronicle* (see, for instance, Bately 1986: 48–50; Taylor 1983: 35–37, 47; O'Brien O'Keeffe 2001: 59–61, 73). The name also appears in the *Durham Liber Vitae*, but only in post-Conquest additions to the manuscript, and John Insley and David Rollason treat this name as being of Scandinavian origin (see Rollason and Rollason 2007: 2.224). Besides these sources, a *dux* of this name appears in the tenth-century (or purportedly tenth-century) charters S 407, 425, 428 and 679, and a *princeps regis* bearing this name appears in S 952, a charter of Cnut. The name is also not uncommon in the *Domesday Book*. This name is also not to be found on the Continent, with the exception of a single instance in the confraternity book of the abbey of Reichenau (Piper 1884: 341 (col. 636, l. 20)), where it appears in the vicinity of various clearly Scandinavian name forms such as *Suein*, *Durchil*,

Arnchetil and *Toki*. This confraternity book, recording names from the eleventh and twelfth centuries, is notable for its inclusion of large numbers of Scandinavian personal names (Jónsson and Jørgensen 1923; Melefors 2002: 965). All of this is consistent with this name deriving solely from Scandinavian onomastic traditions.

Healfdene's son Halga also has a name that suggests that he originated in Scandinavian tradition. His name does not appear to be attested in early medieval England; it occurs neither in *PASE* nor in the *Durham Liber Vitae*. Peterson (2004: 38) treats this name as one of those names in *Beowulf* that can be characterised as Proto-Scandinavian and, indeed, this is a very common name in later Scandinavian sources (see, for instance, Peterson 2007: s.v. *Hælgi*; Benediktsson 1968: 1.50, 1.186–87, 2.250, 2.320 *inter alia*). This name is also found on the Continent, although it is not very common (Förstemann 1900: s.v. *HAILAGA*). It could, then, have developed either in Scandinavia or on the Continent, although the former is a good deal more likely in view of the enormous popularity of this name in Scandinavia.

Halga's son Hroðulf also has a name that is likely to have developed in Scandinavia, although here the evidence is slightly more complicated. Peterson (2004: 39) treats this name as one of the Proto-Scandinavian names in *Beowulf*, noting that both of its component elements occur in her corpus of names from early Scandinavian runic inscriptions. These two elements are attested in combination in the Viking Age, appearing in the form *Hrólfr* as the name of three of the earliest settlers of Iceland mentioned in *Landnámabók* (Benediktsson 1968: 1.104, 2.266, 2.358) and in runic inscriptions from this period (Peterson 2007: s.v. *Hroðulfr*). The contracted form of the name *Hrólfr* is, however, the more common form in Viking Age material (Peterson 2007: s.v. *Hrōlfr*) and it is worth remarking that this contracted form would be far less likely than the full form to be interpreted by an Old English speaker as corresponding to an Old English form *Hroðulf*. The same observation could be made in relation to a speaker of a Continental Germanic dialect; this name is fairly common on the Continent (Förstemann 1900: s.v. *HROTHI*), but the continental forms of the name (forms such as *Hrodulf*, *Chrodulf*, *Hrotulf* and *Hruodolf*) suggest that a Continental Germanic speaker would have had some difficulty in identifying Old Norse *Hrólfr* with this name. There is, then, good reason to think that the figure who bears this name, if he originated in Scandinavian tradition, did so relatively early on, before *Hrólfr* became the more common form in Scandinavia, and was also passed into continental or English tradition fairly early on. This is a very imprecise dating mechanism, however, given that there was clearly a period of overlap between the uncontracted and contracted forms, and it would be extremely difficult to establish a precise date when the uncontracted form could be said with certainty to be entirely obsolete.

That the figure in *Beowulf* who bears this name appears in later Scandinavian tradition with the contracted form of the name (Jónsson 1959: 1.25 *et passim*) suggests that his name came into existence at an early stage, wherever in the Germanic-speaking world this took place. We could envisage the importation of this figure into Scandinavia from England or the Continent at a period before the contractions took place in Scandinavia that produced the form *Hrólfr*. Yet it is a good deal more likely, in the present author's view, that this figure originated in Scandinavia and was transmitted from there to other parts of the Germanic-speaking world at an early date in its uncontracted form. This is consistent with the generally Scandinavian character of the names *Healfdene* and *Halga* that we have already noted, and which contrasts, as we are beginning to establish, with the non-Scandinavian character of many of the other names in *Beowulf*. While other narrative traditions that have fed into the poem seem unlikely to be Scandinavian in origin, Healfdene and his descendants do seem good candidates for a place of origin in Scandinavia. As to whether this particular name was transmitted directly to England from Scandinavia, or via an intervening Continental Germanic tradition, the form of the name offers no clear evidence. It is true that the Continental Germanic forms noted above lack initial /w/ in the second element, but, as we shall see in our discussion of the name *Heorogar* below, late Old English spellings of personal names in *-wulf* frequently indicate loss of the initial /w/ as well. We can therefore say only that the balance of probability is that this figure was originally Scandinavian, and his name found its way into *Beowulf* either directly from Scandinavia or via the Continent.

Healfdene's other two sons and their children bear names that do exist outside Scandinavia, but which are also consistent with origins in Scandinavian tradition. To begin with Heorogar and his son Heoroweard, Peterson (2004: 38) includes both names among those she regards as plausibly Proto-Scandinavian, noting the presence of their shared first element in her early runic data and the second element of each name in her corpus of early Scandinavian place-names. The particular combination of elements in *Heoroweard* is also attested in Viking Age Scandinavian runic inscriptions (Peterson 2007: s.v. *Hiǫrvarðr*), but the combination in *Heorogar* is not attested in the Scandinavian Viking Age runic inscriptions surveyed in Peterson (2007), although both elements are (Peterson 2007: s.v. *-arr, Hiǫr-*; note that in the case of the second element, it falls together with some other elements due to phonetic developments in Old Norse). These names could certainly, therefore, have developed in Scandinavia. These combinations of elements can also be found in the Continental Germanic materials assembled by Förstemann (1900: s.v. *HIRU*), and although the first element is not very common on the Continent, it is clearly attested, while both second elements are very common across the Germanic-speaking world. A Continental Germanic origin is thus also possible, but Scandinavian origin is probably to be preferred in view of the evidence for Scandinavian origin of other members of Healfdene's family.

It seems unlikely, moreover, that these names could have arisen in an English context; in Old English naming traditions the first element *Heoru-* is not clearly attested. *PASE* offers no clear instances of names formed with this element (the headform *Heoruwulf 1* in *PASE* refers to instances of this name in *Domesday Book*, but these could all represent Scandinavian or Continental Germanic forms). The name form *Heruuald* in the *Durham Liber Vitae* has been interpreted (Müller 1901: 91) as possibly containing this first element but, as Insley, Rollason and McClure point out, the first element of this name form could very well be *Here-*, which is common in Old English personal naming (Rollason and Rollason 2007: 2.127). They also point, however, to the name of Harleston in Suffolk as containing a personal name formed with this first element, referring to Ekwall (1960: s.v. *Harleston Sf*) for details concerning the history of this place-name. The evidence here is, however, not entirely straightforward. There are a number of place-names that could contain personal names formed with this element; Ekwall (1960: s.v. *Harlaston St, Harlaxton Li, Harlescott Sa, Harlesden Mx, Harleston D, Harleston Nf, Harleston Sf, Harlestone Np, Harston Ca*) notes *Harlaston* in Staffordshire, *Harlaxton* in Lincolnshire, *Harlescott* in Shropshire, *Harlesden* in Middlesex, *Harleston* in Durham, *Harleston* in Norfolk, *Harleston* in Suffolk, *Harlestone* in Northamptonshire and *Harston* in Cambridgeshire. To these we can also add *Hardmead* in Buckinghamshire (Mawer and Stenton 1925: 36). It is not, however, clear that all of these place-names do contain a personal name formed with a first element *Heoru-*; in some cases, it is difficult to distinguish between the Old English name element *Here-* and the possible Old English name element *Heoru-* in these names, while in other cases a single element personal name, unrelated to the putative element *Heoru-*, may be involved.

In the cases of *Harlaxton*, *Harlescott* and *Harleston* in Durham, the early attestations only include forms where the first element of the personal name is realised as *Her-* or *Har-*. There is no way to decide whether these forms represent *Heoru-* or *Here*. In the cases of *Hardmead*, *Harlesden* and *Harlestone*, the early forms *Herulfmede*, *Herulvestune* and *Herolvestune*, respectively, all from the *Domesday Book*, do not provide clear evidence for a first element *Heoru-* as opposed to *Here-*. In these forms, the second element *-wulf*, phonetically reduced by the loss of the semi-vowel /w/, obscures the final vowel of the first element, leaving us unable to decide between *Heoru-* and *Here-* (as Mawer and Stenton 1925: 36 note). The use of <e> rather than <eo> for the root vowel in these forms also tends to suggest *Here-* rather than *Heoru-*. This leaves us with *Harlaston* in Staffordshire, first attested in the early eleventh-century will of Wulfric, in the form *Heorlfestun*, and *Harleston* in Norfolk, *Harleston* in Suffolk and *Harston* in Cambridgeshire. According to Ekwall (1960: s.v. *Harleston Nf*, *Harleston Sf*, *Harston Ca*), the *Harlestons* in Norfolk and Suffolk and *Harston* in Cambridgeshire are all potential candidates for the place attested in the will of Ætheling Æthelstan (1014 AD) in the form *Heorulfestun*. These forms with the root vowel represented as <eo> have a stronger claim to be considered as instances of names containing a first element *Heoru-*, although neither of these early forms is decisive.

To begin with *Harlaston* in Staffordshire, the will of Wulfric (1002 x 1004 AD) is extant in a copy made 'towards the end of the eleventh century' (Sawyer 1979: xx). The form *Heorlfestun* that appears in this document is puzzling, on the face of it, since the second element of the underlying personal name is not clearly represented. We might wonder, for example, whether the second element was *-lāf* or *-wulf* (possibly in a reduced form *-ulf*), and indeed Horovitz (2003: 2.351) offers both possibilities as interpretations of the origins of this name. The later attestations of the name noted by Horovitz are, however, largely consistent with a second element *-lāf*; apart from the form *Horuluestone* in the *Domesday Book*, suggesting *-wulf*, the twelfth- and thirteenth-century forms Horovitz lists are *Herlaueston*, *Herlaveston'* and *Herlaweston*, all of which suggest *-lāf* rather than *-wulf*. The name also appears in the form *Heorlauestun* in a note of lands in Offlow Hundred on the dorse of the document in which Wulfric's will appears, although this note could be late eleventh century or early twelfth century (Sawyer 1979: xxxvii; see Figure 2.2); this form is also consistent with a

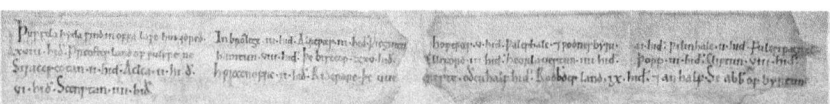

Figure 2.2 Note of the lands in Offlow Hundred, Staffordshire (Burton-on-Trent, Burton-on-Trent Museum, Muniments 1, dorse). Note *Heorlauestun* in line 2, four words to the right of the break. (Accepted in lieu by HM Government in 2019 and allocated to Staffordshire Archives. Reproduced courtesy of Staffordshire Record Office).

second element *-lāf* in the personal name. It therefore seems considerably more likely that this is a name containing the element *-lāf*, rather than the element *-wulf*.

Heorlfestun is, in fact, readily explicable as a form in which the second element of the personal name is a miscopied form of the element *-lāf*. The copy of the charter on the face of Burton-on-Trent, Burton-on-Trent Museum, Muniments 1 (see Figure 2.3) is notable for the relatively large number of scribal errors in its text. In line 1, we find the phrase 'hleofan hlaforde', which must originally have read 'leofan hlaforde'. This would appear to result from eye-skip, caused by the scribe looking forward too soon to the opening letters of the word *hlaforde*, before returning to the <l> of *leofan* and completing this word. In line 17, the name of Appleby Magna in Leicestershire appears in the form *æppeb byg*. The form *æppeb* is very obviously an error for *æppel* occasioned by the scribe's eye skipping forwards to the <b> of *byg*. Yet another eye-skip occurs in line 22, where the form *ealdermoder* appears in place of *ealdemoder*, indicating that the scribe skipped from the <d> of *ealde* forward to the <d> of *moder* and wrote the <er> that should conclude the word *moder*. In the light of these examples of eye-skip in the scribe's performance, it seems likely that the form *heorlfestun* is the result of a similar error. This form occurs immediately after the form *rolfestun* (referring to Rolleston, Staffordshire). If the scribe were copying a form such as *heorlafestun, but, on reaching the <l>, accidentally

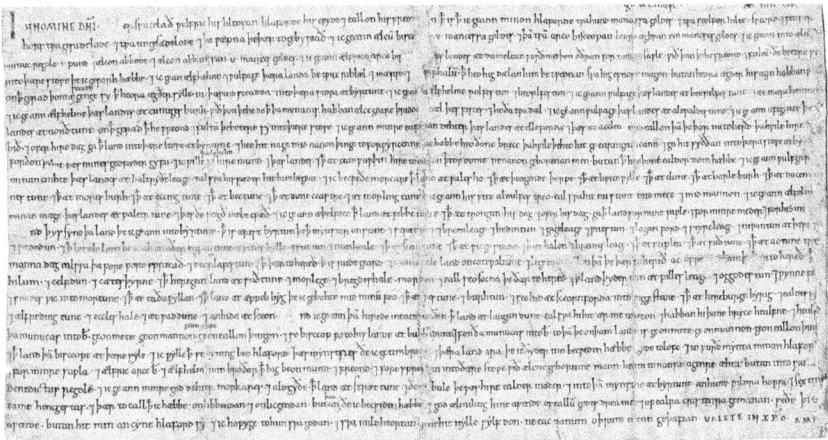

Figure 2.3 The will of Wulfric (1002 x 1004 AD; Burton-on-Trent, Burton-on-Trent Museum, Muniments 1, face). Note *Heorlfestun* in line 5. (Accepted in lieu by HM Government in 2019 and allocated to Staffordshire Archives. Reproduced courtesy of Staffordshire Record Office.)

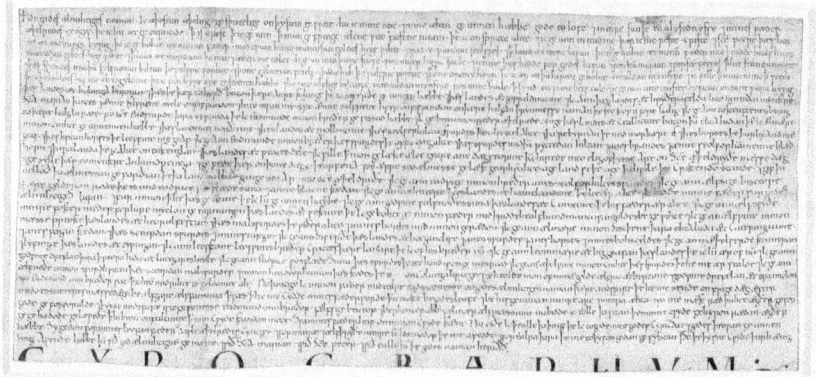

Figure 2.4 London, British Library, Stowe Charters 37, face (© The British Library Board).

looked back to the <l> of the immediately preceding name *rolfestun*, then the scribe would have continued writing at the <f> of *rolfestun*, thus omitting the <a> of **heorlafestun*. It is thus plausible, not only on the basis of the later attestations of this place-name in medieval documents, but also in view of the pattern of scribal errors in this document, that the name of Harlaston in Staffordshire originally contained a personal name that a late Old English scribe could represent as **Heorlaf*. It remains to be considered whether this could represent evidence for an Old English name **Heorulaf*, formed with the first element *Heoru-*.

In the case of S 1503, the will of Ætheling Æthelstan, we have a chirograph that is clearly the original (1014 AD) and which contains the form *heorulfestun* (see Figure 2.4). This shows the loss of the initial /w/ of the second element *-wulf*, noted above, that is common in place-names containing personal names in the charter corpus from early medieval England. A search of the *Electronic Sawyer* reveals no instances of names of places or landmarks containing personal names with the second element *-wulf* represented with the initial <w>. However, forms without <w> are fairly common:

S 887 (996 AD) *aculfes*
S 883 (995 AD) *Eardulfes lea*
S 842 (982 AD) *aðulfes hylle*
S 673 (958 for 959 AD) *eadulfes pytte*
S 657 (958 AD) *ordulfes*
S 607 (956 AD) *cuðulfes cotstowe*
S 542 (948? for 947 AD) *aþulfes*

S 535 (948 AD) *eadulfes mearce*
S 529 (947 AD) *ordulfes gemære*
S 526 (947 AD) *heardulfes hlæwe*
S 479 (942 AD) *Roðulfeston*
S 453 (924 x 939 AD) *Eadulfes næsa*
S 447 (939 AD) *ecgulfes setl*
S 422 (933 AD) *ecgulfes treow*
S 366 (901 AD) *audulfes cnol*
S 360 (900 AD) *ecgulfes treow . . . eadulfes hamm*
S 1536 (1002 x 1004 AD) *Aldulfestreo*
S 1503 (1014 AD) *Heorulfestune.*

We should, then, expect the loss of the initial /w/ of the second element -*wulf* in this context, and with the loss of /w/ the final vowel of a first element *Heoru*- would be expected to fall together with the /u/ of -(*w*)*ulf*. The form *Heorulf would therefore be a plausible form for an Old English name *Heoruwulf to assume in this context. As we have seen, however, this is not the most plausible explanation for the form *Heorlfestun* discussed above. In this case, it seems likely that the underlying personal name form is *Heorlaf. In this instance, the absence of the final -*u*/-*o* of the first element of the personal name cannot be accounted for by its coalescence with an initial vowel of the second element of the name. If we compare the well-attested Old English name element *Heaðu*-, which is similar in having a final vowel usually represented as <u> or <o>, we find that the loss of this final vowel in phonetic contexts other than before /w/ does not seem to take place. Examining all the names containing this element recorded in *PASE*, the present author has been unable to find an instance where the vowel is not represented, although in documents from the late Old English period it is sometimes represented by <e>, probably as a result of phonetic reduction of this vowel.

While the form *heorulfestun* might be taken, therefore, to provide evidence for an otherwise unattested late Old English name *Heorulf, deriving from a putative earlier *Heoruwulf, the form *Heorlfestun* does not appear to provide clear evidence for an Old English *Heorulaf. This form is, then, more readily explicable as an Anglicised form of the securely attested Old Norse name *Hjǫrleifr* (Lind 1905–1915: s.v. *Hiǫrleifr*; see also the attestations of the separate elements forming this name recorded by Peterson 2007: s.v. *Hiǫr-, -læifr*/-*lafr*). When we consider, moreover, that Harlaston in Staffordshire lies on the edge of the Danelaw, while all three places that may appear in the will of Æthelstan as *Heorulfestun* lie within the Danelaw, we might reasonably ask whether in both cases we are dealing with Old Norse personal names rather than Old English. The second element represented as <ulf> in *Heorulfestun* could just as easily be the common Old Norse second element *-ulfr* as a reduced form of Old English *-wulf*.

The possibility that are dealing with Scandinavian names is further complicated by the name *Heorstan*, which, according to *PASE*, occurs as the name of two tenth-century individuals, one of them the father of St Dunstan, whose name appears in the forms *Heorstan*/*Heorstanus*/*Heorstanum* in B's *Vita Sancti Dunstani* (Winterbottom and Lapidge 2012: 10–13), and the other a witness to a charter (S 1417) conveying land in Wiltshire (*PASE: Heorstan 1–2*). On the face of it, it seems somewhat unlikely that two individuals both associated with the southwest (as Lapidge (2004) notes, Dunstan appears to have grown up somewhere near Glastonbury) should have names of Scandinavian origin. It is worth, therefore, considering the possible origins of this very rare name form. Brooks (1992: 6–7) argues from the rarity of this name that the witness in S 1417 could, in fact, be Dunstan's father (see also Lapidge 2004), and this seems very plausible. He also suggests that the lack of the qualifying title *minister* with the name might indicate the low social status of the Heorstan in the charter, and Lapidge (2004) argues that this fact, together with the absence of his name from all other extant charters of Æthelstan, indicates that he may have been 'a person of lowly social standing' although he qualifies this with the observation that Dunstan's brother is likely to be the same individual called Wulfric who was the recipient of royal grants of large estates in the 940s. This is intriguing in relation to the will of Wynflæd (S 1539), which mentions a slave called *Herestan* and his unnamed wife in connection with Chinnock in Somerset, which lies around twenty miles south of Glastonbury. One might wonder whether this reference to an individual called *Herestan* could represent a reference to Dunstan's father at an early stage in his life, before the family's fortunes improved. The date of Wynflæd's will is difficult to determine. While Dumville (1994: 146 n. 75) states that the script of the document cannot be dated as early as the middle of the tenth century, it is clear that the document we have is a copy; Rumble (1984: 50) points out scribal errors that are undoubtedly the product of misreading of individual letters in the process of copying. Since the will mentions granting 'ðæs worþiges gif his hyre se cing an swa swa Eadweard cing ær his Byrhtwynne hyre meder geuþe' ('the homestead if the king grant it to her as King Edward granted it to Brihtwyn her mother'; Whitelock 1930: 14–15), it would seem plausible that Wynflæd's mother received a grant from Edward the Elder (as Whitelock 1930: 114 supposes), but Wynflæd's will was produced under a later king, quite probably Æthelstan. It is thus not impossible – although it does seem decidedly unlikely – that Dunstan's father could have been a slave of Wynflæd early in Æthelstan's reign but have seen a significant change in fortunes over the next ten to fifteen years. If this were the case, however, it would not significantly alter the problem posed by the name form *Heorstan*. On the one hand, we should hardly be surprised that an Old English scribe, whose work can be shown to contain some errors, should produce a form *Herestan*, formed from two well-attested Old English name elements, when confronted with the unusual form *Heorstan*. That the name *Herestan* should have been miscopied as *Heorstan* in two entirely different contexts, S 1417 and B's *Vita Sancti Dunstani*, on the other hand, seems distinctly implausible.

We have, then, to take seriously the possibility that *Heorstan* is an accurate representation of the name of Dunstan's father, and to consider how this name might have arisen. It is interesting in this connection that S 1417 includes a number of personal names that appear to be of Continental Germanic origin. Keynes (1996: 21) points out that the names *Waltere*, *Gundlaf* and *Hildewine* that occur as a group early in the witness list (see first line of the witness list in Figure 2.5) suggest that their bearers 'may have been of continental origin'. He

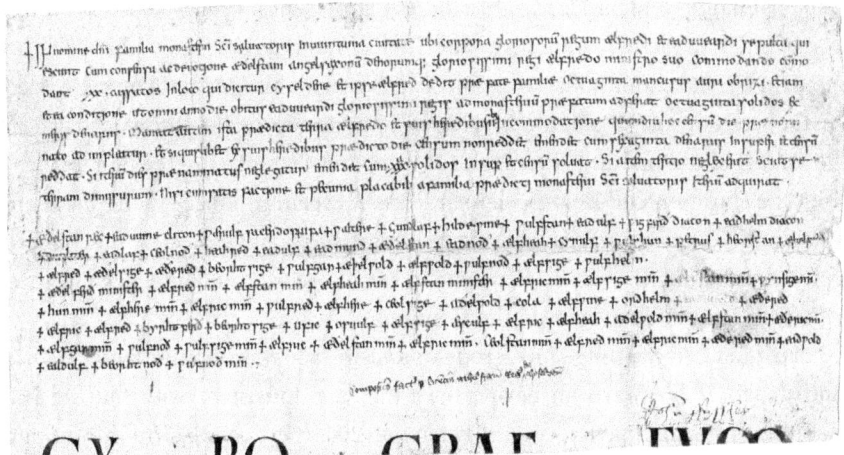

Figure 2.5 Lease of land at Chisledon, Wiltshire, from the New Minster, Winchester, to Alfred, minister of King Æthelstan (Winchester, Winchester College Muniments 12092; S 1417). (Reproduced courtesy of the Warden and Scholars of Winchester College).

also notes the name *Petrus*, that appears in the second line of the witness list, as potentially suggesting continental origins for its bearer. In this case, of course, the name is of Latin origin and therefore does not indicate continental origins as unequivocally as the other three but, given the rarity of Latin names among tenth-century English individuals, Keynes' suggestion certainly seems plausible. It seems significant, moreover, that *Petrus* occurs immediately before *Heorstan*. The earlier non-English group of names suggests, perhaps, that we should see these two names, neither of which is common early medieval England, as another such group. A Continental Germanic name formed with the first element *Hiru-* could conceivably have been Anglicised as *Heorstan* but, in general, this first element in Continental Germanic names ends in a vowel (see Förstemann 1900: s.v. *HIRU*); we might therefore expect Anglicisation to produce a form such as **Heorustan*. This brings us back to the observation that an Old English form *Heorstan* is most readily explained as an Anglicisation of a Scandinavian name with the first element *Hiǫr-*.

That the father of St Dunstan should have borne a Scandinavian or Anglo-Scandinavian personal name is difficult to accept as a conclusion. We might suggest instead that both instances of the form *Heorstan* should be treated simply as scribal errors for a putative Old English **Heorustan*, or as evidence for a form of this name with an unusual loss of the final vowel of the first element, or for an anomalous name of some other, unknown origin. Yet none of these explanations is compelling. It is difficult to be certain that there was not an Old English personal name element *Heoru-*, but there is at present no clear evidence for the use of such an element in native Old English naming practices. That such an element might be unfamiliar to an Old English scribe also seems to be reinforced by the fact that the this figure is referred to by the form *Heregar* at line 467 of *Beowulf* (Fulk, Bjork and Niles 2008: 18), apparently replacing the first element with the common Old English element *Here-*. It seems unlikely, then, that there was an Old English personal naming element *Heoru-*, but we can be much more confident that names such as *Heorogar* and *Heoroweard* could have been formed originally in Scandinavia or on the Continent.

Healfdene's remaining son, Hroðgar, and his sons Hroðmund and Hreðric and daughter Freawaru all have names that are consistent with but are not definitely of Scandinavian origin. Peterson (2004: 39) counts *Hroðgar* among those names from *Beowulf* she regards as Proto-Scandinavian. The elements used in forming this name are attested in her early runic and place-name material, although this combination of elements is not. That such a combination was used, however, seems extremely likely, especially as it occurs in later

Scandinavian evidence. The name is not very common but is solidly attested in the onomastic material from Viking Age Scandinavian runic inscriptions assembled by Peterson (2007: s.v. *Hróðgæirr*). *Hróðgeirr* also occurs as the name of three individuals in *Landnámabók*, two of them among the initial settlers of Iceland (Benediktsson 1968: 1.68, 2.289, 2.374). We can, therefore, be certain that this name formed part of Scandinavian naming traditions.

On the Continent, this name is also fairly common, judging by the various instances listed by Förstemann (1900: s.v. *HROTHI*). In England, this particular combination of elements is attested only as the name of a number of tenth-century moneyers (*PASE*: *Hrothgar 1–7*) and, as noted above under *Hreðel*, many of the forms of these individuals' names suggest continental origins. While we cannot identify a clear instance of this combination of elements in use as a native Old English name, however, both elements are separately attested. For a discussion of the evidence for an Old English first element *Hroð-*, see under *Hreðel* above. The second element *-gar* is extremely common in Old English personal naming; the most frequently recorded names in *-gar* in *PASE* are *Ælfgar*, *Æthelgar*, *Edgar*, *Leofgar*, *Ordgar*, *Wihtgar* and *Wulfgar*, all of which *PASE* identifies as having been borne by ten or more attested individuals. In the *Durham Liber Vitae*, *Hroð-* occurs a few times as a first element, as does *-gar* as a second element in names attested in the ninth-century sections of the *Liber Vitae* such as *Cuðgar*, *Cynegar*, *Eadgar* and *Wulfgar* (Rollason and Rollason 2007: 2.129–30, 2.100, 2.102, 2.105, 2.162). It is entirely possible, then, that the name *Hroðgar* could have been in use in early medieval England, but it does not appear to have been common.

This name does not, then, provide strong evidence for the geographical origin of the figure called *Hroðgar*, although the onomastic evidence presented here would be more consistent with Scandinavian or continental origin than with English origin. The presence of a cognate figure in Scandinavian sources (Jónsson 1959: 1.1-23; Guðnason 1982: 21–26), however, demonstrates that a Scandinavian origin for this figure (along with other members of Healfdene's family) is overwhelmingly likely.

Hroðgar's son Hroðmund also has a name that could derive from anywhere in the Germanic-speaking world. Peterson (2004: 39) treats his name as Proto-Scandinavian, noting that the two elements used in forming it are attested in her corpus of early Scandinavian runic inscriptions. This name also occurs a few times in the corpus of personal names from Scandinavian Viking Age runic inscriptions assembled by Peterson (2007: s.v. *Hróðmundr*). It is, therefore, unproblematic to view this as an early Scandinavian personal name. On the

Continent, however, this name is also common (Förstemann 1900: s.v. *HROTHI*). In England, this particular combination of elements is not certainly attested; *PASE* records (*Hrothmund 1–2*) the name as that of an ancestor figure of the East Anglian royal house in the Anglian collection of royal genealogies (Dumville 1976: 31, 34, 37) and as the name of an individual recorded in the *Domesday Book*. In the *Durham Liber Vitae*, this combination of elements is also unattested, although names in *Hroð-* and names in *-mund* are attested (Rollason and Rollason 2007: 2.129–30, 2. 139). This name could, therefore, have been coined almost anywhere in the Germanic-speaking world, although Scandinavian or Continental Germanic origin seems rather more likely than English origin.

When we come to Hroðgar's other son, Hreðric, the situation is broadly similar, although, as we shall see, the form in which his name appears (in comparison to the forms of the names of his father and brother) might point towards Scandinavian influence on the Old English spelling of his name. Peterson (2004: 39) includes *Hreðric* among those names in *Beowulf* that she considers plausibly Proto-Scandinavian, noting the presence of the first element of the name in her runic material and the second element in her place-name evidence. Both elements are also attested in the Viking Age Scandinavian runic material assembled by Peterson (2007: s.v. *Hrōð-*, *-rīkr*), although not in combination. On the Continent, this combination of name elements is common (Förstemann 1900: s.v. *HROTHI*). This name could, then, derive from a Scandinavian tradition, or could reflect either a continental version of a Scandinavian tradition, or a tradition developed on the Continent.

In early medieval England, the situation is slightly more complex. Names formed with *-ric* are very common (e.g., to note just the most numerous names with this second element, *PASE* records 490 individuals called *Ælfric*, 172 individuals called *Æthelric*, 140 called *Beorhtric*, 274 called *Eadric* and 261 called *Leofric*). Names formed with the first element *Hroð-/Hreð-*, however, are very much less common, and this specific combination of elements is not attested. It is also possible that a number of the names attested in England that are formed with this first element are, in fact, Continental Germanic names. In the case of the tenth-century moneyers called *Hroðgar* (*PASE*: *Hrothgar 1–7*), we might suspect the possibility that these are individuals from the Continent (cf. Clark 1992: 465; Smart 1986) and this suspicion is reinforced by the fact that most of these individuals' names are spelt with initial <f> rather than <h> (*PASE*: *Hrothgar 1, 4, 5–7*). Development of Germanic initial /xr/ to /fr/ is particularly a feature of Germanic naming in areas of intensive contact with Proto-Romance dialects such as the northern parts of what had been Gaul (Kaufmann 1965: 202–4), so we should expect this in the name of an individual from the Continent. The other name with the first element *Hroð-* borne by a moneyer in early medieval England appears in the form HROÐVLF (*PASE: Hrothulf 1*), which could represent an Old English name, although it could also be a form of a Continental Germanic name. The eighth-century abbess labelled *Hrothwaru 1* in *PASE* is also potentially problematic as evidence for an Old English name element, as her name appears in S 1429 in the form *Hrotuuari*, which could represent a Continental Germanic name form with <t> representing the final consonant of the first element (consider the many examples of spellings of this kind in Förstemann 1900: s.v. HROTHI), although <t> spellings for the dental fricative in early Old English are not unknown (Shaw 2013a: 122–25). There are, then, varying degrees of doubt as to whether these are, in fact, Old English names.

Nevertheless, there are some indubitably English individuals who bore names with the first element *Hroð-/Hreð-*, such as a relative of Archbishop Lull of Mainz called *Hrothuin* and the individual called HROETHBERH[TE] whose niece or nephew set up a commemorative sundial to him found at Falstone in Northumberland (*PASE*: s.v. *Hrothberht 1*; Okasha 1971: 71–72 (no 39)). There is also no obvious reason to doubt the Englishness of the early tenth-century Archbishop of York labelled *Hrothweard 1* by *PASE*. The various individuals bearing names formed with this first element in the *Durham Liber Vitae* are also presumably mainly of English extraction, although Insley, Rollason and McClure note the possibility that some of these represent forms of continental or Scandinavian names (Rollason and Rollason 2007: 2.129–30). While *Hroð-/Hreð-* is rare as a name element in early medieval England, then, it does nevertheless appear to have formed part of the Old English naming tradition.

The fact that the name *Hreðric* appears with <e> representing the vowel of the first element requires some consideration, given that the stem vowel of this name element is usually represented <o> in the early medieval sources from England noted above. An exception to this is the *Durham Liber Vitae*, in which there are a number of forms in which the element is *Hroð-*, without i-mutation, but also several forms in which it is spelt *Hroeð-*, with i-mutation of the vowel; this i-mutated form, which is also present in the sundial inscription from Falstone, may be a specifically Northumbrian form of this name element (Rollason and Rollason 2007: 2.10). The form we should expect in West Saxon, if forms with i-mutation of the vowel appeared in this dialect, would be *Hreð-* (Hogg and Fulk

2011: 1.121-22 §5.77). One possibility, then, is that the form *Hreðric* in *Beowulf* represents a West Saxon realisation of a name form derived from a Northumbrian tradition. This seems unlikely, however, as Hreðric is just one of several members of the Scylding dynasty whose names are formed with this first element, but he is the only one whose name appears with i-mutation in the first element. We might expect these figures to have formed part of the same tradition and to have travelled together, so if one appeared in a Northumbrian form, it would be surprising to find that the others did not. In the Northumbrian name forms discussed above, the i-mutation that produces *Hroeð-* must be conditioned by the compositional vowel at the end of the first element, rather than by the vowel of the second elements, which have various different vowels, not just /i/, and therefore cannot all provide the conditions for i-mutation. A putative Northumbrian version of the Scylding dynasty might, then, be expected (after West Saxonisation of its spellings) to include not just *Hreðric* but also **Hreðgar*, **Hreðmund* and **Hreðulf*.

It is perhaps not entirely impossible, therefore, that the form *Hreðric* derives from a Northumbrian tradition, but this seems highly unlikely. The pattern of i-mutation that produces *Hreðric* but does not affect the other *Hroð-* names of the Scylding dynasty is the same pattern that appears in Old Norse, where i-mutation caused by the stem vowel of the second element in this name produces forms such as *Rørik* and *Hrørikr* (Peterson 2007: s.v. *Hrørīkr*; Lind 1905–1915: s.v. *Hrǿrekr*) in contrast to forms without i-mutation where the stem vowel of the second element is not /i/, such as *Hróðgeirr* (Peterson 2007: s.v. *Hrōðgæirr*; Lind 1905–1915: s.v. *Hróðgeirr*). As Björkman (1920b: 71–73) points out, however, there is a lack of clear evidence for i-mutation in Scandinavian varieties before around 900 AD, rendering problematic any suggestion that this pattern in the names of the Scyldings is the result of their having been borrowed from Scandinavian tradition in forms already affected by Old Norse i-mutation. Björkman supposes on these grounds that the form *Hreðric* results from i-mutation conditioned by the /i/ in *-ric* taking place in an Old English context. Alternatively, we could suppose that the forms in the extant manuscript of *Beowulf* do not reflect the earliest forms of this name in this text, but rather forms influenced by a tenth- or eleventh-century scribe's knowledge of the contemporary Scandinavian forms of these names, in which i-mutation might then have taken place. There is a lack of evidence for parallel developments to support Björkman's view, but the alternative is also complex. In either case, however, although this name could plausibly have been created anywhere in the Germanic-speaking world, the likelihood of its having been developed in

Scandinavia as part of the tradition of Healfdene and his descendants seems very high.

The question remains whether this Scandinavian tradition was transmitted directly to early medieval England, or whether it could have travelled via the Continent, given the evidence for continental origins for many of the other names in *Beowulf*. Taking the names of Healfdene and his descendants in isolation, the simplest explanation would undoubtedly be direct importation from Scandinavia, but we would then have to suppose that this royal family was pressed into service in England as the backdrop for a narrative of monster-slaying derived from continental sources. We should not, then, rule out the possibility that the Scylding dynasty formed the narrative backdrop in a continental version of the narrative that went on to become the basis for *Beowulf*. Since the Scylding dynasty was known independently in England (as evidenced by the mention of Hroðgar and Hroðwulf in *Widsith*; see Malone 1962: 24 (l. 45)), a narrative derived from the Continent that involved this dynasty would naturally use the Old English forms of the names of the Scyldings. The forms of the names, then, would in all likelihood be the same whether the *Beowulf* poet drew on materials directly from Scandinavia, or only on materials from the Continent, although it would seem entirely possible that the Scylding dynasty was known in England through direct contacts with Scandinavia.

Hroðgar's daughter Freawaru also bears a name that is consistent with the view that Healfdene's family derives from Scandinavian tradition, although her name could be continental as well as Scandinavian in origin. Peterson treats her name as Proto-Scandinavian (2004: 37), interpreting the second element as a feminine *Movierung* (i.e., a feminine form derived directly from, in this case, a pre-existing masculine form) of *-waraz or *-warjaz. This element is also well attested in Viking Age runic inscriptions from Scandinavia (Peterson 2007: s.v. -vǫr), as is the Scandinavian cognate of the first element *Frøy*- (Peterson 2007: s.v. *Frøy*-). There is, therefore, little reason to doubt that this could be a name of Scandinavian origin. The name would also be readily explicable as a Continental Germanic name. The first element is common on the Continent (Förstemann 1900: s.v. *FRAVI*), as is the second element, which is often used in forming women's names (Förstemann 1900: s.v. *VAR*). This name could, in principle, then, have been coined either in Scandinavia or on the Continent.

The name is harder to account for as an Old English name, however, since the first element *Frea*- is not well attested in Old English. It occurs in the name *Frealaf*, borne by the father of Woden in the royal genealogies (Dumville 1976:

30–37), but does not appear to occur in the names of historical individuals from early medieval England, unless this is also the first element of the name *Frehelm*, borne by an eighth-century abbot according to the northern annals as recorded in Symeon of Durham's *Historia Regum* (Arnold 1882–1885: 2.42). The form *Freowin(us)* also occurs as the name of an individual in the *Domesday Book* for Suffolk (Rumble 1986: 7.121) and the form *Freuuin(us)* in the Essex *Domesday Book* (Rumble 1983: 20.64). Given the late date of both of these sources, the forms *Fre-* and *Freo-* for the first element of these names do not necessarily militate against an interpretation of this element as being identical to the element *Frea-* in *Beowulf* and in the royal genealogies, but the late date also makes other possibilities likely. In the case of *Frehelm*, we might reckon with the possibility of scribal error in the transmission of a name form such as *Freðohelm, and in the case of *Freowinus* we should also consider whether this might not be an imported name, rather than a native Old English name.

The second element *-waru* is more straightforwardly attested in early medieval England. PASE lists the following names containing this second element as occurring in English contexts: *Ælfwaru, Beorhtwaru, Cynewaru, Ealhswaru, Ealhwaru, Hrothwaru, Leofwaru, Oswaru, Ringwaru, Sigewaru, Sæwaru* and *Wulfwaru*. These names are sufficiently numerous that we can be fairly certain that *-waru* was a productive name element in Old English, but it seems unlikely that *Frea-* was, and it therefore seems more likely than not that this name in *Beowulf* derives originally from a continental or Scandinavian milieu. This could be interpreted as indicating that Freawaru formed part of the Scandinavian tradition of Healfdene's family, but we should also consider the possibility that she really forms part of the tradition surrounding the marriage of Ingeld, who is depicted as her husband in *Beowulf*. While later records of Scandinavian tradition suggest that many of the male figures in the dynasty originated in Scandinavia (an origin that is consistent with their names, as discussed above), a name cognate with *Freawaru* does not feature in these traditions. While we find *Hálfdanr*, cognate with *Healfdene*, *Helgi*, cognate with *Halga*, *Hrólfr*, cognate with *Hroðulf*, and *Hjǫrvarðr*, cognate with *Heoroweard* in Scandinavian texts (for a summary of these, see Garmonsway and Simpson 1968: 124–27, 141–206), we cannot be certain that Freawaru formed part of the Scandinavian tradition (indeed, Malone 1930: 258 suggests that her name is, in fact, an epithet that in *Beowulf* replaced the name *Hrut*, which she bears in Scandinavian tradition) and it must remain an open question whether she, in fact, belongs with the Continental Germanic tradition of Ingeld and the Heathobards, to which we now turn.

The Heathobards

Freawaru links the Scyldings to the Heathobards through her marriage to Ingeld. The name *Ingeld* appears a few times in early medieval England (*PASE*: s.v. *Ingeld* 2–4; Rollason and Rollason 2007: 2.133) and, on the face of it, can therefore be considered a native Old English personal name, albeit a rare one. Förstemann (1900: s.v. *IN, INGVI*) notes a number of occurrences in Continental Germanic contexts that demonstrate that this was also a rare Continental Germanic personal name. Peterson (2004), however, does not identify this name as plausibly Proto-Scandinavian. Although Peterson (2007: s.v. *Ingialdr*) notes a fair number of instances of this name in the Viking Age runic inscriptions of Scandinavia, she identifies this name as a borrowing from West Germanic personal naming practices. Two of the earliest settlers of Iceland recorded in *Landnámabók* bore this name (Benediktsson 1968: 1.182, 2.268), but here again it seems plausible to see this name as a borrowing from West Germanic. The geographical distribution of the name would, therefore, suggest that the figure named *Ingeld* in *Beowulf* and in *Widsith* (Malone 1962: 24 (l. 48)) originated either in England or on the Continent.

The picture becomes slightly more complicated, however, when we consider whether the first element of this name is to be interpreted as *In-* or *Ing-*. Names in *Ing-*, although rare, certainly occur in Old English (see, e.g. *PASE*: s.v. *Ingwald 1–2*; Rollason and Rollason 2007: 2.133). Names in *In-*, on the other hand, are less certainly attested. Leaving aside *Ingeld* itself, the *Durham Liber Vitae* appears to yield one instance in the ninth-century name form *Infrith*, although Insley, Rollason and McClure treat the ninth-century form *Inuald* and the thirteenth-century form *Inuard(us)* as forms of *Ingweald* and *Ingweard*, respectively (Rollason and Rollason 2007: 2.133). The logic for this is presumably that the name *Ingweald* is otherwise attested in early medieval England and, in the case of *Inuard(us)*, the late date of the name makes it difficult to rely on the spelling as a clear indicator of whether *In-* or *Ing-* is the first element. Since *Infrith* is otherwise unattested in early medieval England, but is, as Rollason and Rollason (2007: 2.133) point out, attested on the Continent, it seems open to question whether this should not be regarded as one of the Continental Germanic personal names found in the *Durham Liber Vitae*. The evidence from textual records of personal names in early medieval England is therefore inconclusive as to the existence of an Old English personal name element *In-*, although *Ing-* does appear to be securely attested.

In addition to textual records of personal names, we must also consider place-names. The place-name *Inwinesburg* in S 114, a probably original single-sheet charter of 779 AD, has also been adduced as evidence for an Old English first element *In-* (Forssner 1916: 163; Kaufmann 1968: 216 s.v. *In-*; Rollason and Rollason 2007: 2. 132–3). Unfortunately, this place-name does not seem to have survived, so we cannot confirm whether it was *Inwinesburg* or *Winesburg*; the text of S 114 could be read either 'usque Inwinesburg' ('up to Inwinesburg') or 'usque in Winesburg' ('up to Winesburg'). *Wine* is an exceedingly common Old English personal name (*PASE* identifies 36 individuals with this name; even allowing for the probability of some errors and duplication of individuals, then, this was clearly a very popular Old English name). The use of *usque* with the preposition *in* in specifying bounds in early medieval English charters is also not uncommon (consider, for example, S 111, S 1182, S 268, S 37). The present author therefore accepts the interpretation in *LangScape* of this phrase as 'usque in Winesburg' ('up to Winesburg [= Wine's fortification]'; *LangScape*: bound L114.0.00). This place-name does not, then, provide clear evidence for an Old English personal name *Inwine* formed with a first element *In-*.

The lack of evidence for an Old English name element *In-* would be of no consequence if the name *Ingeld* in *Beowulf* and *Widsith* were formed with the first element *Ing-*, which is clearly attested in Old English personal naming. There appears, however, to be an additional reference to this figure that demonstrates that his name should be interpreted as containing a first element *In-* rather than *Ing-*. In a lengthy letter to an individual he calls *Speratus*, Alcuin famously poses the rhetorical question 'Quid Hinieldus cum Christo?' ('What has Ingeld to do with Christ?'; Duemmler 1895: 183). There is no linguistic difficulty with the view that *Ingeld* in *Beowulf* and *Widsith*, and *Hinieldus* in Alcuin's letter represent the same name, and Alcuin's association of the figure he calls *Hinieldus* with 'carmina gentilium' ('songs of pagans'; Duemmler 1895: 183) suggests that he is probably the same figure mentioned in *Beowulf* and *Widsith*. The form *Hinieldus*, however, requires some careful linguistic analysis. Alcuin's letter is preserved in two manuscripts: London, British Library, Harley 208, produced on the Continent sometime in the ninth century after 814 AD; and Vatican, Reginae Christinae 272, a tenth-century production. The form *hinieldus* is that of the earlier manuscript, while the later manuscript gives the form *himeldus*, which is clearly a scribal error based on misreading the sequence of three minims forming <ni> as <m>. Both manuscripts, therefore, seem to indicate a palatal approximant or fricative by the use of <i> at the beginning of the second element, rather than a stop. As Alcuin was an Englishman, we should expect this in his realisation of the name element *-geld*, in which the Primitive Old English palatal fricative [ɣ] immediately followed by a front vowel, as in this name element, regularly developed into an approximant [j] (Hogg and Fulk 2011: 1.253–57 §7.15–7.17). Here, Alcuin uses <i>, which frequently represents an approximant [j] in Latin, to represent this sound. This does not demonstrate, however, that the name of this figure was of English origin; it would not be surprising if Alcuin had Anglicised a Continental Germanic name form by identifying the second element with the cognate Old English second element and representing it accordingly.

What is very clearly lacking from the form *Hinieldus*, however, is any letter representing the stop that we should expect at the end of the first element *Ing-*. Fulk, Bjork and Niles (2008: 470) treat this as evidence for the lack of an affricate at the end of the first element of the name. One might quibble that the development of an affricate in this phonological environment had perhaps not occurred by the date Alcuin was writing, but this in no way affects the validity of their claim that this spelling constitutes evidence that the first element is not *Ing-* but *In-* (although the present author remains decidedly puzzled that they make reference here to Frank (1991: 91), who says nothing whatsoever about the form *Hinieldus*). Unless both manuscripts are in error in omitting a <g>, <c> or combination of these letters from the end of the first element of this name, we must interpret this as a Continental Germanic name formed with the first element *In-*, not *Ing-*. In assessing the likelihood of such an error in the manuscript transmission of this letter, it is perhaps worth remarking that the initial <h>, used without phonetic value, is unlikely to have derived from the pen of the Englishman Alcuin, and must be the result of scribal enterprise on the part of later copyists. Since both manuscripts preserving this letter post-date Alcuin's death and were produced on the Continent, however, the introduction of this form by a copyist seems unremarkable. That a continental scribe should omit a <g> or <c> from a form such as *(*h*)*ingieldus* or *(*h*)*incieldus*, however, is surprising; the first element *Ing-* appears not uncommonly in Continental Germanic forms as (*h*)*ing-* or (*h*)*inc-* (Förstemann 1900: s.v. *INGVI*), so a Continental Germanic-speaking scribe would be likely to copy such a form as it appeared. Obviously we cannot absolutely rule out a scribal error early in the manuscript transmission of this letter, but much the most straightforward reading of the evidence provided by this letter is that the tradition surrounding a figure called *Ingeld* in *Beowulf* and *Widsith* derived from a continental Germanic milieu.

There is one more piece of evidence in Alcuin's letter that might also be taken to point in the same direction. While the 'carmina gentilium' of which Alcuin complains could be taken to be Old English heroic poems, we should consider to whom his complaint is addressed. The traditional view has been that the individual Alcuin calls *Speratus* was Bishop Hygebald of Lindisfarne (Duemmler 1895: 181; *PASE*: s.v. *Hygebald 3*). However, Bullough (1993) has very cogently argued that the recipient of this letter was, in fact, Bishop Unwona of Leicester (*PASE*: s.v. *Unwona 2*). This identification seems to the present author a compelling one, and it has important implications for how we read Alcuin's complaint. The name *Unwona* is not an Old English personal name, but rather a Continental Germanic personal name. Förstemann (1900: s.v. *UN*) notes several continental instances of this name and, as we shall see in relation to the name *Wonred* in *Beowulf*, the element *won(a)* is most plausibly explained as an Anglicisation of Continental Germanic *wan* (for which, see Förstemann 1900: s.v. *VAN*). The first element *Un-*, moreover, seems to be a Continental Germanic personal naming element, and not an Old English one (see discussion under *Unferð*, below). That Bishop Unwona was of continental origin is also evidenced by the use of *-o* as the weak masculine nominative ending of his name in S 128 and S 1184, both probably original single-sheet charters or contemporary copies (and also in S 153, although opinion is divided on whether this is an original or contemporary copy on the one hand, or a later fabrication on the other hand). In Old English, this ending would be *-a*, but in Continental Germanic personal names *-o* is the usual form. The Old English *-a* is used in Unwona's name in S 123, S 139, S 155 and S 1186a, all of which are originals or contemporary copies, but it is not surprising to see English scribes Anglicising a Continental Germanic name in this way; the striking fact is that two or three contemporary witnesses to his name from England use a form with a Continental Germanic ending.

Given that Bishop Unwona bore a clearly Continental Germanic personal name, it seems likely that he was a continental immigrant in England. North's suggestion (2006: 141), therefore, that Alcuin met him at a church council in England, may not be necessary. It is possible that Alcuin could have first met Unwona on the Continent, before he travelled to England to take up the role of Bishop of Leicester (although we do not know the details of Unwona's career prior to this). In any case, recognising that Unwona was of continental origin presents us with a new context for understanding Alcuin's letter; rather than complaining about the performance of Old English heroic poetry, Alcuin may, in fact, be expressing his distaste for Continental Germanic heroic narratives, including those involving the figure *Ingeld*. This is consistent with the linguistic evidence for the origin of the name *Ingeld* discussed above, and it is also suggestive in relation to the broader evidence for Continental Germanic origins of many of the names in *Beowulf*. This is a point to which we will return in due course.

There is one other potential early witness to the narrative tradition surrounding Ingeld which we must consider. Fulk, Bjork and Niles (2008: 470) claim that the name *Ingcél*, borne by a character in the Middle Irish *Togail Bruidne Da Derga* ('The Destruction of Da Derga's Hostel'), 'is almost certainly a borrowing of' *Ingeld*. They base this claim on a similar claim by Henry (1966: 220–21), who points to the fact that both figures carry out killings at a feast as evidence for the creation of Ingcél from Ingeld. Henry's position, in turn, appears to have been prompted by Knott's passing observation (1936: 80 n. 404) that she 'is tempted to connect *Ingcél* with the Hingiald of Alcuin's letter, but I have no evidence to justify this'. Knott's view seems very much more defensible than Henry's. In the first place, the supposed narrative parallel that Henry adduces must carry only very limited weight, given the prevalence of killings at feasts in heroic narratives. Henry (1966: 221) argues, moreover, that 'the Anglo-Irish milieu of Northumbria attested by Alcuin's rebuke provides the key to one source of these correspondences'. As we have seen, however, Alcuin's rebuke is directed not at an Anglo-Irish milieu in Northumbria, but rather at a Continental Germanic milieu in Mercia. The apparent evidence for a specific path of transmission is thus illusory. It is also worth remarking that *Ingcél* stands alone in *Togail Bruidne Da Derga* as a name bearing a passing resemblance to *Ingeld*; were this figure and his story borrowed from England, we might perhaps expect other figures in the narrative to bear names resembling those of figures associated with Ingeld, most obviously his father Froda. On balance, the present author is inclined not to regard this as a compelling case for influence of English heroic narrative on Irish heroic narrative. There is, then, no strong reason to treat the name *Ingcél*, as Fulk, Bjork and Niles (2008: 470) do, as potential evidence for the name *Ingeld* having had a first element *Ing-* rather than *In-*.

The likelihood of a Continental Germanic source or sources for the figure of Ingeld in English literary tradition must also be considered in light of the potential evidence for this figure in the ninth-century Scandinavian poem *Ynglingatal* (Marold 2012: 44 (stanza 20)), in which an individual called *Ingjaldr* is mentioned as dying in a fire. Since *Beowulf* provides no clear indication of how Ingeld died, it is difficult to assess the possible relationship between the figure in *Ynglingatal* and the figure in *Beowulf*. The death of a figure called *Ingialldus* in Arngrim's epitome of *Skjǫldunga saga*, moreover, provides no indication of death by fire (Guðnason 1982: 23; Miller 2007: 16). When Saxo Grammaticus comes to treat the son of Frothi he calls *Ingellus*, he provides no indication as to the manner of his death, although the slaughter of his guests at the urging of Starkather clearly recalls the passage concerning Ingeld in *Beowulf* (Friis-Jensen and Fisher 2015: 1.416–43; Fisher and Davidson 1979–1980: 1.184–94). Saxo includes two other figures bearing this name. One appears as the father of a bridegroom who dies in a duel arising at his own wedding feast (Fisher and Ellis Davidson 1979–1980: 1.54–55), again recalling to some degree the narrative presented in *Beowulf*, while the other is simply introduced as the father of a figure called Ring, whose exploits are treated in some detail (Fisher and Ellis Davidson 1979–1980: 1.226–28). That these various later Scandinavian versions of Ingeld derive from English or continental tradition seems entirely possible, and it is not clear that we must assign the figure in *Ynglingatal* to native Scandinavian tradition either; at any rate, we can be quite sure from Alcuin's pronouncement on the subject that this figure was known in Continental Germanic tradition some considerable time prior to the composition of *Ynglingatal*.

As we have noted, Saxo records a figure called *Ingellus* whose father is called *Frothi*; this appears to reflect Ingeld's parentage in *Beowulf*, where his father is called *Froda*. This name is attested across the Germanic languages. In early medieval England, it is not at all common; *PASE* records only one bearer of the name, a late seventh- to early eighth-century abbot (*PASE*: s.v. *Froda 1*). The name is also attested but quite rare on the Continent (Förstemann 1900: s.v. *FRODA*), and the same is true in Scandinavia, judging by the names found in Viking Age runic inscriptions (Peterson 2007: s.v. *Fróði*) and from *Landnámabók*, in which (aside from the legendary king himself; see Benediktsson 1968: 2.246) only one individual, an Icelander from the generation following the initial settlement, is recorded as bearing this name (Benediktsson 1968: 2.369). This name, therefore, cannot provide any evidence for the development of the narrative materials of *Beowulf*, since it could come from almost anywhere in the Germanic-speaking world. That his son Ingeld has a name that suggests an origin in Continental Germanic narrative tradition, however, should incline us to view both figures as belonging to this milieu.

This view is also reinforced by the one other named Heathobard in the poem, Wiðergyld. Although he is not presented explicitly as a blood relative of Froda and Ingeld, his central role as the figure whose death catalyses Ingeld's renewal of hostility with the Danes suggests that he probably originally formed part of the narrative tradition surrounding Ingeld and his ill-fated bride. It is, therefore, telling that his name, like that of Ingeld himself, is most readily explained as originating in a Continental Germanic context. Förstemann (1900: s.v. *VID*) treats names such as *Widrebold, Widargelt* and *Widerolf* as having first elements formed by extension of the name element *wid* (related either to the adjective meaning 'wide' or to the noun meaning 'wood'), but admits that, in some cases in his corpus, the first element may relate to Old High German *widar* 'against'. Björkman (1920b: 119) interprets the name *Wiðergyld* in *Beowulf* in terms of the latter interpretation, treating it as a meaningful compound with the sense 'payer back, avenger'. In advancing this claim, Björkman suggests, despite the fact that both elements in the name are attested as variation elements, that in this case, they should not be interpreted in this way. This is, perhaps, a necessary stage in the argument if we are to build a case for treating this name as a meaningful compound rather than as an ordinary variation name. It seems far from clear, however, that we should seek to interpret the name in this way. Even if the character called *Wiðergyld* is to be interpreted as an avenger – and the allusive reference to him at line 2051 of the poem hardly provides conclusive evidence that he is – his name would be no more appropriate to him that it might have been to other, more clearly avenging characters in the poem, such as Beowulf himself. In a poem riddled with acts of revenge, calling a character 'avenger' does not seem a particularly effective form of characterisation.

There is, in fact, no particular reason to insist on interpreting *Wiðergyld* as a meaningful compound. As the evidence assembled by Förstemann (1900: s.v. *VID*) demonstrates, in Continental Germanic names the first element *Widre/Widra/Wider/Widar* occurs in combination not only with *-gild/-gelt*, but also with second elements realised in the forms *-bold, -vert, -gasius, -had, -olt* and *-olf*. There is, therefore, some reason to suppose that there was a variation element derived from the Proto-Germanic preposition **wiþra(n)* 'against, opposite' (see Orel 2003: s.v. **wiþra(n)*). Schramm (1957: 71) notes in relation to the range of first elements with which this element is combined that it perhaps bore various meanings, including both 'the sacrificer' and 'the avenger'. While the name element may have borne such meanings (or at least one of them) in its earliest development, it seems quite likely that by the earliest possible date for the *Beowulf* narrative it was already simply an ordinary variation element. The antiquity of this element is demonstrated by its occurrence in the name *Widragasius*, borne by an individual named in the shorter version of the will of Saint Remigius as recorded in Hincmar of Reims' *vita* of the saint (Krusch 1896: 337 (l. 24)). Since the arguments of Krusch (1895) against the authenticity of this document have been convincingly disposed of by Jones, Grierson and Crook (1957), we can see this as evidence for the existence of this name element in the early sixth century. The dating can perhaps be pushed even earlier, moreover, by the name *Vitrodorus*, borne, according to Ammianus Marcellinus, by a king of the Quadi who was in power around the middle of the fourth century AD (Seyfarth 1978: 1.126). A name such as *Wiðergyld* need not represent a deliberately meaningful formation by the Old English poet, but could simply be an ordinary variation name.

The use of *Wiðer-* as a variation element in Old English, however, is not attested, unless the eleventh-century provost of Worcester called *Witheric* (*PASE*: s.v. *Witheric 1*; Hearne 1723: 1.261 and 1.268) can be considered as having this element as the first element of his name. This is possible, but since the second element -*ric* begins with /r/, it is not clear whether the first element is *wiðer-* with assimilation of the final /r/ to the initial /r/ of the second element, or simply *wiðe-*. The latter would not be an unproblematic name element, but it is perhaps paralleled in the name of Withburg, sister of Æthelthryth, whose name appears in the form *Wyðburh* in S 958 (*PASE*: s.v. *Withburg 1*). There is, in short, no clear evidence for the use *Wither-* as a variation element in Old English. However, *PASE* does list a number of individuals called *Wither*, but this seems indecisive; the first of these is a figure from the legendary reaches of English royal genealogy as represented in Æthelweard's *Chronicon* (Campbell 1962: 9, 18). Æthelweard's forms of the name *Vuithar* and *Wither* appear to be the result of an attempt by Æthelweard to harmonise English genealogical material with Scandinavian traditions (Shaw 2002: 133; Townend 2002: 123–25) as the corresponding figure in Bede's genealogy of Hengest and Horsa, and in the Kentish regnal list in London, British Library, Cotton Vespasian B. vi, fols 104–9, is called *Uitta* (Plummer 1896: 1.32; Colgrave and Mynors 1969: 50 (book 1, chapter 15); Dumville 1976: 31). The other individuals bearing this name appear in the *New Minster Liber Vitae* (*PASE*: s.v. *Wither 2*), in the charters S 911, S 922 and S 1503 (*PASE*: s.v. *Wither 3* and *Wither 4*) and in the *Domesday Book* (*PASE*: s.v. *Wither 5*). Given the late date of all these sources (both the charters and the relevant section of the *New Minster Liber Vitae* date to the eleventh century; on the dating of the latter, see Keynes 1996: 94), it is not clear whether they represent English or Scandinavian names. It is worth noting, however, that in the *New Minster Liber Vitae* the name form *Wiþer* appears on the same folio as four names explicitly identifed in the manuscript as being borne by Danes (*Þored* twice and *Toui* and *Toca* once each; see Keynes 1996: fol. 25r nos 47–50) as well as several certainly or very probably Danish names which, like *Wiþer*, are not explicitly identified as the names of Danes (*Þored, Swegen, Vlf, Þurgysl, Ðurhild, Toui*; see Keynes 1996: fol. 25r, no. 20 and fol. 25v, nos 75, 93, 94 and 96). Even if some or all of these instances of the name *Wiðer* represent a native Old English name, however, the existence of a single element name of this form need not necessarily indicate that this element was employed in forming names consisting of two elements.

In Scandinavia, too, we lack clear evidence for a variation name element corresponding to Old English *Wiðer-*. Peterson (2004) finds no evidence in *urnordisk* for such a name element in her corpus of early Scandinavian personal names. In Viking Age runic inscriptions, Peterson (2007: s.v. *Við-*) does note a name element *Við-*, which she interprets as related to the noun *viðr* 'wood'. This element could conceivably represent a reduced form of Proto-Germanic **wiþra-*, reflecting the common reduction of *viðr* 'against' to *við* in Old Norse (Cleasby, Vigfússon and Craigie 1957: s.v. *við* (preposition)). This does not seem particularly likely, however, especially as names in *widu-*, which must derive from the noun meaning 'wood', are attested in Scandinavian runic inscriptions in the older futhark (Peterson 2004: 18). It seems a great deal more likely that all these names are to be explained, as Peterson notes, as containing an element related to the noun meaning 'wood'. Moreover, the Old Norse name *Viðarr*, which may be the source of the name *Wither* in Viking Age England (discussed above), could be interpreted as containing the element *við(r)-* derived from the noun meaning 'wood', although Peterson (2004: 34) also notes a possible derivation from the adjective *víðr* 'wide'. Overall, there seems little, if any, reason to suppose that the Old English or the Old Norse onomastic traditions included a name element derived from Proto-Germanic **wiþra*.

It seems, then, that England and Scandinavia are unlikely to have had native names formed with a first element deriving from Proto-Germanic **wiþra*, whereas the Continental Germanic onomasticon does appear to contain this name element from an early stage. The natural interpretation of the evidence is that this name element existed in early Germanic naming practices but fell out of use in the ancestors of Old Norse and Old English. However, it continued to be used on the Continent, and it therefore seems reasonable to suppose that the name *Widergyld* in *Beowulf* found its way into this text from a continental source of some sort. Taken together with the probably Continental Germanic origin of *Ingeld*, and the fact that the name *Froda* could have arisen in a Continental Germanic milieu as well, this suggests that the entire Heathobard episode represents a Continental Germanic narrative tradition, albeit one that influenced later Scandinavian authors. It may well be that Freawaru, whose name could derive from either Scandinavia or the Continent, also formed part of that narrative tradition rather than coming into being as part of the Scandinavian tradition of Healfdene's family.

The Helmings

The Helmings are represented in *Beowulf* by Wealhþeow, Hroðgar's queen, and thus feature in this chapter devoted to the Scyldings and their satellites. As noted above (p. 46), however, it is possible that the Helmings and the Wylfings are, in fact, the same tribal group; in *Widsith* (line 29), we learn that a figure called *Helm* ruled the *Wulfingum*, and Chambers (1912: 198) plausibly connects Helm with the Helming family of *Beowulf*, to whom Wealhþeow belongs, and identifies the *Wulfingum* of *Widsith* with the Wylfings of *Beowulf*. It is not implausible, then, that we should consider Wealhþeow as belonging to the Wylfings, and, if we do so, then this might incline us to view the Wylfing Heaðolaf as probably forming part of the Continental Germanic element in the narrative materials of *Beowulf*, since Wealhþeow herself must have originated in a Continental Germanic context.

The name *Wealhþeow* has been identified as a meaningful name by a number of scholars, and the supposed meaning 'foreign slave' has prompted a good deal of discussion around the problem of a queen having a servile name (Wessén 1927: 110–18; Gordon 1935; Robinson 1964; Hill 1990; Breen 2009; Neidorf 2018a). This debate is, however, unnecessary if we regard *Wealhþeow* – like other names that have often been identified as meaningful, such as *Unferð* – as an ordinary variation name, whose elements are not intended to be understood as forming a meaningful compound. Jurasinski (2007) does just this, arguing that *Wealhþeow* is not to be understood as a meaningful compound, on the grounds that onomasticians view two-element variation names as non-meaningful. Curiously, he nevertheless argues that the name element *-þeow* may have come into being as a meaningful nickname that was later adopted as a variation element. While there is no way of disproving (or, indeed, proving) this hypothesis, it is hard to see how it helps to explain the main difficulty presented by the name *Wealhþeow*. The difficulty is that, where names in *-þeow* are attested in Old English (and they are actually only attested as names of legendary figures in *Beowulf* and in royal genealogies, as discussed at p. 27), they occur only as male names. It is therefore potentially problematic to find a prominent female character in an Old English poem bearing a name that Old English-speaking audiences would presumably have regarded as applicable only to men – if, indeed, they did not find the name element *-þeow* quite unfamiliar. Jurasinski (2007: 710) notes Gordon's (1935: 174) argument that *Wealhþeow* is a name of an older type in which a feminine variant of the Proto-Germanic name element **-þewaz* existed. While the masculine name element is attested in pre-Viking

Age Scandinavian names (Peterson 2004: 13, 19) and Continental Germanic (Förstemann 1900: s.v. *THIVA*), the feminine *Movierung* is attested only in Continental Germanic personal naming (Förstemann 1900: s.v. *THIVA*). For Gordon (1935: 174), this constitutes evidence that there was a feminine form of this name element that existed across the Germanic languages but fell out of use early in England and Scandinavia. On this view, the name *Wealhþeow* could represent either a Scandinavian or an English coinage of a very early date, but of course there is no evidence to support this view; it is entirely possible that the feminine form of the element *-*þewaz* developed only on the Continent, and that the name *Wealhþeow* thus represents another instance of a personal name in *Beowulf* that must derive from a Continental Germanic source.

The first element of the name *Wealhþeow* is less informative as to the origins of the name, but nevertheless deserves some comment. Shaw (2013b: 61–63) notes that this name element is securely attested in the West Germanic languages (see also Förstemann 1900: s.v. *VALHA*), including Old English (see also *PASE*: s.v. *Æthelwalh 1, Cenwealh 2–3, Dunwalh 1–2, Merewalh 1–2, Penwealh 1, Wealh 1–2, Wealheard 1–2, Wealhheard 1, Wealhhere 1–6, Wealhhun 1; Wealhberht 1* is attested only in S 68, a post-Conquest forgery, in the ambiguous form *Walbert*), but in North and East Germanic dialects it is impossible to be sure that this name element is attested. Neidorf (2018a: 78–86) argues for interpreting the first element of this name as deriving originally from a different element */wala/ 'chosen, beloved', which may be attested in North and East Germanic dialects as well as West Germanic (but not in Old English). Whichever of these elements we suppose underlies the first element of this name, we cannot rule out the possibility that a Scandinavian name formed with that element could have existed at the time *Beowulf* was composed, but the use of the second element -*þeow* in a female name clearly points to a Continental Germanic origin as the most plausible explanation for the name.

Hroðgar's courtiers

Thus far, we have considered the Scyldings and their in-laws the Heathobards and Helmings, and the picture that emerges is one of a mixing of traditions. The Scylding dynasty itself appears to represent a composite; a Scandinavian heroic tradition surrounding Healfdene and his descendants has been combined with an English genealogical tradition which itself has Continental Germanic elements. The Scylding dynasty has also been tied into a Continental Germanic narrative tradition surrounding Ingeld, perhaps through the creation of a daughter for Hroðgar, although we cannot rule out the possibility that Hroðgar's daughter formed part of the Scandinavian tradition of Healfdene and his descendants. This suggests that the narrative of Healfdene's descendants was joined with that of Ingeld and the Heathobards in a Continental context, and Hroðgar also gained his wife on the Continent, while the addition of Scyld and Beow to Healfdene's genealogy was a narrative development by the Old English poet. We have not yet, however, considered the other figures in the poem who form part of Hroðgar's court. These are Unferð and his father Ecglaf, Æschere and his brother Yrmenlaf, and Wulfgar. While Wulfgar could have been created in any part of the Germanic-speaking world, the others in this group have names that tend to point towards Continental Germanic origins. Since these characters all play roles in the narrative of Beowulf's interactions with Hroðgar, this would be consistent with a reading of them as having been developed as part of the central narrative of the poem concerning Beowulf's monster fights – a narrative, moreover, that must have developed on the Continent before being taken up by the Old English poet. As we shall see, one of these figures provides an intriguing clue to the way in which the Old English poet may have received this narrative, or parts of it.

To begin with the most famous of Hroðgar's courtiers, the name *Unferð* is surely one of the most discussed names in *Beowulf*. This name above all others has frequently been treated as a name coined by the poet as a meaningful name that characterises its bearer. To give just a few examples of this approach, Bloomfield (1949: 410–12) interprets the name as a deliberate coinage by the poet with the meaning 'mar-peace'; Hulbert (1951: 15–16) and Eliason (1963: 267) accept this interpretation of Unferð's name as a given; Ogilvy (1964) nods very briefly to this view in suggesting that 'he may be considered a type character as his name (Malvolio?) implies'; Clover (1980: 467), more cautiously, raises the possibility that the name has a meaning of this sort, without committing to this view. Fulk (1987), however, has shown conclusively the weakness of such claims, and there seems no reason to suppose that *Unferð* was anything other than a normal variation name, formed on the usual principles of Germanic name formation. Despite this, some scholars have continued to treat this name as a meaningful coinage; for example, Owen-Crocker (2007: 276) espouses this view, while Niles (1994: 458–59) – apparently taking the view that personal names are generally meaningful – appears to see the name's lack of meaning, as demonstrated by Fulk, as evidence that we should, in fact, retain the manuscript reading *Hunferð* on the grounds that this produces a meaningful name. Since personal names in the Germanic-speaking world in the early Middle Ages do not generally appear to be meaningful, the present author does not accept this line of argument, but the form of the name in the manuscript is nevertheless an important issue, to which we now turn.

The etymology of this name is, however, not entirely straightforward. The *Beowulf* manuscript in fact gives the name of this figure as *Hunferð*, which is a fairly well-attested Old English personal name (see *PASE*: s.v. *Hunfrith 1-11*). This name form is usually amended in editions of the text to the more familiar *Unferð* (see discussion in Fulk, Bjork and Niles 2008: 150), because the form *Hunferð* would break the metrically required alliteration in three lines:

Unferð maþelode,   Ecglafes bearn, (499)
æghwylc oðrum trywe.   Swylce þær Unferþ þyle (1165)
Ond þu Unferð læt   ealde lafe, (1488)

In these lines, it is absolutely clear that this name must have been understood by the Old English poet to begin with a vowel sound, so that it could alliterate with the initial vowel sounds of *Ecglafes*, *æghwylc oðrum* and *ealde*, as the patterns of Old English poetic metre require. The emendation that replaces *Hunferð* with *Unferð* is plausible both because it is the simplest emendation that produces from *Hunferð* a form capable of vowel alliteration, and, as Fulk (1987: 120-21) points out, because an Old English scribe encountering the form *Unferð*, which is not otherwise attested in Old English, might very readily attempt to correct this unexpected form to produce the familiar and very similar Old English name *Hunferð*.

It seems very highly probable, then, that the archetype of *Beowulf* contained the name *Unferð*. This leaves us with the puzzle of the origins of this name form. Fulk (1987: 121-25) argues cogently that this is not a name formed with the negative particle *un-*, preferring to interpret the first element of the name as deriving from a Proto-Germanic element *$\bar{u}n(i)$-*. The evidence that Fulk presents for the existence of this element seems open to question, however. He notes that in Old High German sources we find names such as *Hunbert* and *Hunwald*, evidently formed with the element *Hun-* that is common across the Germanic-speaking world (see Neuß 2008 for a valuable re-assessment of the origins of this name element), but also, much less commonly, forms such as *Unbert* and *Unwald* (Fulk 1987: 122). The latter forms, he suggests, cannot have a first element *Hun-* since 'etymological antevocalic initial *h* is almost never lost in Old High German' (Fulk 1987: 122). His authority for this claim about loss of initial /h/ is the work of Braune and Eggers (1975: 146-47 §153 note 2), who, in fact, note that careful scribes rarely omit to represent this sound by <h> in spelling, but a few less careful scribal performances do sometimes do so (see also the somewhat updated treatment in Braune and Heidermanns 2018: 202 (§153 note 2)). In principle, then, it is certainly possible that Old High German name forms such as *Unbert* and *Unwald* simply represent less than careful spellings of names with the first element *Hun-*. When we consider scribal practices in relation to personal names in sources for the eighth century, moreover, we find that omission of an etymologically required initial <h> is actually not uncommon; Henning (1874: 141) in his study of the St Gall charters notes a number of instances before 760 AD as well as a few instances in later charters, when the representation of initial /h/ becomes more regular. Braune and Heidermanns (2018: 202 (§153 note 2b)) suggest that such spellings in early charters are the result of Latin scribal practice. One might, then, wonder whether there is any need to posit a Proto-Germanic element *ūn(i)-, or if there is simply the element *Hun-*, which sometimes appears in Old High German contexts in the spelling <un>.

Fulk (1987: 123) also points, however, to evidence from outside the Old High German speaking area; he notes an Ostrogothic (or, according to Reichert (2009: 86 (§89), Vandalic) name form *Untancus* and the Frisian place-name forms *Untank* (Ondank) and *Unwaerskamp* (Onweerskamp). In particular, the Frisian form *Untank*, he suggests, confirms that the Ostrogothic *Untancus* is not simply a spelling lacking initial <h> due to Latin orthographic influence. This argument seems tenuous. The Frisian place-name is paralleled by several English places called *Unthank*, which Armstrong *et al* (1950–1952: 1.193) explain, not implausibly, as being related to the Old English word *unþanc*, suggesting that they usually originally indicated 'a squatter's holding' (see also Cameron 1959: 2.265; Ekwall 1960: s.v. *Unthank*). It seems highly likely that the Frisian place-name is to be explained in the same way, and it therefore does not shed any light on the Ostrogothic *Untancus*, a form which occurs within a Latin memorial text (Wilmanns 1881: 738 (no. 8650); see also Reichert 2009: 86 (§89), who notes another instance of the same name) and which we might, therefore, expect to show the influence of Latin orthographic practice (as Reichert 2009: 86 (§89) points out), in which <h> might readily be dropped because of its lack of phonetic value in Latin. There is, then, a lack of compelling evidence for Fulk's putative Proto-Germanic element *ūn(i)-. In the absence of clear evidence for the existence of this element, it seems simplest to suppose that ordinary variation names with a first element spelt <un> are, in fact, names formed with the well-attested element *Hun-*.

The implications of this for our understanding of the name *Unferð* are considerable. If Fulk was right to identify this name as formed with an element *Un(i)-*, then we could see this name as having been transmitted to England in either oral or written form, as the Old English poet would have identified it in either form as requiring vowel alliteration. If we discount Fulk's view, however, then we must explain the name as the result of a Continental Germanic spelling of the name that appears in Old English in forms such as *Hunferð* and *Hunfrið* without the initial <h> that appears very consistently in Old English forms of names with initial /h/. For an Old English poet to have received this name and to have identified it as requiring vowel alliteration, that poet would have to have had a written exemplar containing the Continental Germanic spelling without initial <h>. The *Beowulf* poet, it would appear, worked with at least one Continental Germanic written text, in which a form without initial <h> was employed for the name of this figure, and, in reading this source, the poet did not identify the name with Old English *Hunferð*, but treated it as a name beginning with a vowel sound. Only in the course of the manuscript transmission of the Old English poem did an Old English scribe then decide that the unfamiliar form *Unferð* required correction to the familiar *Hunferð*. This furnishes a very significant clue to the composition of the Old English poem, suggesting that the poet very probably had one or more written texts in a Continental Germanic dialect (quite probably a High German dialect) before them when they composed *Beowulf*.

When we turn to Unferð's father, Ecglaf, it is curious that Peterson (2004) does not include *Ecglaf* in her corpus of pre-Viking Age Scandinavian personal names. This may be because the two elements used in forming this name appear in names in *Beowulf*, but not in the runic material or place-names that form the rest of Peterson's corpus. Since *Ecgþeow* does appear (Peterson 2004: 37), however, along with *Oslaf, Guðlaf, Heaðolaf* and *Wiglaf* (Peterson 2004: 37, 38, 40), the logic of omitting *Ecglaf* seems unclear; if one is content to accept that all of these are early Scandinavian names, then *Ecglaf* is formed with elements used in early Scandinavian naming practices and should, therefore, be included in Peterson's material. It is far from clear, however, that *Ecgþeow* should feature in Peterson's Scandinavian personal names. As we have already seen in our consideration of Beowulf's father Ecgþeow (see pp. 26–29), it is not clear that there was a Scandinavian name element derived from Proto-Germanic *$a_3jō$ 'blade', cognate with Old English *Ecg-*, and we cannot, therefore, be certain that *Ecglaf* could represent an Anglicisation of a Scandinavian personal name.

The situation on the Continent is distinct from that in Scandinavia. Förstemann (1900: s.v. AG) groups under the headword *AG* names containing elements that he believes could derive from a number of different roots, including *aʒjō* 'blade'. Distinguishing between these possible roots is challenging, but *aʒjō* can be distinguished from the others on the basis that the /ʒ/ undergoes West Germanic consonant gemination before /j/, yielding forms such as *ecg* in Old English and *ekke* in Old High German (Hogg and Fulk 2011: 1.71 §4.11–4.13). Felder (2003: 48) argues that there is no clear evidence, in his dataset drawn from Merovingian coins, of forms in which West Germanic consonant gemination has taken place. In the broader dataset gathered by Förstemann (1900: s.v. *AG*), on the other hand, it seems clear that there are forms which reflect this sound change; alongside forms such as *Agebald* and *Agabert* we also find numerous instances of forms with <gg> or <kk> such as *Eggibald*, *Eggibert*, *Ekkeburg* and *Eggideo*. It would be perverse to dismiss all of these spellings with a double consonant symbol as not indicating a geminate consonant in speech, thus arguing that *aʒjō* 'blade' did not produce a personal name element in Continental Germanic dialects, but only in Old English. The most straightforward explanation of the evidence available is that *aʒjō* did indeed provide a name element used in Continental Germanic and in Old English personal names, but in all probability did not form part of Scandinavian personal naming practices.

The combination that appears as *Ecglaf* in Old English (*PASE*: s.v. *Ecglaf*) and in forms such as *Eggileib* and *Eckileip* in Old High German (Förstemann 1900: s.v. *AG*) is not particularly frequently attested either in England or on the Continent. It is, nevertheless, clearly a name that was in use in both areas. Since it was not in use in Scandinavia, we can be confident that the character called *Ecglaf* did not feature under this name in Scandinavian tradition. Moreover, he features in the poem solely as the father of Unferð, never appearing himself, and, as we have seen, Unferð is himself a character whose name is clearly not Scandinavian in origin. There is, then, no way in which the character Ecglaf is anchored to Scandinavian tradition, and he serves no narrative function in the Scandinavian dynastic narratives that provide the backdrop to the central action of the poem. We can be fairly certain, on this basis, that Ecglaf was created either on the Continent or in England and, given that he is inextricably linked with Unferð, whose name marks him out as a continental creation, a Continental Germanic origin seems by far the more likely.

If Unferð and his father represent part of the Continental Germanic narrative woven around the Scandinavian core represented by Hroðgar and his lineage, then we should not be surprised to find that Hroðgar's counsellor Æschere and his brother Yrmenlaf also belong to the continental central narrative of the poem. The name *Æschere* consists of one name-forming element that is very common in the early Germanic languages, the reflex of Proto-Germanic */xarjaz/ 'army', and another name-forming element that is less common but still well attested, the reflex of Proto-Germanic */askaz/ 'ash-tree'. The name element derived from */xarjaz/ is attested across the Germanic languages, although sound changes in the Scandinavian dialects render it difficult to distinguish this from some other similar elements when it appears as the second element in names (see discussion under *Ælfhere* at p. 36). The element derived from */askaz/, on the other hand, does not appear to be attested in Scandinavia, which is no doubt why this name does not feature among the plausibly Proto-Scandinavian names in *Beowulf* identified by Peterson (2004). This element is quite well attested in Old English, although the specific combination *æsc* + *here* does not appear before the *Domesday Book* (*PASE*: esp. s.v. *Æschere*). On the Continent, not only is the element derived from */askaz/ attested, but this particular combination of elements is not uncommon (Förstemann 1900: s.v. *ASCA*). There is, therefore, strong evidence for this as a Continental Germanic name, but the evidence for this name in early medieval England is less clear.

It is not straightforward to assess the significance of the absence of the exact name *Æschere* from the Old English onomasticon. Its presence in the *Domesday Book* could be the result of importation of the Continental Germanic name, rather than evidence for a native Old English form of the name. The *Domesday Book* includes numerous instances of Continental Germanic personal names that are readily identifiable as continental based on their forms. For example, forms of the name *Ansgar* are common; the first element of this name is in the Continental Germanic form *ans-*, which regularly corresponds to the form *os-* in Old English. While *Osgar* is an attested Old English personal name (*PASE*: s.v. *Osgar*), the name *Ansgar* is the Continental Germanic cognate of this name and clearly reflects increased importation of Continental Germanic personal names around the period of the Norman Conquest. In the case of the name *Æschere*, however, the form of the name does not allow us to distinguish between a putative Old English name and its Continental Germanic cognate. Since both elements of this name were certainly in use in other combinations in Old English, it is entirely possible that *Æschere* was in use in the Old English onomasticon but no instances happen to have survived. On the other hand, it is also possible that this particular combination was not in use in England, and that this particular combination of elements was used only on the Continent.

It is interesting to note that this name is unlikely to be a Scandinavian name. The character bearing this name is a peripheral character, in the sense that he is not part of the royal houses whose scions are attested in other texts besides *Beowulf*. He is peripheral also in the sense that he appears (explicitly at least) only after his death, when he is mentioned as the Dane killed by Grendel's mother. This would tend to suggest that the narrative detail of his name did not form part of any Scandinavian tradition that informed the poem, but was instead an addition at a later stage, outside Scandinavia. On the basis of the English and Continental Germanic evidence discussed above, the most straightforward interpretation is that this figure was created in a continental milieu, and this would be consistent with the hypothesis that the central narrative of Beowulf's monster fights – of which Æschere forms part – was woven around the Scandinavian tradition of Hroðgar's court in a continental milieu.

This conclusion is reinforced by the name of Æschere's younger brother, *Yrmenlaf*, as this name is attested on the Continent (Förstemann 1900: s.v. *ERMIN*), but not in Scandinavia or England. While the second element is well attested across the Germanic languages, the first element is more limited in its distribution. In Scandinavia, this name element occurs only, to the best of the present author's knowledge, in the Old Norse form of the name of the Gothic king Ermanaric (see Lind 1905–1915: s.v. *Iǫrmunrekr*). This is clearly a borrowed name, however, and is not evidence of native Scandinavian use of the name element. In England, on the other hand, the situation is more complicated. While this name element is very common on the Continent (see Förstemann 1900: s.v. *ERMIN*), in England *PASE* records only the names *Eormenburg*, *Eormengyth*, *Eormenhild*, *Eormenred*, *Eormenric* and *Eormenthryth* (*PASE*: s.v. *Eormenburg 1*, *Eormengyth 1*, *Eormenhild 1*, *Eormenred 1–3*, *Eormenric 1* and *Eormenthryth 1*). Besides these, *PASE* also includes entries for individuals called *Ermenfrid* and *Ermenfridus*, but neither of these is an Englishman (*PASE*: s.v. *Ermenfrid 1* and *Ermenfridus 1*). The *Durham Liber Vitae* includes instances of the names *Eormenburg* and *Eormenhild* (Rollason and Rollason 2007: 2. 116). We will return to the former shortly, but it is worth remarking at this point that the name form *Hermenild* occurs in a twelfth-century section of the *Durham Liber Vitae*. While this name is treated by Insley, Rollason and McClure as an English personal name (Rollason and Rollason 2007: 2.116), there seems no strong reason to regard this name as English rather than Continental Germanic, given the date of its entry into the *Liber Vitae*, and we can, therefore, discount this as evidence for an English name. Nevertheless, the Old English name element *Eormen-* is clearly not poorly attested, so one might, at first glance, think it possible that *Yrmenlaf* is an English name that simply happens not to be attested outside *Beowulf*.

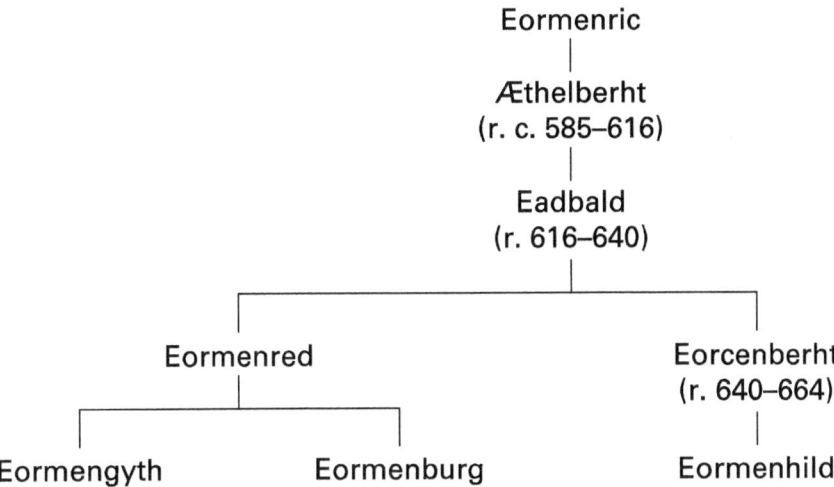

Figure 2.6 Partial family tree of the royal house of Kent, showing sixth- and seventh-century individuals whose names contain the first element *Eormen-*, and their immediate relatives.

If we consider only the mere existence of the Old English names in *Eormen-*, however, we are liable to be misled. With the exception of the names *Eormenred* and *Eormenthryth*, these names were all borne, according to *PASE*, exclusively by members of the Kentish royal house who lived in the sixth and seventh centuries (see Figure 2.6). The *Iurminburg* recorded in the *Durham Liber Vitae* is in all probability the same individual as *PASE*'s *Eormenburg 1*, whose name forms part of this group of Kentish royal names (Briggs 1987: 27). *PASE* records two other bearers of the name *Eormenred* besides *Eormenred 1*, the member of the Kentish royal house noted in Figure 2.6. *Eormenred 2* is a witness to a Kentish charter in 679 AD (S 8), while *Eormenred 3* is mentioned in a charter of around 690 AD (S 14) as a previous owner of some land in Thanet. It is entirely conceivable that both *Eormenred 2* and *Eormenred 3* were, in fact, the same person as *Eormenred 1*, given that *Eormenred 1* was the brother of King Eorcenberht of Kent, whose rule extended into the 660s. These Kentish royal names are probably also to be understood as borrowings from Continental Germanic. The tendency of the early Kentish royal house to choose Continental Germanic personal names is evidenced in other names as well, such as the names of Hloðhere, king of Kent (*PASE*: s.v. *Hlothhere 1*), Eorcenberht, king of Kent (*PASE*: s.v. *Eorcenberht 1*) and his daughter Eorcengota (*PASE*: s.v. *Eorcengota 1*), and Swæfheard, king of Kent (*PASE*: s.v. *Swæfheard 1*), and it seems likely that the *Eormen-* names provide more evidence of this family tradition.[1]

It seems quite plausible, then, that the only individual who does not fit in this Kentish royal group is *Eormenthryth 1*, and she does not appear to have a native English name. Although she was a granddaughter of King Alfred, she was the daughter of Baldwin II, Count of Flanders (*PASE*: s.v. *Baldwin 2*), so it seems likely that her name was a Continental Germanic name, as was that of her brother Arnulf (*PASE*: s.v. *Arnulf 2*). She is mentioned in Æthelweard's *Chronicon*, where her name appears in the form *Earmentruth*, with the <truth> spelling of the second element (in contrast to the spelling <dryde> for the same element in her English mother's name) representing an obviously Continental Germanic form of this second element (Campbell 1962: 2). We can therefore discount her name as evidence for an English tradition of use of *Eormen-* as a name element. There is, then, no particular reason to suppose that *Eormen-* was ever employed as a native English variation element.

Here again, we have evidence for the use in *Beowulf* of a personal name that is formed with a variation element that is common on the Continent but not in England or Scandinavia. The presence of this name in *Beowulf* is not readily explicable in terms of borrowing of Scandinavian narrative traditions, or invention by an Old English poet. If some of the narrative material of *Beowulf* made its way to England from the Continent, however, this name is readily explained as a Continental Germanic name that came into being in a Continental Germanic narrative about Scandinavia. Once again, it seems plausible to see these peripheral figures at Hroðgar's court not as part of the Scandinavian tradition of Hroðgar and his family, but as part of a continental narrative of Beowulf's exploits that was set against this Scandinavian backdrop.

The last of Hroðgar's courtiers to consider is Wulfgar, who describes himself at line 336 as Hroðgar's 'ar ond ombiht' ('herald and officer') when he greets Beowulf and his men before going to announce them to Hroðgar. Unlike the other courtiers discussed above, his name provides no clue as to his origins. The name *Wulfgar* is extremely common in Old English, with *PASE* presenting 70 distinct entries for it; even allowing for the possibility that some distinct entries relate to the same individual, this was clearly a very popular name. *Wulfgar* also occurs twice in the *Durham Liber Vitae* (Rollason and Rollason 2007: 2.162). This name is equally plausibly an early Scandinavian name, with Peterson (2004: 35, 40) noting the use of the individual elements used in forming this name in either her runic or her place-name data. Similarly, in *Landnámabók* we find both elements frequently attested, although never in combination with one another; just among the earliest settlers, we find the names *Úlfarr* and *Úlfljótr*, *Álfgeirr*, *Arngeirr*, *Ásgeirr*, *Hallgeirr*, *Hróðgeirr*, *Jólgeirr*, *Oddgeirr* and *Þorgeirr*

(Benediktsson 1968: 1.126, 2.229, 2.230, 2.285, 1.86, 2.354, 1.68, 2.367, 1.68, 1.72). In Viking Age runic inscriptions, however, not only are both elements common in other combinations, but they are also paired to form the name *Ulfgæirr*, cognate with Old English *Wulfgar* (Peterson 2007: s.v. *Ulf-*, *-gæirr*, *Ulfgæirr*). This name would, therefore, be entirely plausible as a Scandinavian or as an Old English name. On the Continent, moreover, this name is also well attested; Förstemann (1900: s.v. *VULFA*) records numerous instances of this name. There is, then, no reason to see this name as geographically restricted within the Germanic-speaking world. We could, then, suppose that Wulfgar was a figure closely associated with Hroðgar who travelled with him from Scandinavia, but it is also possible that he represents an innovation on the Continent or in early medieval England. Given that Hroðgar's other courtiers in the poem appear to represent part of the continental narrative surrounding Beowulf, however, it is certainly tempting to suppose that Wulfgar was similarly created in this context, although we also cannot rule out the possibility that he represents an additional flourish on the part of the Old English poet.

3

The Scilfings

The Swedish Scilfing dynasty deserves its own chapter as it represents a significant part of the framing narrative of conflict between the Geats and the Swedes in *Beowulf*. This dynasty presents interesting challenges of interpretation, both because, like Healfdene's family, it is represented in later Scandinavian texts, and because the names borne by figures in this dynasty suggest a puzzling mixture of Scandinavian and Continental Germanic origins. While the names *Ohthere* and *Onela* could be interpreted as Scandinavian in origin – although Continental Germanic origins are also possible – *Ongenþeow*, *Eadgils* and *Eanmund* are not readily explicable as deriving from Scandinavian tradition. This might suggest that the Scilfing dynasty, as represented in *Beowulf*, is the result of a combination of Scandinavian narrative tradition with additional elements created either on the Continent or in England as part of the development of the central narrative of *Beowulf* itself. It is perhaps more likely, however, that the Scilfing dynasty was an early import from the Continent into Scandinavia.

As represented in *Beowulf*, this dynasty consists of Ongenþeow, his sons Onela and Ohthere, and Ohthere's sons Eanmund and Eadgils. This family tree must be compared with the representation of this dynasty in *Ynglingatal*, which features figures called Óttarr (cognate with *Ohthere*), Aðils (corresponding to *Eadgils*) and Áli (cognate with *Onela*). The relationships between these figures are not explicitly stated in *Ynglingatal*, however, leaving us to puzzle over the extent to which the dynastic relationships depicted in *Beowulf* underlie the accounts in the Scandinavian poem. It seems reasonable to suppose that *Ynglingatal* presents its sequence of Scilfing kings in essentially chronological order, so that the placement of Aðils in the stanza after Óttarr is consistent with an identification of Aðils as Óttarr's son. The identification of Áli as the enemy of Aðils, however, does not demonstrate that the author or audience of *Ynglingatal* knew Áli as Óttarr's brother and Aðils's uncle. If, however, the *cyning* who is deprived of life by Eadgils with Beowulf's aid at line 2396 of *Beowulf* is identified with Onela, then this would fit with the treatment of Áli and Aðils as enemies in

Ynglingatal. In the Scandinavian poem, however, the head of the dynasty in *Beowulf*, Ongenþeow, is lacking, as is his grandson Eanmund. The implications of this are difficult to assess. Possibly Ongenþeow and Eanmund do not belong to the main narrative tradition of this dynasty and represent additions made by the *Beowulf* poet or in a source or sources used by the poet. However, insofar as we can date *Ynglingatal* and *Beowulf*, the latter appears to be the older text (see discussion of the dating of *Ynglingatal* in Marold 2012: 5–6); we might, therefore, suggest that *Beowulf* represents a more complete form of the narrative tradition of this group of figures. The implications of these two models will be considered below, but we turn first to the potential origins of the names of figures in this dynasty, on which any assessment of the origins of the dynastic tradition must be built.

We begin with those members of the dynasty who are attested in both *Beowulf* and *Ynglingatal*. The brothers Onela and Ohthere both have names that are consistent with Scandinavian origin, although they could also have been formed on the Continent. Peterson (2004: 37) regards *Onela* as plausibly Proto-Scandinavian, noting that the root element of this name occurs in her data from early Scandinavian place-names. This name is also well attested on the Continent, appearing in forms such as *Anila*, *Anilo* and *Anulo* (Förstemann 1900: s.v. *AN*). In early medieval England, there is no evidence for the use of this name, although the name *Anna* is perhaps formed on the same root element (Rollason and Rollason 2007: 2.167), and names such as *Beccel*, *Boisil* and *Pichil* are formed with the -*ila*- suffix that we see in the name *Onela* (*PASE*: s.v. *Beccel 1*; Rollason and Rollason 2007: 2.170, 2.182). It is not impossible, then, that a name of this form could have been created in early medieval England, although Scandinavian or continental origins are more plausible.

The situation is similar with regard to the name *Ohthere*. Peterson (2004: 40) identifies this as a Proto-Scandinavian name, noting that it also appears in her early Scandinavian place-name material. In later Scandinavian sources, including *Ynglingatal*, this name appears as *Óttarr* (see Peterson 2007: s.v. *Óttarr*; Benediktsson 1968: 1.109 n. 9, 1.123, 2.224, 2.275, 2.318, 2.356). It is important to bear in mind, however, that the form *Óttarr* need not be cognate with *Ohthere*; the second element that appears as -*arr* in Viking Age personal names could derive from Proto-Germanic */xarjaz/, */ʒaizaz/ or */warjaz/ (see Peterson 2007: s.v. -*arr*), and thus need not always correspond to Old English -*here* (from Proto-Germanic */xarjaz/). It is difficult to date the loss of initial /x/ in the second elements of Scandinavian personal names; Voyles (1992: 106) points to the inscription on the Svarteborg medallion, dating to around 450 AD, as an instance of loss of initial /x/ in a second element, in a name form *sigaduz*, deriving from **sigahaduz*. It is not, however, certain that this is a name whose second element did have initial /x/; various interpretations of the inscription have been advanced, and while some, such as Krause (1966: 107) and Salberger (1987: 19–21) interpret the inscription as consisting of a name in which the initial /x/ of the second element has been lost, others, such as Andersen (1973: 115–17) and Wagner (2009) provide interpretations that do not involve loss of /x/, while Antonsen (1975: 49 no 36) presents a reading of the text as a name in which /x/ was never present to be lost. Peterson (2004: 15) also attests to the difficulty of interpretation of this inscription, presenting two of the previously advanced interpretations (one of which involves loss of /x/ and one of which does not) without indicating a preference between them. The evidence for loss of /x/ in such cases only becomes clear in the Viking Age runic materials noted by Peterson (2007: s.v. *Ōttarr*), but these inscriptions generally cannot be dated very precisely, and may well belong mainly or wholly to the later part of the Viking Age.

It is thus difficult to know when the Proto-Scandinavian name **Ōhta-harjaz* would have lost the initial */x/ of its second element, and it is therefore difficult to assess the significance of the differing representations of this Scandinavian name (or the others that come to be identical in form with it) in Old English sources. In *Beowulf*, the name appears twice in forms in which the second element is explicitly represented as *-here* (lines 2928 and 2932) and three times in forms without an initial <h> in the second element (lines 2380, 2394 and 2612). We also find instances in the account of Ohthere's voyage in the Alfredian *Orosius* (Bately 1980: 13, 16) and in the *Anglo-Saxon Chronicle* (see, for instance, Bately 1986: 65; Taylor 1983: 47, 48; O'Brien O'Keeffe 2001: 73, 74). In the Alfredian *Orosius* the second element is represented as *-here*, whereas in the *Chronicle* the name occurs in forms such as *Ohtor* and *Ohter*, in which the second element is represented without an initial <h>. The *Orosius* pre-dates the relevant *Chronicle* entries, which are for 911 and 914 AD, although the timespan between the production of the *Orosius* and the first of the *Chronicle* entries could be as short as twelve years or as long as forty years (on the dating of the Old English *Orosius*, see Bately 1980: lxxxvi–lxxxix). In *Beowulf*, we have to reckon not only with the date of original production of a manuscript text of the poem, but also with the date of the extant manuscript; given the late date of the extant manuscript, we might surmise that the forms with <h> in the second element represent an earlier stage in the transmission of the text, while the forms without could have been introduced by the early eleventh-century copyist. While this idea is attractive, however, it is far from clear that we should treat this as an issue of chronology. It is entirely possible that loss of /h/ in *Ōhta-harjaz pre-dated even the earliest manuscript form of Beowulf, and that the spellings with <h> in Old English texts merely represent an effort at Anglicising the name Óttarr that takes Old English -here as a plausible guess at the identity of the Old Norse second element -arr. The spellings without <h> would then simply represent efforts at Anglicisation that do not attempt to find an equivalent Old English second element, but instead simply represent the Old Norse second element more or less phonetically.

These considerations are important if we treat the name Ohthere as deriving from Scandinavia, but it is worth noting that it could also be of continental origin. On the Continent, a name cognate with Proto-Scandinavian *Ōhta-harjaz is attested occasionally. Förstemann (1900: s.v. AHT) notes some examples in the Traditiones Corbeienses (Wigand 1843: 58 (nos 279, 280) and 102 (no. 461)) which, although preserved only in a later medieval manuscript, probably record land grants from the later ninth century. To these we might wish to add the name form Ohtcarius, which is given as that of a bishop of Chur, Switzerland, in a fourteenth-century addition to the Liber anniversariorum ecclesiae maioris Curiensis (Baumann 1888: 634). Given the late date of this attestation, however, we might also consider the possibility that the second element of this name derives from Proto-Germanic *ʒaizaz 'spear' with the devoicing of Proto-Germanic initial */ʒ/ characteristic of High German dialects. A clearer case is the name form Ohteri, which occurs in the necrology of Magdeburg in an addition of the early eleventh century to the entry for 30 September (Althoff and Wollasch 1983: facsimile p. 60; see also p. XXXI on dating). This was apparently not an enormously popular name on the Continent, but it is nevertheless securely attested as a Continental Germanic personal name. In principle, then, we could see this name as originating either in Scandinavia or on the Continent.

The name of Ohthere's son, Eadgils, provides greater insight into the origins of this dynastic tradition. This name presents interesting problems, as it is attested as the name of a legendary Swedish king not only in this form in Beowulf, but also in various forms not cognate with Old English Eadgils in Scandinavian texts (in both Old Norse and in Latin). Scandinavian forms of the name include: Atislus and Athislus, applied to two distinct Swedish kings in Saxo Grammaticus's Gesta Danorum, although it seems likely that Saxo here created two kings out of a single legendary figure (Friis-Jensen and Fisher 2015: 1.108–18, 1.142, 1.156, 1.222–42); Aðils in Hrólfs saga kraka (Jónsson 1959: 1.26–43, 1.73–90) and in Ynglingatal (Marold 2012: 36 (stanza 16)) and the alternative possibilities Adils and Athisl offered in the Latin rendering of Ynglingatal in the Historia Norwegiae.

The Scandinavian forms can be explained as deriving from a Proto-Germanic form */aþa-ʒīslaz/, which is not cognate with the Old English form *Eadgils*, deriving from Proto-Germanic */auða-ʒīslaz/. The first element */aþa/ is not well attested in Scandinavia but is fairly common on the Continent (Förstemann 1900: s.v. ATHA) and is uncommon but not poorly attested in Old English (*PASE*: s.v. *Athulf, Æthelm, Ætheric, Æthred, Æthulf, Æthwine*). That a name containing this element continued in use in Scandinavia into the Viking Age (Peterson 2007: s.v. *Aðīsl*) may be a result of the influence of the legendary tradition surrounding this Swedish king on personal naming practices. The name element may appear in some early place-names in Scandinavia (Peterson 2004: 22–23) but given the later medieval dates of attestation of these place-names, this interpretation of their origins is open to doubt. Otherwise the sole evidence for the existence of this name element in Scandinavian naming practices appears to be the phonetically reduced name form *Aðisl* itself. The phonetic reduction may well reflect a transmission of this name as a complete item, rather than a continuing creation of the name from the two variation elements of which it was originally composed. It is possible, then, that the element */aþa/ never formed part of Scandinavian naming practice and that this name was imported from elsewhere in the Germanic-speaking world and fossilised in this form. This name *Aðisl* then continued in use as a complete name, because of its use in legendary narrative.

This presents difficulties for our interpretation of the name form *Eadgils* in *Beowulf*. Although not cognate with *Aðils/Aðisl*, the fact that both figures form part of the Swedish dynasty as the son or at least an immediate successor of *Ohthere* suggests that we should view them as reflexes of the same figure. How, then, are we to account for the development of two different – albeit quite similar sounding – names for the same figure? There is no reason why an Old English **Æðgils* should not have been formed as an English cognate of the Scandinavian name *Aðils/Aðisl*, given that both of the necessary elements were in use in Old English. If the Scandinavian figure had been imported from England into Scandinavia, moreover, we should not expect *Eadgils* to yield *Aðils*, given that Old Norse did have a name element directly cognate with Old English *Ead-* (see, for example, Peterson 2007: s.v. *Auð-*). In order to account for the development of these two distinct names, we must posit a Continental Germanic origin for this figure. Only on the Continent, and specifically in the Old Saxon area, do we find a name element in the form *Âd-*, which Kaufmann (1968: 44; see also Schlaug 1962: 136–37, but note Kaufmann's criticisms of Schlaug's analysis) regards as a side form of *Auda-*, cognate with Old English *Ead-*. A Scandinavian encountering this element *Âd-* would be highly likely to render it as *Að-*, which would account for the name form *Aðils/Aðisl*. If this were a side form of a Continental Germanic name in *Auda-*, moreover, then this name would have been readily identified by the Old English poet as a cognate of Old English *Eadgils*. Alternatively, if the archetype of *Beowulf* had simply transcribed a Continental Germanic spelling such as <adgils>, then a later scribe might well have identified this as a misspelling of the familiar name *Eadgils*. The hypothesis of a continental origin for this figure helps us to account in a fairly simple fashion for the apparently different names he bears in Scandinavian tradition as compared with *Beowulf*, and it does so without requiring us to accept that the Proto-Germanic element */aþa/ existed in Scandinavian naming practice, despite the lack of clear evidence for it in this region. This might suggest that Eadgils and his father Ohthere and uncle Onela are all derived ultimately from a Continental Germanic tradition.

The Scilfings who appear both in *Beowulf* and in *Ynglingatal* are, then, perhaps to be seen as originating ultimately somewhere on the Continent. When we turn to the Scilfings who feature in *Beowulf* but not in *Ynglingatal*, we find that a Continental Germanic origin is also possible in both cases. The head of the dynasty in *Beowulf* bears the name *Ongenþeow* (but note the possibility that this name is also applied to a king of the Angles in the poem; see discussion in relation to *Eomer* at pp. 145–46), which is unlikely to be an English name and presents interesting problems of interpretation as a Scandinavian name. The first element *Ongen-* corresponds to *Angan-* in Continental Germanic names such as *Anganhilda* (Waitz 1887: 260 (l. 42)), *Anganulfus* (Loewenfeld 1886: 26), *Anganricho* and *Anganberto* (Piper 1884: 238 (col. 279, l. 11, 19)). This name element is well attested on the Continent, but considerably less so in England and Scandinavia. Björkman (1920b: 91–92) notes the scarce English and Scandinavian evidence, and suggests that this is a name element that fell out of productive use in these areas before the period when written evidence began to appear in any quantity. This may be the correct explanation of the situation in Scandinavia, to which we will return shortly, but there is no evidence to suggest that this name element was ever in use in English naming practices.

The only instances of this name element in English sources appear to be in the names of figures associated with the Continent in the royal genealogical tradition and in *Widsith*. The various versions of the English royal genealogies seem to reflect considerable confusion about the name of the individual who comes between Offa and Eomer. This individual is variously named *Angelgeot* (Dumville 1976: 36) and *Angengeot/Angengiot* (Dumville 1976: 30, 33) in the Anglian collection of royal genealogies, *Angelþeow* in the *Anglo-Saxon Chronicle* (O'Brien O'Keeffe 2001: 37 (s.a. 626), 48 (s.a. 755)), *Ongen* in the *Historia Brittonum* (Mommsen 1898: 203; Dumville 1975: 1.241, 3.698) and *Angengeat* in the *Chronicle* of John of Worcester (Darlington and McGurk 1995: 86). As discussed in relation to the name *Ecgþeow* above (pp. 26–29), *-þeow* does not appear to have existed in Old English naming practices, occurring only in the name of this figure from the legendary reaches of the genealogical tradition and in *Beowulf*. The same is true of *Angen-/Ongen-*, and it would, therefore, not be entirely surprising to find forms of the name *Angenþeow* in which one or other of these elements had been adjusted. Indeed, it seems highly probable that the name *Incgenþeow* in *Widsith* (Malone 1962: 26 (l. 116)) represents an Anglicised form of the name that appears in *Heiðreks saga* as *Angantýr*; in this line of the Old English poem, we find *Incgenþeow* alongside *Heaþoric, Sifecan* and *Hliþe*, apparently corresponding to *Heiðrekr, Sifka* and *Hlǫðr* in the saga (see Turville-Petre [1956] 2014: 19, 30 and Jónsson 1959: 2.24, 2.30 for the first appearances of the figures bearing these names in the saga). Tolkien (1960: xxv–xxvi) argues convincingly that this passage in *Widsith* reflects knowledge in early medieval England of a reflex of the narrative tradition of the battle of the Goths and Huns that is also attested in *Heiðreks saga*. In *Widsith*, therefore, we have a clear instance of an adjustment of the name element *Angen-* in an Old English text.

In the royal genealogies, something similar appears to have taken place; *Angen-* is adjusted to *Angel-* in some cases, while in other cases *-þeow* is adjusted to *-geat* or simply removed. An interesting aspect of the adjustments to the first element is that it does not involve the swapping of a name element for a more common Old English element. The name element *Angel-* or *Engel-* does not appear to have been in use in Old English; besides the royal ancestor *Angelþeow* (*PASE*: s.v. *Angeltheow 1*), *PASE* has the phantom headforms *Engelbald* and *Engeler*, which do not link to any entries, and the headforms *Engelbert* and *Engelric*, which refer only to names in the *Domesday Book* that could well be Continental Germanic names. The *Durham Liber Vitae* yields no instances of names formed with this element. The element *-geat*, on the other hand, is very common, although restricted to names from the tenth century onwards (*PASE*: s.v. *Ælfgeat 1–18, Æthelgeat 2–3, Earngeat 1, Leofgeat 1, Mergeat 1–2, Osgeat 2–4, Sægeat 1, Ufegeat 1–2, Wulfgeat 1–19* and *21–31; Wurgeat 1* is probably to be identified as bearing a Welsh name). The royal genealogies, moreover, contain two more individuals with *-geat* names besides *Angengeat: Siggeot* and *Weoðulgeot/Weoþolgiot/Weoðogeot* (Dumville 1976: 30, 32, 33, 35, 36). One could, then, explain the replacement of *-þeow* by *-geat* in terms of attraction of a problematic name element towards one that was moderately common in Old English personal naming (at least in the later Old English period) and in evidence elsewhere in the genealogical material. It seems plausible, then, to suppose that the name *Ongenþeow* was not in use in early medieval England, and the uses of its constituent elements in English genealogical tradition reflect the engagement of that tradition with the continental past from which the English royal houses sought to trace their descent.

The situation is more complex when we turn to the Scandinavian evidence. The only Old Norse evidence for a name element cognate with *Ongen-* consists of the name *Angantýr*, which Björkman (1920b: 92) views as a corruption or transformation of an original Old Norse form **Anganþér*. This seems problematic, as although the second element is attested in early runic inscriptions in its Proto-Norse form *-þewaz* (Peterson 2004: 13, 19), there is no particular reason to expect that it would undergo corruption or transformation to *-týr*. The expected reflex of *-þewaz* is *-þér*, which does, in fact, occur, although only (to the best of the present author's knowledge) in the names of fictional characters such as Eggþér and Hjálmþér (Lind 1905–1915: s.v. *Eggþér*, *Hiálmþér*). The form *Angantýr* might, however, readily arise as a borrowing of a Continental Germanic form in which the second element had become *-tio* or *-teo*, as in forms such as *Erlenteo*, *Godestio* and *Walateo* (Förstemann 1900: s.v. ERLA, GUDA, VALHA). This would account for the use of <t> rather than <þ> as a representation of the initial sound of the element, while the termination in <r> might well have been added as part of the adaptation of the name to Old Norse. This is consistent with the fact that *Angantýr* in Old Norse is found only in the narrative of Gothic dynastic strife presented in *Heiðreks saga* (Jónsson 1959: 2.2, 2.23). This would appear, then, to provide evidence not for a Scandinavian name, but for the Scandinavianisation of a Continental Germanic name.

In addition to the Old Norse evidence for the use of *Angan-*, we must also consider the evidence of continental Latin sources for a name cognate with *Ongenþeow* in Scandinavia. A name form *Ongendus* is attributed to a king of the Danes in Alcuin's *Vita Sancti Willibrordi* (Krusch and Levison 1920: 123) and Krusch and Levison (1920: 123 n. 3) identify this as a form of the name *Ongenþeow*. The *Annales regni Francorum* for the year 811 AD, moreover, makes reference to a brother of a king Hemming of the Danes called *Angandeo* (Kurze 1895: 134), which is clearly cognate with *Ongenþeow*. This might suggest that this name was in use within at least the uppermost echelon of Danish society in the eighth and ninth centuries, but a degree of caution is required here. The spelling *–deo* for the second element of this name is consistent not with the expected Old Norse form *-þér*, but with Continental Germanic forms as noted above; indeed, this form is identical with that used for a bearer of this name who attested a land grant to Fulda (Dronke 1850: 164 no. 343). This might simply be a case of a Frankish individual silently translating a Scandinavian name into the corresponding Continental Germanic name. Given that *Angan-* features in various different Continental Germanic names but only in these two instances of *Angandeo* in Scandinavia, however, it seems quite possible that this name represents a Continental Germanic import adopted by Danish royalty (cf. Hammer 2005: 44), just as early Kentish royalty adopted Frankish names (see above pp. 99–100). There is also a figure named *Anganterus/Anganturus* in Saxo's *Gesta Danorum* who is depicted as a son of the *dux* of *Sialandia*, present-day Sjælland (Friis-Jensen and Fisher 2015: 1.402, 1.408). This name appears to correspond to the Old Norse form *Angantýr* discussed above, raising questions about the possibility that Saxo derived this name from Continental Germanic tradition, although we might also consider the possibility that this reflects some tradition deriving from one or other of the royal individuals noted in the *Vita Sancti Willibrordi* and the *Annales regni Francorum*.

The name *Ongenþeow* in *Beowulf* clearly presents some complexities of interpretation. It could plausibly be an Anglicised form of the Continental Germanic name *Angandeo*, but it is also possible that it reflects Scandinavian use of this name, whether as a native name or as an import from the Continent. As noted above, it is perhaps more likely that this name was an import from the Continent in Danish royal circles than a native Scandinavian name that is otherwise unattested. We might also wonder whether the Ongenþeow of *Beowulf* could have derived from the individual called *Ongendus* in the *Vita Sancti Willibrordi*. This is not a chronological impossibility, but we also cannot rule out the possibility that Ongendus was named under the influence of Continental Germanic narrative traditions in Danish royal circles. We might, then, see *Ongenþeow* as potentially deriving either from Denmark or the Continent, but the probably Continental Germanic origins of *Eadgils/Aðils* might incline us somewhat towards the view that Ongenþeow and his sons also originated on the Continent.

The final figure to consider in the Scilfing dynasty as represented in *Beowulf* is Eanmund, son of Ohthere, who appears just once in the text as a previous owner of Wiglaf's war gear (l. 2611). While Ohthere and his other son Eadgils appear in Scandinavian tradition (see Garmonsway and Simpson 1968: 214–21 and discussion above), Eanmund does not (*pace* Garmonsway and Simpson 1968: 216; the figures called *Eymundr* and *Hömothus* to whom they point cannot certainly be identified as a son of Ohthere, and the first element of their names appears to be the element *Øy-* identified by Peterson (2007: s.v. *Øy-*), which is not cognate with Old English *Ean-*). This should come as little surprise, however, as the name *Eanmund* does not appear to have existed in Scandinavia. The second element *-mund* is unproblematic, in that it is a widespread personal name-forming element in the Germanic languages. Förstemann (1900: s.v. *MUNDA*) lists 172 different names formed with this as a second element. *PASE* has 67 headforms containing this as a second element, although here we have to bear in mind that some of these may be different forms of the same name (e.g. *Freothomund* and *Frithumund*, *Sigemund* and *Sigmund*) and there are undoubtedly some Scandinavian (e.g. *Agmundr*) and Continental Germanic (e.g. *Trasmund*) personal name forms included. Nevertheless, this name element was clearly very common in Old English naming practices. In Scandinavia, this name element crops up in the corpora of names in early runic inscriptions and in early place-names assembled by Peterson (2004: 43). It is also very well attested in the Viking Age Scandinavian runic inscriptions surveyed by Peterson (2007: s.v. *-mundr*). In *Landnámabók* names with the second element *-mundr* are fairly common; just among the initial settlers of Iceland named in the text, for example, we find the names *Ásmundr*, *Friðmundr*, *Geirmundr*, *Hrómundr*, *Ingimundr*, *Sigmundr*, *Sæmundr* and *Vémundr* (Benediktsson 1968: 2.218, 2.218, 1.87, 1.85, 2.218, 1.88, 2.228, 2.307). We can, therefore, be very confident that the second element of the name *Eanmund* was a common Germanic name element that was in use across England, Scandinavia and the Continent.

The first element, which appears in Old English as *Ean-*, is more locally distributed, however. This element is well attested on the Continent, and there are a number of instances of bearers of Continental Germanic forms of the name *Eanmund* such as *Aunimund* and *Aunemund* (Förstemann 1900: s.v. *AUN*). *PASE* identifies eleven individuals bearing the name *Eanmund* in early medieval England, and the element *Ean-* appears as the first element of some eighteen distinct names in the *PASE* corpus. At first glance, there appear to be twenty distinct names in *Ean-* in the headforms in *PASE*, but two of these should be discounted. *Eanfric 1*, the sole bearer of this name, is a product of a spurious charter and we should probably, therefore, discount this particular name, especially as the second element *-fric* that it appears to imply is not otherwise attested. In contrast, the very suspicious *Eandberht 1* proves, on closer inspection, to be a clear instance of a name in *Ean-* that should, in fact, appear under the headform *Eanberht*. The individual labelled *Eandberht 1* by *PASE* is an individual whose name appears in the form *EONBERECH[T]* on an eighth- or ninth-century lead plate from Flixborough in Lincolnshire (Okasha 1992: 46–47 (no. 193)). Discounting these two names from the *PASE* headforms, one because it is probably not genuine, and the other because it is a genuine form that is already represented by another headform, we arrive at this figure of eighteen distinct name forms. This element is thus quite well attested in England and on the Continent. In Scandinavia, in contrast, there is no clear evidence for the use of this name element.

It seems clear that *Eanmund* is not a Scandinavian name. That a supposedly Scandinavian character bears this name might, therefore, appear to be a puzzle. It is worth remarking, however, that although this character forms part of the Swedish Scilfing dynasty – a dynasty that is well attested in the legendary literature of Scandinavia – he is, as noted above, a figure who does not actually appear himself in the Scandinavian texts. Moreover, he appears in *Beowulf* in what is essentially a self-contained micro-excursus on the origins of Wiglaf's war-gear (lines 2609–2625):

> hond rond gefeng,
> geolwe linde,   gomel swyrd geteah;
> þæt wæs mid eldum   Eanmundes laf,
> suna Ohtere[s];   þam æt sæcce wearð,
> wrǽcca(n) wineleasum   Weohsta*n* bana
> meces ecgum,   ond his magum ætbær
> brunfagne helm,   hringde byrnan,
> ealdsweord etonisc;   þæt him Onela forgeaf,
> his gædelinges   guðgewædu,
> fyrdsearo fuslic —   no ymbe ða fæhðe spræc,
> þeah ðe he his broðor bearn   abredwade.
> He frætwe geheold   fela missera,
> bill ond byrnan,   oð ðæt his byre mihte
> eorlscipe efnan   swa his ærfæder;
> geaf him ða mid Geatum   guðgewæda
> æghwæs unrim   þa he of ealdre gewat
> frod on forðweg.

his hand seized his shield, the yellow linden wood, he took up his ancient sword; that was his inheritance from Eanmund, son of Ohthere, among his ancestors; Weohstan killed him as a lordless exile in battle with the sword's edges, and carried away to his kinsmen the bright-patterned helmet, the ringed mail-shirt and the ancient, giant-made sword; Onela gave him that, his kinsman's battle-clothing, his readied armour — he spoke not about that feud, though he had killed his brother's child. He possessed that treasure, the sword and mail-shirt, many half-years until his son could perform acts of heroism like his father; then he gave him among the Geats a countless number of every battle-garment when he departed this life, wise on the way forth.

This appears within the main narrative at the point at which Wiglaf goes to help Beowulf in his final fight against the dragon. The insertion of a narrative of this sort helps to anchor Wiglaf – a character unknown to the Scandinavian textual tradition – to a dynasty that forms an important part of Scandinavian tradition. This could suggest that Eanmund is a character created as part of a conscious effort to place the central narrative of *Beowulf* against the backdrop of legendary history against which the story of the hero Beowulf is told.

The Scilfings provide an important part of the Scandinavian legendary history that contextualises the life and exploits of Beowulf himself, yet their names suggest that they need not have originated in Scandinavia but may have arisen somewhere on the Continent. If so, they were imported quite early into Scandinavia, and flourished in the heroic tradition of that region, although we could also see Ongenþeow and his sons as forming the core of a native Scandinavian tradition that was enlarged by the addition of the figure *Eadgils/Aðils* from a continental source. Eanmund could have formed part of an original continental tradition which was simply not transplanted into Scandinavia, but could also represent an innovation by the *Beowulf* poet; he seems minimally anchored into the traditions surrounding the rest of the dynasty, and may simply serve to tie Wiglaf into the heroic backdrop of the poem. Taken as a whole, however, the Scilfings appear to represent a set of figures who moved more or less as a group in Germanic heroic traditions, either originating on the Continent and travelling from there to Scandinavia and to England, or originating in Scandinavia, but with input from the Continent.

4

The Finnsburh episode and the non-Scylding Danes

The Finnsburh episode represents a self-contained narrative concerning the interactions between the Frisians and the Hocings, who are represented as Danes but who have no obvious connection with the Scylding dynasty which provides the backdrop to the earlier parts of Beowulf's story. This episode also appears to involve some Jutes, although it is hard to identify any named characters in the episode as Jutes. Since the episode is only loosely linked to the main narrative of the poem through the device of presenting it as a narrative performed by the *scop* in Hroðgar's hall, this could, in principle, have come into being at any point in the development of the narrative materials of *Beowulf*, either in Scandinavia, on the Continent, or in England during the composition of the Old English poem itself. The personal names of the characters in the episode present a complex picture; some, such as *Hoc, Hnæf* and *Folcwalda*, suggest Continental Germanic origins for the episode, but the figure named Hengest instead appears to reflect English genealogical tradition, while the Frisian king Finn has a name that, oddly enough, appears to be Scandinavian in origin, although, here too, a link with English royal genealogical traditions must be considered.

The Danish dynasty concerned with the Finnsburh episode is represented by Hoc and his children Hnæf and Hildeburh. Their names, taken together, suggest a Continental Germanic origin for this dynasty, but also a layer of Old English influence in the development of the forms of their names that we encounter in *Beowulf*. We will begin with Hnæf, whose name is most straightforwardly to be identified as of Continental Germanic origin. There is no evidence for this name in early medieval England, to judge from its absence both from *PASE* and the *Durham Liber Vitae*. On the Continent, one bearer of this name is known, the father of a *Rotbertus comes* who gave land to St Gall in 770 AD (Wartmann 1863–1866: 56; Bruckner and Marichal 1954: 76–77 (no. 71)). Förstemann (1900: s.v. *Hnabi*) argues that the more common forms without initial <h> such as *Nebi* and *Nebe* represent the same name, claiming in support of this contention that a father called *Hnabi* with a son called *Nebi* appears in a St Gall charter of 774 AD. The present author can find no trace of this document, however, although the Hnabi mentioned in the charter of 770 AD is identified by von Arx as the same individual as a *dux* called *Nebi* mentioned in the ninth-century *Vita S Galli* by Wettinus of Reichenau (von Arx 1829: 23 n. 2). Jänichen (1976) takes this identification further, arguing that Hnabi can be identified with the Nebi, son of an individual called *Huoching*, mentioned by Thegan (Tremp 1995: 176) and that the Finnsburh episode derives from a feud between Hnabi and the Alamannic prince Berthold which must have taken place in the early eighth century. In order to support this argument Jänichen (1976: 34) makes the case that the name *Berthold* was misinterpreted by an Old English-speaking recipient of the story of Hnabi and Berthold's feud as a form of the title *Bretwalda*, and that he was then identified with the figure called *Finn* in the English royal genealogies. Jänichen (1976: 35) also provides Hnabi with a putative sister called *Hiltburg*, married to Berthold, in order to match with the Hildeburh of *Beowulf*. Jänichen's reading of the evidence is ingenious and not without its attractions, but it does not seem clear to the present author that he should so readily dismiss the possibility that Hnabi and his father Huoching derived their names from a version of the Finnsburh narrative, rather than providing the inspiration for that narrative themselves (Jänichen 1976: 32). Jänichen's objection to the possibility that this father and son pair were named for the heroic figures is based on the fact that the narrative involving Hnæf and Hildeburh is extant only in English texts. Yet this objection is not decisive, since we have very little evidence for the contents of Continental Germanic heroic poetry, despite knowing that it must have existed. In other words, it is entirely possible that the Finnsburh episode derived from a Continental Germanic narrative that also influenced the naming of these Alamannic noblemen.

In addition to the Continental Germanic forms *Hnabi*, *Nebi* and *Nebe*, Förstemann also refers to an Old Norse form *Hnefi*, but the forms that appear in Viking Age runic inscriptions, and which Peterson (2007: s.v. *Hnefi (?)*) tentatively ascribes to a putative Old Norse name *Hnefi are **nafa** and **nfa**. Neither of these forms compels us to accept the existence of an early Old Norse name *Hnefi, given the lack of evidence for initial /h/ in these forms. The name does occur in later Scandinavian sources, as the name of a twelfth-century inhabitant of the Orkneys, a sea-king mentioned in a verse in the *Prose Edda* and a companion of Hialmar in *Örvar-Odds saga* (see Lind 1905–1915: s.v. *Hnefi*). Whether these later instances stem from an older Scandinavian name for which earlier evidence is lost, or represent a borrowing from Continental Germanic, is unclear. What little clear evidence there is for this personal name, then, points to a Continental Germanic origin.

Hnæf's sister Hildeburh bears a name that could conceivably come from anywhere in the Germanic-speaking world, but which is much more common on the Continent than in England or Scandinavia. Peterson (2004) does not include her name among those in *Beowulf* she identifies as plausibly Proto-Scandinavian, although both elements of the name (but not in combination) are attested in the Viking Age runic inscriptions of Scandinavia (Peterson 2007: s.v. -bjǫrg/-borg, Hild-). These elements are also attested among the names of the earliest Scandinavian settlers in Iceland recorded in *Landnámabók* (see, e.g. Benediktsson 1968: 1.90, 1.104). It therefore seems possible that a figure bearing this name could have originated in Scandinavian tradition, although this particular combination of name elements does not appear to have been common in Scandinavia in the Viking Age and before.

PASE records one instance of a bearer of this name in early medieval England, a sister of Romsey Abbey whose name was recorded in the form *Hildeburh* in the *New Minster Liber Vitae* in the first half of the eleventh century (*Hildeburg 1*). There is also an individual with this name (in the form *Hildiburg*) recorded in an early ninth-century section of the *Durham Liber Vitae* (Rollason and Rollason 2007: 2. 128). This demonstrates clearly that this name was used in early medieval England, although it does not appear to have been very common. On the Continent, in contrast, this name is fairly common (Förstemann 1900: s.v. *HILDI*). The figure named *Hildeburh* in *Beowulf* could, then, have derived from Scandinavian tradition or have been created in England, but is certainly consistent with derivation from a continental narrative tradition, and perhaps slightly more likely to have derived from such a tradition. Taken together with the evidence for the continental origins of the name *Hnæf*, this seems to suggest that these siblings both represent part of a narrative tradition originating on the Continent.

The situation is more complex with their father Hoc, whose name as represented in the poem is best explained as an Old English name. Peterson (2004) does not include *Hoc* among the names in *Beowulf* that she identifies as Proto-Scandinavian, and Björkman (1920b: 67) suggests that this name is lacking in Scandinavia, although he points out the name *Haki* as a parallel formation from a word with the sense 'hook'. This parallel may suggest the plausibility of derivation of a name from a word with this sense, but Old Norse *haki* and Old English *hoc* are not directly cognate (the Old English cognate of *haki* is *haca*). It would appear, then, that Hoc is unlikely to have been a character derived from Scandinavian tradition. This begs the question, of course, of what the name *Hoc* might indicate about how and where this character came into the narrative tradition represented in *Beowulf*.

This name is attested in the form *Hooc* in three seventh-century English charters (S 1171, 1246 and 1248; see *PASE*: s.v. *Hooc 1*, which fails to note S 1171). Although there is room for some doubt about the authenticity of S 1246 and S 1248, S 1171 is in all probability an original, and we can therefore be fairly confident that there was at least one bearer of this name in late seventh-century England. This name does not appear in the *Durham Liber Vitae*. On the Continent, the evidence for this name is unclear; Förstemann (1900: s.v. *HOC*) lists some name forms (e.g. *Huohhi* and *Hoccho*) that appear to represent weakly inflected names with a geminate consonant; these would then be cognate with Old English *Hocca*, a similarly rare name borne by an individual who appears briefly in the *Vita Wilfridi* by Eddius Stephanus (Krusch and Levison 1913: 213; Colgrave 1927: 40 (chapter 18)). It is difficult, then, to establish that a strongly inflected name cognate with Old English *Hoc* existed on the Continent. This would appear to militate against Björkman's (1920b: 67) argument that Hoc, along with Hnæf, Hildeburh and Hengest, must form part of a narrative of Continental Germanic origin:

> *Hōc, Hnæf, Hengest*, die im Beowulf als Dänen bezeichnet werden, fehlen sowohl als Namen wie als Appellativa dem Nordischen; *Hildeburg* ist auch kein sicher nordischer Name. Somit müssen die Sagen, in denen diese Personen begegnen, kontinentalgermanischen (zunächst westgerm.-jütischen) Ursprungs sein.

> Hoc, Hnæf and Hengest, who were described as Danes in *Beowulf*, do not exist as names or appellatives in Scandinavia; *Hildeburg* is also not certainly a Scandinavian name. Thus the narratives in which these figures are found must be of Continental Germanic (first of all West Germanic-Jutish) origin.

While Björkman may be broadly correct to identify a Continental Germanic element in the narrative materials of *Beowulf*, the name *Hoc* seems most readily explicable as an Old English innovation. The nature of this innovation is, however, something that requires some careful consideration. As noted in relation to *Hnæf*, above, there is the possibility of a connection between the early eighth-century Alamannic nobleman Huoching and his son Hnabi and the figures called *Hoc* and *Hnæf* in *Beowulf* (Jänichen 1976). Jänichen's suggestion that these historical individuals inspired the Finnsburh episode lacks compelling evidence to support it, but the possibility remains that their name-giving was influenced by some version of this narrative. If a continental version of the narrative knew the father of the figure called *Hnæf* in *Beowulf* as *Huoching*, then this could readily have been misidentified in England as a patronymic form implying the existence of a figure called *Hoc*. The fact that *Huoching* is a well-attested name on the Continent tends to support this view (see Förstemann 1900: s.v. *HOC*); it would not be surprising to find a narrative that developed in a continental milieu employing this name for one of the figures involved. Given the Continental Germanic origins of the name of Hoc's son, *Hnæf*, and the probably continental origins of the name *Hildeburh* for his daughter, it seems plausible to suppose that this family group of figures developed in a continental milieu. The use of the Old English name form *Hoc*, then, can be plausibly explained as the result of a misinterpretation of the Continental Germanic name *Huoching* as a patronymic. This would fit with an interpretation of Hoc and his children as forming a dynastic unit that developed in continental heroic tradition.

The Frisian adversaries of the Hocings are represented by the names of the Frisian king Finn and his father Folcwalda. The names of this father and son present an interesting challenge of interpretation, given that the son's name appears most likely to be Scandinavian in origin; if we see the Finnsburh episode as a narrative that developed as a whole, with its current cast of characters from the outset, then it is difficult to reconcile the probably Continental Germanic origins of the names *Hoc*, *Hnæf* and *Hildeburh* with a Scandinavian origin for *Finn*. The name *Folcwalda* would fit with a Continental Germanic origin, although it could also be consistent with Scandinavian or English origins. Perhaps, then, we must consider the possibility that the Finnsburh episode represents a narrative combining a Continental Germanic heroic dynasty – the Hocings – with characters developed elsewhere in the Germanic-speaking world. As we shall see, the other key characters in the Finnsburh episode all have names that link them with English royal genealogical traditions, suggesting that perhaps the Finnsburh episode was created in an English milieu albeit, in part, based on Continental Germanic tradition.

The name *Finn* is not well attested as an Old English name; it occurs in the legendary reaches of royal genealogies, appearing a few generations before Woden in the Lindsey genealogy (Dumville 1976: 31, 34 and 37), and it also appears once in a post-Conquest record relating to land in Suffolk (*PASE*: s.v. *Finn* 2), where it might well represent a Scandinavian name. This does not provide strong evidence for the currency of this name in early medieval England. The evidence on the Continent is also not unproblematic; Förstemann (1900: s.v. *FIN*) notes some possible uses of this simplex name in place-names, as well as a few two-element names in which *Fin-* may be the first element. This stands in marked contrast to the Scandinavian sources, in which the name *Finnr* is very well attested. In *Landnámabók* there are some four or five bearers of this name: Finnr enn skjálgi, a contemporary of the earliest settlers (Benediktsson 1968: 2.348), Finnr enn auðgi Halldórsson, one of the earliest settlers (Benediktsson 1968: 1.64), Finnr Hallsson, a later Icelander (Benediktsson 1968: 2.395), Finnr Otkelsson, a contemporary of the children of one of the earliest settlers (Benediktsson 1968: 2.344) and the later Icelander Finni enn draumspaki, whose name appears as *Finnr* in one of the manuscripts (Benediktsson 1968: 2.275). In the Viking Age runic inscriptions of Scandinavia the simplex is certainly attested, as are a number of two-element names formed with this element (Peterson 2007: s.v. *Finn-*, *Finnr/Fiðr*, and *-finnr*). That this name element should be particularly common in Scandinavia is perhaps unsurprising in view of its probable connection with the ethnonym *Finn*, referring to the Scandinavians' non-Germanic-speaking neighbours.

If *Finn* is, in all probability, a Scandinavian personal name, then this raises questions about the origins of the character who bears this name in *Beowulf*. He is a king of the Frisians, but his name is perhaps not one that we should expect to have been borne by a Frisian, although we cannot, given the sparse evidence for early Frisian naming practices, rule out the possibility that this name had currency in Migration Age Frisia. At the same time, we should note the presence of this name in the Lindsey genealogy. This might suggest a Scandinavian component in the genesis of this genealogical tradition and a role for the genealogical tradition in the creation of *Beowulf*. That the Finn of *Beowulf* is related in some way to English royal genealogical tradition, moreover, is also suggested by the name of his father *Folcwalda* and by the occurrence of a figure called *Hengest* in the Finnsburh episode.

Turning first to Finn's father, Folcwalda, the form of his name is somewhat puzzling, in that the second element *-wald* or *-weald* is well attested in Old English (see, e.g. *PASE*: s.v. *Ælfwald*, *Æthelwald*, *Beorhtwald*, *Eadwald* and *Oswald*), but is not inflected according to the pattern of weak nouns. It is worth noting, however, that a weak form of this element exists in Scandinavian naming practices; Peterson (2007: s.v. *-valdi*) interprets this as a weak variant of the common strong form *-valdr*. Noting this, Schramm (1957: 42–43) suggests that the names *Catualda* and *Chariovalda* in Tacitus's *Annals*, when taken together with the Scandinavian *-valdi*, provide evidence for an old variant of the common element derived from Proto-Germanic **waldaz* that inflects according to the weak noun pattern. This weak variant, he claims, must have derived from poetic language, noting the Old High German compounds *lantwalto* and *sigiwalto* alongside Old Norse *fólkvaldi* (Schramm 1957: 43). As Schramm notes, however, Scandinavian naming practice includes other weak variant forms, whereas outside Scandinavia such forms do not generally occur (Schramm 1957: 43). This is an argument with some merits, but the fact that the case for a Common Germanic weak variant of this name element rests entirely on two names in a single classical text leaves it open to some doubt.

When we turn to other sources that mention this figure, moreover, we find forms that appear to be – or at least could be – regular strongly inflected names. In *Widsith*, we find reference to a 'Fin Folcwalding' who ruled the 'Fresna cynne' (Chambers 1912: 197 (l. 27); Malone 1962: 24 (l. 27)). The patronymic ending *-ing* in this case obscures whether Finn's father was called *Folcwalda* or *Folcwald* but were it not for the form *Folcwaldan* in *Beowulf* we would naturally suppose that underlying *Folcwalding* in *Widsith* is a regular, strongly inflected name *Folcwald*. In the genealogy provided for Hengest and Horsa in the *Historia Brittonum*, moreover, we find clear evidence for the currency of such a strongly inflected name for the father of an individual called *Finn*; this is best represented in the form *Folcpald* (in which wynn has been misread as <p> by a scribe) in the 'Chartres' recension of this text (see Dumville 1975: 2.321, 2.331; for the forms *Fodepald* in the 'Harleian' recension and *Folegualz* in the 'Vatican' recension, see Dumville 1975: 1.199 and 3.683, and 2.408, respectively, and Dumville 1985: 82; Mommsen 1898: 171 prints in his main text the blundered form *Fodepald* from London, British Library, Harley 3859, fol. 180r). It should be noted that all the variants Dumville records reflect a regular, strongly inflected Old English name form *Folcwald*, albeit with varying degrees of misreading of the name. This would appear to suggest that the Welsh author of the *Historia Brittonum*, writing around the year 830 (see Dumville 1974; Dumville 1985: 3), knew some English tradition of a Finn, son of Folcwald, similar to that reflected in *Widsith* and in *Beowulf*.

We should probably, then, regard the form *Folcwaldan* in *Beowulf* as suspect. There is a lack of clear evidence for a weak variant form *-walda* of the second element *-wald* in Old English personal naming, and the *Historia Brittonum* suggests that this figure had a regular, strongly inflected name, while the evidence of *Widsith* is also consistent with this view. The evidence of Tacitus' *Annals*, moreover, is perhaps not enough for us to insist that there was a Common Germanic weak variant form of this name element. We might, then, reasonably interpret the form *Folcwaldan* in *Beowulf* as a scribal correction, taking a regular, strong name *Folcwald* and replacing it with the noun **folcwalda* 'ruler of a people', cognate with Old Norse *fólkvaldi*, which is, to the best of the present author's knowledge, unique to *Skírnismál* (Dronke 1969–2011: 2.377 (stanza 3); Kristjánsson and Ólason 2014: 1.380 (stanza 3). Since there is evidence elsewhere in the transmission history of *Beowulf* for scribal replacement of personal names with words (e.g. *geomor* for *Eomer*; see also discussion in Neidorf 2013b), this seems a very plausible interpretation of the evidence. Intriguingly, this would also represent a unique instance of an Old English word **folcwalda*, raising the possibility that the scribe who made this correction was familiar with the Old Norse word *fólkvaldi* and formed an Old English cognate for this term.

The possibility that *Folcwalda* in *Beowulf* derives from an epithet *folcwalda* ('ruler of a people') has been raised before. Chambers (1921: 200) suggested that the father of Finn was, in fact, originally named *Godwulf*, which is the name of the father of a figure called *Finn* in the Lindsey royal genealogy (see Dumville 1976: 31, 34, 37), and that an epithet *folcwalda*. which was applied to Godwulf, then replaced his name. Tolkien made a similar claim in lectures delivered in the 1920s and 1930s (see Tolkien 1982: 46), but Malone (1953: 160), reflecting on Chambers' presentation of this idea, expressed some scepticism, although he did think it plausible that the personal name *Folcwalda* had originally derived from such an epithet. The positions taken by Chambers and Tolkien seek to reconcile the genealogy of Hengest and Horsa in the *Historia Brittonum* with all the other versions of English royal genealogies in which the father of Finn is called *Godwulf*. The evidence of the *Historia Brittonum*, however, seems to speak against the idea of the development of a name *Folcwalda* from an epithet, pointing instead to a tradition of a Finn, son of Folcwald, who appears in *Beowulf* and in *Widsith*, although his name has been misunderstood as an epithet in the course of the transmission of *Beowulf*. It seems more likely, then, that the replacement of *Godwulf* by *Folcwald* in the Kentish genealogy in the *Historia Brittonum* is due to knowledge of an English heroic tradition involving Finn, son of Folcwald. On the basis of the various spellings of the name *Folcwald* reflecting misreading of Old English wynn in the manuscript tradition of the *Historia Brittonum* (see above), Dumville (1975: 3.683) argues – no doubt correctly – that the author of the *Historia Brittonum* received this genealogical material in written form from an Old English source. The insertion of the name *Folcwald* into this material, then, must have taken place in this putative source, and we can see this as an effort (and perhaps an idiosyncratic one) to harmonise the heroic narrative tradition of the Finnsburh episode with the genealogical tradition.

It seems likely, then, that the father of Finn in *Beowulf* originally had the name *Folcwald*, whose second element is common across the Germanic-speaking world. For England, *PASE* includes 106 different name forms in *-wald* and *-weald* as headwords, showing the huge popularity of this name element, although we must allow for the possibility of some duplicates of names in this count and some names that may not be English. For Scandinavia, Lind (1905–1915: s.v. *-valdr*) notes twenty-one first elements appearing in combination with this second element, while Peterson (2007: s.v. *-valdr*) notes ten clear-cut combinations with this second element. Förstemann (1900: s.v. *VALD*) lists 347 different combinations with this second element in masculine names from Continental Germanic sources. Clearly, this second element provides no indication as to the origins of this name. The first element of this name, however, is substantially more common on the Continent than elsewhere in the Germanic-speaking world; Förstemann (1900: s.v. *FULCA*) lists a very large number of instances of names with this first element, including many in which it is combined with the second element derived from Proto-Germanic **waldaz*. This is not to say that this element did not exist in Scandinavia and in England. Lind (1905–1915: s.v. *Fólkungr, Fólkvarðr*) notes two names that could contain this first element, although the bearers of these names all seem to belong to the Middle Ages rather than the Viking Age, raising the possibility that these names reflect Continental Germanic linguistic influence in Scandinavia, rather than being native Scandinavian names. Peterson (2007: s.v. *Folkaðr, Folkbiǫrn, Folkgæirr, Folkgærðr, Folkmarr, Folkstæinn, Folkvī, Folkviðr*) notes a handful of names with this first element in her runic material, which may be enough to suggest that this was a native Scandinavian element, although it was certainly very rare if it was. Turning to England, *PASE* has nine headforms in which this element occurs, and although some of these (e.g. *Folcard, Folcrad*) appear to be Continental Germanic names, it seems probable that others are native Old English names. Rollason and Rollason (2007: 2.117) argue that *Folc-* is likely to be 'a genuinely English element', although they also suggest that the sole instance of *Folcuald* in a ninth-century part of the *Durham Liber Vitae* 'may be a Frankish name'.

The evidence, then, suggests that *Folcwald* could derive from any part of the Germanic-speaking world, but is more likely to derive from the Continent than elsewhere. Taken together with the name *Finn* for Folcwald's son, we may have to do here with an eclectic English royal genealogical tradition that mixed figures from different sources. The connections of the Finnsburh episode with such genealogical traditions are, moreover, reinforced by the central role of a figure called *Hengest* in the episode. This name does not appear to be attested outside of *Beowulf* other than as the name of one of the two brothers who were the legendary founding figures of the kingdom of Kent in English tradition. Peterson

(2004) does not list this name among those in *Beowulf* that she identifies as plausibly Proto-Scandinavian, nor does it appear in later Scandinavian contexts (Lind 1905–1915; Benediktsson 1968; Peterson 2007). This name is also not attested on the Continent. Förstemann (1900: s.v. *Hengist*) notes the English legendary figure Hengest and also suggests that there is one instance of an individual bearing this name in a royal land grant of 1042 (*Diplomata Imperatorum Authentica* 1831: 76). This is an error on Förstemann's part, however, as the name *Hengest* in the land grant is the name of an area, not a person. *PASE* also records only the legendary figure as a bearer of this name, and it does not feature in the *Durham Liber Vitae* (Rollason and Rollason 2007). While names consisting of a single element derived from the word for an animal are not a rare feature of the Germanic naming system (consider, e.g. names such as Old Norse *Ormr* and *Úlfr*, and Continental Germanic *Arn* and *Hraban*), *Hengest* does not appear to be a normal name of this type.

The legendary founding figure Hengest clearly has a name that relates to his brother's name, *Horsa*, in that both names appear to relate to terms for horses. The name *Horsa*, however, is perhaps a little less problematic. It differs from *Hengest* in that there is a name element formed on the Proto-Germanic root */xrussan/ that produces Old English *hors*, Old High German *hros* and Old Norse *hross* (Orel 2003: s.v. **xrussan*); this element is rare, but does occur in a few instances in Continental Germanic personal naming (Förstemann 1900: s.v. *HORSA*). The evidence for the use of this name element in forming a single element name is a little complex, in that Förstemann groups no instances of such a name under his headword *HORSA* apart from the name of the legendary English founding figure. Förstemann (1900: s.v. *URSA*) does, however, suggest that the names grouped under his headword *URSA* are formed with the same element, albeit in a different spelling, and Kaufmann (1968: 370) agrees with this analysis. If we accept this view, then the Continental Germanic name forms *Urso* and *Orso* are direct cognates for the Old English form *Horsa*. That Horsa should have an ordinary name, while his brother bears the otherwise unparalleled name *Hengest*, might suggest that the figure of Hengest represents an elaboration based on the name *Horsa*. Alternatively, this pair of personal names could represent an etymological fantasy derived from place-names such as *Horsmonden* and *Hinxhill* in Kent (Ekwall 1960: s.v. *Horsmonden K* suggests that the early forms of this name may derive from a stream name **Horsburna* 'horse stream'; Ekwall 1960: s.v. *Hinxhill K* offers the possible interpretations 'Hengest's hill' or 'the hill of the stallion'). Whatever origin we assign to the name *Hengest*, however, the fact that it seems to be restricted to the figure in *Beowulf* and the Kentish founding figure suggests quite strongly that these are one and the same, as several scholars have (on various grounds) previously claimed (see, e.g. Tolkien 1982: 66-67; Stanley 1990: 59-60; Gwara 2008: 186; Vickrey 2009: 142; Neidorf 2015: 619). The origins of this name in *Beowulf* are, then, most plausibly to be sought in English legends of ethnogenesis and royal genealogical traditions.

The central figures of the Finnsburh episode present a complex picture. The Hocings appear to represent a Continental Germanic heroic dynastic tradition but, in this episode, they interact with characters who appear elsewhere in English royal genealogical traditions. Perhaps the most straightforward model for the development of the episode is that the Old English poet drew on the native genealogical tradition (itself perhaps a product of drawing together names of heroic figures from across the Germanic-speaking world) and on a Continental Germanic dynastic tradition to create this narrative of the ill-fated Hildeburh.

The remaining names of characters in the Finnsburh episode appear to belong to a family with names in *-laf*, who may not be blood relations of the Hocings, but who appear to fight on the Danish side. The pairing Oslaf and Guðlaf in the Finnsburh episode appears to correspond to the pairing Ordlaf and Guðlaf in *The Fight at Finnsburh*, and the fact that this pair (albeit with a minor change in one name due to the vagaries of transmission) appears as part of Hnæf's retinue in both poems tends to suggest that they formed part of the original narrative of Hnæf's battle at Finnsburh. It would seem likely, moreover, that one of these two figures was the *Hunlafing* ('son of Hunlaf') who laid the sword in Hengest's lap at lines 1143-44, spurring him on to avenge Hnæf's death. Given the shared second element *-laf* in all three names, it seems reasonable to suppose that Oslaf and Guðlaf were brothers, and the sons of Hunlaf, although we cannot be certain of this as the texts do not provide explicit statements about the family relationships between them. This group of figures does not add much to the picture we have already established about the development of the Finnsburh narrative, since their names could have originated anywhere in the Germanic-speaking world. For the sake of completeness, however, we should set out briefly the evidence for this view.

The name *Guðlaf* is formed from elements that are common across the Germanic-speaking world; this particular combination is attested in Scandinavia and on the Continent. The name is one of those that Peterson (2004: 38) treats as a Proto-Scandinavian name, and it is also attested in a Viking Age runic inscription (Peterson 2007: s.v. *Guðlafr*), as well as featuring as the name of three different Icelanders from the generations following the initial settlement, as recorded in *Landnámabók* (Benediktsson 1968: 1.100, 1.105, 1.163). Förstemann

(1900: s.v. *GUNDI*) notes a number of instances of this name in continental sources. In England, *PASE* records various names formed with the first element *Guð-*, such as *Guðheard, Guðlac* and *Guðmund*, and with the second element *-laf*, such as *Beorhtlaf, Hunlaf* and *Wulflaf*. There is not, however, a clear instance of this particular combination of elements recorded from early medieval England, although there is no obvious reason to discount the possibility that such a combination could have been used, given the attestation of both of its elements. This name could, then, have originated anywhere in the Germanic-speaking world, although given its probable connection with Hnæf from the start, an origin on the Continent seems likely.

A similar situation obtains with the figure Oslaf or Ordlaf, who is presumably Guðlaf's brother. Peterson (2004: 37) treats *Oslaf* as plausibly Proto-Scandinavian, noting the presence of the first element of the name in her corpus of early Scandinavian runic material. There is also one possible instance of this name in evidence from Viking Age Scandinavian runic inscriptions assembled by Peterson (2007: s.v. *Áslæifr*). The individual elements that form this name also appear among the names of the earliest Scandinavian settlers of Iceland recorded in *Landnámabók*, although this specific combination of elements does not appear except in a form with feminine *Movierung* of the second element, *Ásleif* (Benediktsson 1968: 364). The second element *-leifr* is very common in *Landnámabók*, occurring in the names *Friðleifr, Geirleifr, Guðleifr, Hjǫrleifr, Hrolleifr, Ísleifr, Oddleifr, Óleifr, Véleifr* and *Þorleifr* (Benediktsson 1968: 2.242, 2.244; 1.172, 2.256; 1.100, 1.105, 1.163; 1.41, 1.100, 1.150; 2.220, 2.389; 1.85, 2.226, 2.386; 1.172, 1.182, 2.243; 1.73, 1.136, 2.324, 2.340, 2.380; 1.72, 2.284; 1.54, 1.58, 1.63, 1.92, 1.95, 1.119, 1.127, 1.135, 1.178, 1.201, 2.254, 2.272 n. 3, 2.278, 2.281, 2.310, 2.313, 2.342, 2.355, 2.374, 2.383, 2.385). The first element *Ás-* is similarly common, occurring in names such as *Ásbjǫrn, Ásborg, Ásbrandr, Ásdís, Ásgautr, Ásgeirr, Ásgerðr, Ásgrímr, Áshildr, Áskell, Áslákr, Ásleikr, Ásmundr, Ásólfr, Ásrøðr, Ásvaldr* and *Ásvǫr* (see, e.g., Benediktsson 1968: 2.298, 2.358, 1.112, 1.182, 2.367, 2.376, 2.343, 2.264, 2.377, 2.274, 2.313, 2.241, 2.218, 1.173, 2.298, 1.130, 2.297). This name is, however, also attested in early medieval England (*PASE: Oslaf 1–3*; Rollason and Rollason 2007: 2. 140). In continental sources we also find some evidence for the currency of this name (Förstemann 1900: s.v. *ANSI*). It seems clear, then, that it was in use across much of the Germanic-speaking world.

We should also consider the alternative form *Ordlaf* from *The Fight at Finnsburh*. As with *Oslaf*, the name *Ordlaf* does not appear to have been geographically restricted within the Germanic languages. In early medieval

England, it occurs a few times, including in the *Durham Liber Vitae* (*PASE*: *Ordlaf 1-4*; Rollason and Rollason 2007: 2.139). On the Continent, it is also attested but not very frequently (Förstemann 1900: s.v. *ORTA*). The individual elements used in forming this name, although not this specific combination of elements, are also attested in the Viking Age Scandinavian runic inscriptions (Peterson 2007: s.v. *Udd-, Uddr, -læifr/-lafr*). This specific combination occurs, moreover, in the form *Oddleifr* in *Landnámabók*, where the name is borne by sons of two of the earliest settlers (Benediktsson 1968: 1,173, 2.243) and by a later Icelander (Benediktsson 1968: 1.182). Whichever name for this figure has priority, then, the name itself provides no indication where in the Germanic-speaking world he came into being, although the same logic that applies to Guðlaf also applies to Oslaf/Ordlaf – he appears to be attached to Hnæf's narrative and therefore presumably arose originally in a Continental Germanic context along with the Hocings.

The presumed father of Guðlaf and Oslaf/Ordlaf is referred to in *Beowulf* in the patronymic form *Hunlafing*, implying an underlying name *Hunlaf*. Peterson (2004) does not include *Hunlaf* in her corpus of Proto-Scandinavian names in *Beowulf*, although she does invoke the element *Hūn-* as a possible source of the name **Hūna* in her place-name material (Peterson 2004: 29). Given that *-laibaz* as a second element is not uncommon among the personal names in *Beowulf* that Peterson (2004: 37, 38, 40) does identify as plausibly Proto-Scandinavian (although it is absent from her place-name and runic data), it seems a little odd that she has omitted this name, but this may have been because it occurs in the poem only in the patronymic form *Hunlafing*. The individual elements that make up this name are also evidenced in the Viking Age runic material assembled by Peterson (2007: s.v. *Hūnviðr, -læifr/-lafr*) and in names that appear in *Landnámabók* such as *Húnbogi, Húngerðr* and *Húnrøðr* (Benediktsson 1968: 1.158, 1.75, 2.226) and *Friðleifr, Guðleifr* and *Óleifr* (Benediktsson 1968: 2.242, 1.163, 1.73). Given that both elements are not uncommon, a name combining them would seem possible as a Scandinavian coinage, although the lack of evidence for this specific combination of elements does suggest that, if this combination were in use in Scandinavia, it was not a common name.

In early medieval England, the name *Hunlaf* is attested; *PASE* records twelve individuals bearing this name (*PASE*: s.v. *Hunlaf 2-13*) although seven of these (*Hunlaf 7-13*) are moneyers, and it is not unlikely that in some instances distinct entries for moneyers actually relate to the same individual. Although both elements used in forming this name are attested in the *Durham Liber Vitae* (Rollason and Rollason 2007: 2.130, 2.134), this particular combination of elements is not attested in this source. *Hunlaf* was, therefore, not a hugely common name in early medieval England, but it clearly did form part of the stock of names in use. This name is also attested a handful of times on the Continent (Förstemann 1900: s.v. *HUNI*), although it does not appear to have been at all common. On this evidence, then, it is conceivable that this name was created in Scandinavia, England or on the Continent.

Whether Hunlaf was part of the original tradition surrounding Hnæf – as Guðlaf and Oslaf/Ordlaf appear to have been – is hard to say, but it is intriguing that, as Björkman (1920b: 75) points out, this name (in the form *Hunleifus*), along with the names *Gunnleifus* and *Oddleifus*, corresponding to Guðlaf and Ordlaf in *The Fight at Finnsburh*, appears among the names of the grandsons of the fourth Danish king Herleifus in Arngrim's epitome of *Skjǫldunga saga* (Guðnason 1982: 8; Miller 2007: 11). The significance of this is difficult to assess. These grandsons have three additional brothers called *Herleifus*, *Aleifus* and *Geirleifus*, raising the possibility that, in creating several grandsons with the second element *-leif* in their names, these three names were coined by chance. However, the rarity of the combination *Hunleif* in Scandinavian naming, discussed above, tends to weigh against this possibility. It may be, rather, that these three names in combination represent an intrusion from the narrative tradition of Finnsburh. If this is the case, then perhaps we might take this as some indication that these three names were all created and travelled together. The evidence is, however, too slight for certainty on this point.

The Finnsburh episode represents a self-contained narrative within *Beowulf* that clearly had its own life as a heroic narrative. Whether or not the combination of a Continental Germanic tradition of the Hocings with elements from English royal genealogical tradition was unique to *Beowulf* is impossible to tell, but it may be that this was an innovation of the *Beowulf* poet in treating a narrative in which the Hocings' antagonists were originally differently identified. However, we could also entertain the possibility that the English royal genealogies themselves draw on a heroic tradition that began as part of the continental narrative of Finnsburh, although this is not without its difficulties when we consider the apparently Scandinavian character of the name *Finn*. Whatever the development of this narrative, it is striking to find that, unlike the main Danish dynasty of the poem, the descendants of Healfdene, the Hocings are clearly not a Scandinavian tradition. This also applies to the other Danish dynasty referenced fleetingly in the poem, that of Ecgwela and Heremod.

The link between Ecgwela and Heremod is not immediately clear but, as we shall see, it may well be the case that this is a father and son pair. We will begin with the older of the two, Ecgwela. The name *Ecgwela* supposedly belongs to a figure from the legendary tradition of the Danes, who are referred to in line 1710 as the 'eaforum Ecgwelan'. There is, however, no evidence for this figure elsewhere and Fulk, Bjork and Niles (2008: 214) suggest that the obscurity of Ecgwela might support an emendation of the manuscript text to 'eafora Ecgwelan', making Heremod the son of Ecgwela. They also note as a possibility Malone's (1932) suggestion that *Ecgwela* might be 'another name for Scyld' formed from a kenning ('sword-vexer') for 'shield'. This suggestion would be a unique instance in *Beowulf* of the use of a kenning as a variation on a personal name, and it therefore seems unlikely that we should read the name *Ecgwela* in this way. However, the suggestion that this passage may be describing Heremod as the son of Ecgwela is supported by the consistent use of the word *eafera* in *Beowulf* to mean 'son' in the specific sense of 'immediate offspring'. The poet uses *eafera* on some fourteen occasions in the course of the poem:

Ðæm eafera wæs æfter cenned (12)
Scyldes eafera Scedelandum in. (19)
angan dohtor; is his eafora nu (375)
Wælses eafera; wyrm hat gemealt. (897)
Finnes eafera*n*; ða hie se fær begeat, (1068)
uncran eaferan gif he þæt eal gemon, (1185)
angan eaferan. Him on eaxle læg (1547)
eaforum Ecgwelan, Ar-Scyldingum; (1710)
hild heorugrimme Hreþles eaferan, (1847)
Hreðles eafora hiorodryncum swealt, (2358)
eaforan ellorsið; oðres ne gymeð (2451)
eaferum læfde, swa deð eadig mon, (2470)
oð ðe him Ongenðeowes eaferan wæran (2475)
Hreðles eafora, þa he to ham becom, (2992)

In seven of these instances, *eafera* collocates immediately with the name of the individual's (or the individuals') father. While we could argue that 'Ongenðeowes eaferan' in line 2475 are 'the followers of Ongenþeow' and that a similar sense is intended in line 1068, there is no particular reason to suppose that immediate descendants are not intended here. In no case do we find *eafera* collocating with the name of a distant ancestor figure such as Scyld. Where *eafera* does not collocate with a personal name, moreover, it is evidently used with the sense 'immediate male descendant' in all cases: in line 12, the reference is clearly to Scyld's son; in line 375, *eafera* clearly denotes Beowulf as Ecgþeow's son; in line 1185, Wealhþeow uses *eafera* in reference to her and Hroðgar's sons; in line

1547, *eafera* is used in reference to Grendel as the son of his unnamed mother; in line 2451, *eafera* refers to the hanged son whose father suffers grief comparable to that of Hreðel at the death of Herebeald; and Hreðel then leaves his lands to his sons (*eaferum*) at line 2470. It therefore seems highly probable that we should read *eafora Ecgwelan* at line 1710a and treat *Ecgwela* as the name of one or other of Heremod's parents.

If *Ecgwela* is a personal name, however, it is not a straightforward one. Peterson (2004) does not include this name among her catalogue of plausibly Proto-Scandinavian personal names in *Beowulf* and, in fact, there is no clear evidence for the existence of the second element of this name anywhere in the Germanic-speaking world, although the first element is common. At first glance, there does appear to be one record of this second element, but on closer inspection this proves to be a false positive. Förstemann (1900: s.v. *ERCAN*) records a name form *Erchanwela* which, in his view, is mistakenly identified as a masculine name in a list of Alamannic personal names compiled by Goldast (1730: 2.98). Förstemann presumably bases this view on the termination *-a*, which in Continental Germanic names is usually grammatically feminine. At the same time, however, he also notes that Goldast probably derived this name from the confraternity book of St Gall, where it appears in the form *Erchanwola*; yet the name *Erchanwola* in the older St Gall confraternity book occurs on a page headed 'NOMINA EPISCOPORUM' (Piper 1884: 35 (col. 77, l. 15); Schmid 1986: 110), which suggests that Goldast was not in error in treating this as a male name. It seems Goldast did, nevertheless, err in reading the root vowel of the second element of this name as <e> rather than <o>, so there is therefore no evidence for a second element *-wela*.

There is, then, the possibility that the form *Ecgwela* in the *Beowulf* manuscript represents a similar error to that apparently made by Goldast, misreading <o> as <e>. The plausibility of such an error occurring at some point in the manuscript transmission of the poem is supported by some instances in the manuscript where the similarity in appearance of <e> and <o> has clearly resulted in scribal error. For example, at line 2176, the manuscript reading *brost* must stand for *breost* ('chest'), with the similarity between <e> and <o> having led to a scribe's eye skipping from <e> to <o> in the exemplar. The same sort of error is evident in the manuscript reading *Swona* for *Sweona* 'of the Swedes' at line 2496, and the form *reafeden* at line 1212 could be the result of scribal misreading of *reafedon* or even *reafodon*, although opinions are divided on this (see notes to line 1212 in Fulk, Bjork and Niles 2008: 42). If we suppose that the name in *Beowulf* originally read *Ecgwola*, then this would appear to be a plausible Anglicisation of a

Continental Germanic name formed with the second element -*wola*. This second element is not, however, very common; aside from *Erchanwola* in the older confraternity book of St Gall, it appears to be attested only in the name *Filwola*, recorded in a charter of 799 AD in the Lorsch cartulary contained in the *Codex Laureshamensis* (Würzburg, Staatsarchiv, Mainzer Bücher verschiedenen Inhalts 72; for an edition of the charter see Glöckner 1929–1936: 2.23, no. 211). Förstemann (1900: s.v. *FILU*) expresses doubt as to whether *Filwola* is a female name, and also suggests that it may be corrupt, although it is unclear whether his doubts stem from the questionable gender of the name or from the extreme rarity of its second element. Given its paucity, we might reasonably express some reservations about whether this is a genuine (but exceedingly rare) second element, or whether the forms *Erchanwola* and *Filwola* represent errors or an unusual spelling of one that is better attested.

In the absence of further evidence, it is difficult to arrive at an interpretation of the name *Ecgwela* that we can regard as certain. What little evidence there is, however, points to the existence of a very rare Continental Germanic second element -*wola*, that might have yielded -*wela* in *Beowulf* through a scribal confusion of <o> and <e>. On balance, then, we can suggest that the *Beowulf* poet derived this name from a continental tradition. The possible role of scribal error in the development of the form *Ecgwela* could be taken to suggest written transmission of a Continental Germanic form with the second element -*wola* but, in fact, this need not be the case; if the name had been transmitted orally into Old English and represented in the original manuscript of *Beowulf* as *Ecgwola, then the scribal error could have occurred during the transmission of the Old English poem. Nevertheless, here we have another personal name in *Beowulf* that is most readily explained as deriving from the Continental Germanic onomasticon, and not from England or Scandinavia.

Unlike his probable father, Heremod has a name for which there is abundant evidence. *Heremod* is well attested in early medieval England, with *PASE* identifying six individual bearers of this name. This total excludes moneyers (*Heremod* 8–14) and the figure called *Heremod* who appears in the legendary sections of some royal genealogies. It also appears in an early ninth-century section of the *Durham Liber Vitae* (Rollason and Rollason 2007: 2.127). Peterson (2004: 38) identifies this name as plausibly Proto-Scandinavian, and it is attested in Viking Age runic inscriptions in Scandinavia (Peterson 2007: s.v. *Hærmōðr*). On the Continent, we find this name attested numerous times (Förstemann 1900: s.v. *HARJA*). This name, therefore, provides no indications as to the development of the narrative materials of *Beowulf*, as it is clearly a very widespread name in the Germanic-speaking world. Given that Heremod is probably the son of Ecgwela, however, and given that the name *Ecgwela* is perhaps a Continental Germanic name, it may well be that here, as with the Hocings, we have to do with a legendary Danish dynasty that is actually the creation of Continental Germanic heroic tradition.

It is also possible that Heremod was known quite widely in the Germanic-speaking world. The name *Hermóðr* appears in the *Prose Edda* (Faulkes 1988: 46–7; Faulkes 1998: 2.8, 2.62, 2.113) and in the eddaic poem *Hyndluljóð* (Kristjánsson and Ólason 2014: 1.460 stanza 2) and the skaldic poem *Hákonarmál* (Fulk 2012: 188, stanza 14). It is unclear whether these references all relate to the same figure or not, and it is also difficult to establish their relationship with the figure who appears in *Beowulf*. The figure in *Beowulf* is presented as a Danish king, and this is consistent with the identification of Heremod in the English royal genealogy in the 855 AD entry in some manuscripts of the *Anglo-Saxon Chronicle* as the father of Scyld (Taylor 1983: 33 s.a. 856 AD; Bately 1986: 46 s.a. 855 AD; Cubbin 1996: 23 s.a. 855 AD; O'Brien O'Keeffe 2001: 57 s.a. 856 AD; this genealogy is also used by Snorri Sturluson in the prologue to the *Prose Edda*, for which see Faulkes 1988: 5). We cannot be sure, then, that the tradition in England of a Danish king called *Heremod* is in any way connected with the figure or figures called *Hermóðr* in Scandinavia, although we cannot rule out the possibility that some or all of these figures are reflexes of the same original figure. For our purposes, however, it is telling that Heremod in *Beowulf* is connected with Ecgwela, whose name might suggest a Continental Germanic origin. Heremod and Ecgwela as they appear in *Beowulf* might, then, represent another continental element in the narrative materials from which *Beowulf* was developed.

5

Weland and the Wælsings

Having considered the major dynasties of *Beowulf* and the characters and dynasties associated with them in the poem, as well as the minor Scandinavian dynasties (whether actually Scandinavian in origin or not), we turn now to the characters who are perhaps best attested in heroic narratives outside *Beowulf*, but who play only a minor part in the poem. The legendary smith Weland makes just one appearance in the poem, in reference to a mail-shirt described as his handiwork (line 455a), while Wæls and his relatives Sigemund and Fitela feature in a brief narrative of Sigemund's dragon-slaying feat – a feat that is described in more detail elsewhere in early Germanic literary tradition. As we shall see, both Weland and the Wælsings have names that appear to point towards Continental Germanic origins, and other literary representations of these figures provide some support for this reading of them as originating in a Continental Germanic milieu.

The name *Weland* clearly belongs to a figure widely known in Germanic narrative tradition in various parts of the Germanic-speaking world and this may complicate efforts to discern the geographical point of origin of this figure. Perhaps because of its status as the name of a semi-mythological figure, Peterson (2004) does not include this in her list of plausibly Proto-Scandinavian personal names in the poem. At the same time, the presence in *Beowulf* of the figure Weland may not be very significant in seeking to understand the development of the narrative traditions of the poem, because of the wide distribution of this figure in Germanic tradition. Weland appears in a variety of Old English texts, and was clearly, therefore, a well-known figure in English tradition. At the same time, this figure was also known on the Continent (for useful summaries of the evidence for this figure, see Rosenfeld 1969: 53 and Dronke 1969–2011: 2.269–74). The sole reference to Weland in *Beowulf* – a passing reference to a mail shirt at line 455a as 'Welandes geweorc' – could therefore very well be a conventional description of a piece of fine metalwork introduced by the Old English poet, or it could reflect a similar conventional description from a continental source (compare the use of the phrase 'Wielandia fabrica' in reference to a mail shirt at line 965 of the

Waltharius (Althof 1899–1905: 1.90; Strecker and Vossen 1947: 84; Ring 2016: 120)). Weland also appears in Old Norse texts, in *Þiðreks saga* (Jónsson 1954: 83–116) and in *Vǫlundarkviða* (Dronke 1969–2011: 2.243–54; Kristjánsson and Ólason 2014: 1.428–37), but in these instances we have to do with a text that was based on continental materials (*Þiðreks saga*) and a text produced in all probability in Anglo-Scandinavian England (McKinnell 1990–1993: 1–13; note also the evidence for Continental Germanic, probably Old Saxon, influence on the poem McKinnell discusses at pp. 7–9). We can perhaps suggest, then, that Weland's appearance in *Beowulf* is unlikely to derive from a Scandinavian source, as Weland appears to have been an introduction into Scandinavian milieux from England and the Continent; indeed, Dronke (1969–2011: 2.271–72) suggests that one of the distinctive motifs in some versions of the narrative could have been imported into Scandinavia from England as early as the eighth century. However, Weland might feature in the poem either due to the use of narrative materials deriving from the Continent, or simply because he was a well-known figure in English tradition.

The name *Weland* does not appear to have been in use in early medieval England as a personal name, to judge from its absence from the *Durham Liber Vitae* (Rollason and Rollason 2007) and *PASE* (*Weland 1* in *PASE* relates to a single individual in *Domesday Book* whose name is in fact *Welland*). On the Continent, forms such as *Weland*, *Wieland*, *Welant* and *Wielant* are common from the eighth century onwards (Förstemann 1900: s.v. *VELA 2*). The form *VELANDV*, in a now-lost memorial inscription from Ebersheim near Mainz (Zangemeister 1905: 406 (no. 7260)), that Förstemann (1900: s.v. *VELA 2*) tentatively dates to the fifth century AD, is more plausibly assigned by Rosenfeld (1969: 57) and Terrien (2007: 148) to the seventh century AD. This is consistent with the claim made by Dronke (1969–2011: 2.269–70) that the name *Weland* is found in German sources from the seventh century onwards. Given that the tradition of Weland appears to have passed to Scandinavia from England and the Continent, the evidence of the personal names on the Continent and in England seems to point very strongly towards the view that the legend and the name of its protagonist first came into being on the Continent (a view endorsed by Rosenfeld 1969: 57). Given the currency of the narrative of Weland in England, however, it is unclear whether the *Beowulf* poet was reliant directly on a continental source for this name, or simply knew the name from narratives already circulating in England.

It is also worth considering briefly the possible etymology of this name. Rosenfeld (1969: 53–56) rejects previous suggested etymologies that rely on an

Old Norse verb for the first element and treating the second element as the present participle ending, arguing instead (59-62) that the name *Weland* can most plausibly be derived from a term *wēla/wiela* meaning 'battle', with the second element *-nand*. If this etymology were correct, we should expect the Old English reflex of the name to be *Welnoð, not *Weland*. However, if the name were borrowed into Old English from a Continental Germanic form such as *Weland*, then it would not be surprising if an Old English speaker was unable to identify the second element as Old English *-noð* based on the Continental Germanic form, and simply repeated the Continental Germanic spelling. In principle, then, Rosenfeld's suggested etymology is not impossible, but he advances this proposal because he rejects the possibility that the second element is *-land* (Rosenfeld 1969: 59) on the grounds that the noun *land* is a neuter noun and thus cannot be used as the second element of a male name. It is abundantly clear, however, from the examples assembled by Förstemann (1900: s.v. *LANDA*) that a second element *-land* did exist in at least some Continental Germanic dialects. It is thus possible that the first element of the name *Weland* does not contain an element containing /l/, and the /l/ belongs only to the second element of the name. It is not, however, clear that there is a good candidate for such an element, and it seems quite possible that we should accept Rosenfeld's proposed first element for forms such as *Weland* and *Wieland*, while Förstemann (1900: s.v. *VALHA*) may be correct to identify the first element of forms such as *Waland* with Proto-Germanic **walha-*. If the second element is to be identified with *-land*, then this is also consistent with the Continental Germanic origin of the name, since *land* is generally restricted to Continental Germanic naming practices. Whatever the second element of the name, however, it is very clear that this name does not originally belong to Scandinavian or English naming practices, but to Continental Germanic naming practices. While the figure of Weland may have spread widely across the Germanic-speaking world, it seems reasonable to view his origins as Continental Germanic. This does not, however, necessarily suggest that his presence in *Beowulf* was the result of borrowing from Continental Germanic narrative materials, as we have suggested in other instances above; rather, Weland was, in all probability, near ubiquitous in Germanic-speaking areas by the date of the production of *Beowulf*, and the single reference in the poem to his workmanship might well be the result of the Old English poet's casual use of a commonplace way of referring to fine metalwork.

When we turn to the Wælsings, the situation is clearly different in the sense that the poet does not just allude to them in passing, but gives some indication, albeit brief and incomplete, of the narrative surrounding them. From this we learn that the poet's knowledge of Sigemund involved his descent from Wæls, unspecified exploits in the company of his nephew Fitela, and his lone slaying of a dragon. These details are most closely matched elsewhere in the corpus of early Germanic literature by the account in *Vǫlsunga saga*, which tells us that Vǫlsungr was the father of Sigmundr, who indeed carried out various exploits with his nephew (and, in the saga, also his son by incest) Sinfjǫtli. The dragon slaying, however, belongs in the saga to Sigmundr's son Sigurðr. In considering the names of these figures, then, we must consider not only the geographical spread of the names themselves, but also the possible relationships between the accounts of these figures in *Beowulf* and in other texts.

The name *Sigemund* is the simplest of the three in terms of its geography. Although this name is not to be considered a plausibly Proto-Scandinavian name according to Peterson (2004), it certainly formed part of later Scandinavian naming traditions, as it was borne by three of the earliest settlers of Iceland as recorded in *Landnámabók* (Benediktsson 1968: 1.88, 1.104, 2.333) and is quite common in the Viking Age runic material assembled by Peterson (2007: s.v. *Sigmundr*). The name is also well attested on the Continent, to judge from the various examples collected by Förstemann (1900: s.v. *SIGU*). *PASE* records four individuals called *Sigemund* and the name occurs multiple times in the *Durham Liber Vitae*, although, as Insley, Rollason and McClure point out, some instances of the name assigned to different individuals by *PASE* may, in fact, belong to the same individual, and later instances of the name in the *Liber Vitae* and elsewhere may represent the Continental Germanic form of the name (Rollason and Rollason 2007: 2. 147–48). It is evident that this name was used across England, Scandinavia and the Continent, so in itself it provides no evidence for the geographical origins of this narrative tradition within *Beowulf*.

When we turn to Sigemund's nephew and companion Fitela, however, the situation is very different. The figure called *Fitela* in *Beowulf* corresponds to the character called *Sinfjǫtli* in *Vǫlsunga saga* and *Helgakviða Hundingsbana I*. On the plausible assumption that Fitela and Sinfjǫtli are reflexes of the same figure, we must consider the potential relationship between their names. The key difficulty here is presented by the first syllable of *Sinfjǫtli*; while *-fjǫtli* might very well be a Scandinavianised form of *Fitela* (or *Fitela* an Old English or Continental Germanic form taken from Scandinavian *-fjǫtli*), there is no straightforward way of accounting for the presence of the element *Sin-* in the Scandinavian name and its absence in the name in *Beowulf*. The name *Fitela* can very plausibly be interpreted as an Anglicised form of the Continental Germanic personal name that appears in forms such as *Fizzilo, Fezzilo* and *Fesselo* (Förstemann 1900: s.v. *FIT*). This appears to be a formation based on an element *Fit-* with the diminutive suffix *-ila*. A Continental Germanic name **Sinfizzila*, corresponding to Old Norse *Sinfjǫtli*, however, seems unlikely. Förstemann (1900: s.v. *SIN*) does note the possibility of a rare first element *Sin-* in Continental Germanic personal naming, but the combination of a variation first element with a variation second element followed by a suffix would be extremely unusual. The rare name *Sintarfizilo* has been adduced as a parallel for the name *Sinfjǫtli* (see Björkman (1920b: 32–40) for a summary of early arguments around these names and De Vries (1962: s.v. *Sinfjǫtli*) for discussion of some slightly more recent treatments; despite Björkman's very reasonable doubts on this score, Fulk, Bjork and Niles (2008: 466 s.v. *Fitela*) treat *Sintarfizilo* as if it is simply a cognate of *Sinfjǫtli*), but here the first element *Sintar-* is not obviously identical with *Sin-* in *Sinfjǫtli*. One might, nevertheless, argue that the Scandinavian name represents a form of the Continental Germanic *Sintarfizilo* that has been simplified in transmission, or, conversely, that *Sintarfizilo* is an elaborated form of *Sinfjǫtli*. It is worth noting, however, that the evidence for this name consists solely of charter attestations by probably three different individuals in Bavaria in the ninth and tenth centuries (see Bitterauf 1905–1909: 1.298 (no. 348), 1.326 (no. 383), 1.412 (no. 481), 1.429 (no. 501a), 1.432 (no. 506), 1.455 (no. 532), 1.467–9 (no. 547a, b, g), 1.473 (no. 550a, b), 1.474 (no. 551), 1.480 (no. 557a) for an individual attesting in the early ninth century; Ried 1816: 1.79 (no. 79) for an individual attesting in 900 AD; and Bitterauf 1905–1909: 2.146 (no. 1239) for an individual attesting in the 970s). While we cannot rule out the possibility that there is some connection between these names, the Continental Germanic name appears to have been a regional (and possibly even a familial) peculiarity and is more probably a secondary development from the name of the heroic figure, rather than the source of his name.

There is another possibility that deserves consideration, however. If the name *Sinfjǫtli* represents a Scandinavianised form of a name found in an Old English or Continental Germanic source, then the first syllable of the name might plausibly be explained as the result of a misreading of this putative source. A Scandinavian working with, for example, an Old High German source containing a phrase such as 'neuo sin Fizzilo' ('his nephew Fizzilo') in reference to Sigemund might have misunderstood the possessive *sin* as part of the personal name. The same misunderstanding would also be possible with the cognate Old English phrase 'nefa sin Fitela' ('his nephew Fitela'), although *sin* is comparatively rare in Old English, whereas in Old High German it is the normal possessive form in the third person masculine singular, having supplanted the original form (Braune and Heidermanns 2018: 334 (§ 283 note 1c)). A mistake of this kind is far from unlikely, given the misreading of the Old English demonstrative pronoun form *se* that produces *Seskef* from 'se Sceaf' in the *Prose Edda* (Faulkes 1988: 5). Given that this reading provides a plausible explanation for the creation of the first syllable of the name *Sinfjǫtli*, whereas the proposal that this name is somehow related to *Sintarfizilo* lacks any clear explanation for the alternation between *Sintar-* and *Sin-*, it seems preferable to suppose that the name *Sinfjǫtli* was taken from an extra-Scandinavian source and results from a misreading of that source. If we are to look for a source for this figure, moreover, the Continent is where we find *Fizzilo* in use as a personal name, and it therefore seems likely that the *Beowulf* poet and the Scandinavian tradition both derive this figure and his name from continental traditions.

The third figure in the Wælsing group in *Beowulf* is Wæls himself; again, his name suggests Continental Germanic origins. Björkman (1920b: 113–15) notes that his name is phonologically puzzling, finding the vowel /æ/ difficult to explain by regular phonological processes. He opts, instead of trying to make sense of the Old English form, to argue that it must share its origins with Old Norse *Vǫlsi*, which he relates to Old Norse *vǫlr* 'a staff'. This argument side-steps the fact that the equivalent figure in Old Norse legendary narrative is called *Vǫlsungr*, a form which Björkman dismisses as secondary to a putative *Vǫlsi* (although the term *Vǫlsi* does appear in *Vǫlsa þáttr* as the name of a phallic cult object; see Vigfússon and Unger 1860–1868: 2.331–36). There is, however, no obvious reason why a form such as *Vǫlsungr* should not have priority; personal names formed with the suffix *-ing* are not unknown in the Germanic languages and, in fact, we find on the Continent individuals bearing name forms such as *uuelisung* (Zürich, Zentralbibliothek, MS Rh. hist. 27, fol. 32r; see Figure 5.1. The form *uuelisuug* on fol. 31v of the same manuscript is presumably a miscopied form of this name form), *Welisunc* and *Welisinch* (Müllenhoff 1865: 288), which would appear to correspond very closely to the Old Norse name *Vǫlsungr*. We should, perhaps, consider the possibility that the Old English form in fact derives from a mistaken interpretation of this name as a patronymic formation and an attempt to identify the name of the father referenced in this putative patronymic formation. An Old English speaker confronted with a Continental Germanic name form such as *Uuelisung*, whether in oral or written form, might well misunderstand it as a patronymic and attempt to extract the underlying personal name by removing the patronymic suffix.

The Continental Germanic forms noted above, and Old Norse *Vǫlsungr*, both point towards a form with the root */walis-/. On the Continent, the */i/ causes

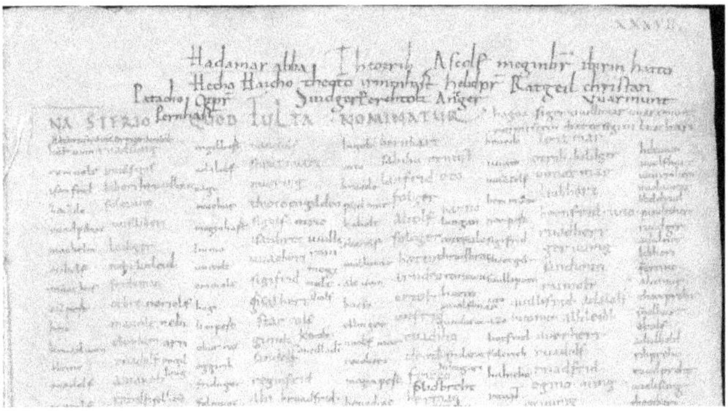

Weland and the Wælsings 139

Figure 5.1 Detail of the Reichenau confraternity book, Zürich, Zentralbibliothek, MS Rh. hist. 27, fol. 32r (www.e-codices.ch), showing the name form *uuelisung* in the bottom right corner.

i-mutation, producing the <e> in the attested forms, while in Scandinavia the */i/ is presumably lost by syncopation and the /u/ in the suffix causes u-mutation to produce <ǫ>. A root */walis-/ would, *pace* Björkman, regularly produce *Wæls* in West Saxon due to i-mutation of the root vowel, followed by loss of the */i/. Phonologically, therefore, there is no way to tell whether this name developed first in Scandinavia or on the Continent, and it is unclear how it came to England. The only other indicator of the name's origins is the fact that it is a fairly well-attested name on the Continent, but not in Scandinavia or England. This suggests, then, that we should see Wæls, Fitela and Sigemund as representing a Continental Germanic tradition that is referenced briefly in *Beowulf* and represented in fuller form in Scandinavian texts such as *Vǫlsunga saga*. This examination of the names of these figures, moreover, suggests that *Beowulf* preserves a form closer to the original Continental Germanic form of Fitela's name, while misinterpreting the *-ing* suffix as a patronymic, to produce the name form *Wæls* from a Continental Germanic form such as *Welisinch*.

6

The continental characters

We have already considered some figures in *Beowulf* who might be considered continental in terms of their tribal affiliations. Figures such as the Frisian king Finn have been treated alongside purportedly Scandinavian figures above, because they belong to the same narratives. It remains to consider the royal house of the Angles, whose tribal area is continental in geographical terms, although we should also bear in mind that it very much formed part of the region surrounding and connected by the Baltic that is the central setting of the poem. Besides this dynasty, we must also consider three figures who are all explicitly associated with the Continent rather than Scandinavia. These figures are the Frankish champion Dæghrefn, and the Gothic king Eormenric and the figure called *Hama* who is associated with him. We begin, however, with the Angles.

The Angles

The dynasty of the Angles – by which we mean, of course, the continental Angles, not the Angles of England – is represented in *Beowulf* by Garmund, his son Offa and Offa's son Eomer, besides a relative called Hemming, whose exact relationship to the central dynasty is not entirely clear. Besides these four figures, it also used to be thought that we had the name of Offa's queen, Modþryð. Weiskott (2011: 5–6) has, however, argued cogently that the queen in *Beowulf* who has often been supposed to be called *Modþryð* is, in fact, unnamed; the form *modþryðo* at line 1931 is, in Weiskott's view, a noun referring to the anonymous queen's arrogance. Weiskott also rightly rejects the attempt by Fulk, Bjork and Niles (2008: 225–26) to generate a name for this queen from *fremu* in line 1932. Given that this is probably not a name, therefore, we need not consider this form in our analysis of the personal names in *Beowulf*. Even if this were a name, however, the elements involved in its formation are attested throughout the

Germanic-speaking world, and it would thus yield no strong indications as to the origins of this figure. The male line of the Angle dynasty and their kinsman Hemming, however, provide important evidence for the relationship between *Beowulf* and English royal genealogical traditions.

The oldest figure in the Angle dynasty mentioned in *Beowulf* is there called *Garmund*. Neidorf (2013b: 257) argues that *Garmund* should, in fact, read *Waermund*, in line with Anglian genealogies and continental sources. *Waermund* is a common Old English personal name, with *PASE* recording 13 individuals bearing this name, and it is also common on the Continent, as Förstemann (1900: s.v. *VAR*) demonstrates, as well as in Scandinavia (see Lind 1905–1915: s.v. *Vermundr*; Peterson 2007: s.v. *Vermundr*). The interesting point here is about scribal error; Neidorf sees this as a result of scribal error, but this cannot be a case of scribal substitution of a common word (or attempt at one) where the scribe fails to recognise a name, which is how Neidorf explains many if not all of the other errors he discusses; this would be a case where the name in the scribe's exemplar would have been well-known to them as a common personal name. Mechanical error is equally implausible, as misreading of *wynn* or <u, uu> as <g> would be highly unlikely in most early medieval scripts. The substitution is therefore rather puzzling, if we consider things only in relation to early medieval English textual culture. However, if we consider the possibility of continental or Old Welsh influence, then the picture becomes clearer.

Förstemann records a number of instances of <gu> spellings for the element that he places under the headword *VAR*, reflecting the continental use of <gu> to represent the reflex of Proto-Germanic */w/. The dating of the development of this spelling is not entirely unproblematic. Kaufmann (1965: 187) suggests that the further development of /gw/ to /g/ is evident in West Frankish as early as the eighth century, but the form *Galter* from around 730 AD, which Kaufmann cites as evidence for this claim (based on Förstemann (1900: s.v. *VALD*)), is, in fact, a form from a spurious Merovingian charter probably actually composed in the late tenth or early eleventh century (see Kölzer 2001: 449–50). The other instances of this spelling noted by Förstemann are, moreover, from eleventh- or twelfth-century sources. While this is not the place for a detailed treatment of the history of <gu> and <g> spellings for the reflex of Proto-Germanic */w/, we should probably look to Lombard Italy for the earliest instances of this spelling; Kaufmann (1965: 190) notes Paul the Deacon's treatment of the name of the god Wodan 'quem adiecta littera Godan dixerunt' (Waitz 1878: 53), but puzzlingly fails to mention that this form of the name also appears in the seventh-century *Origo Gentis Langobardorum* (Waitz 1878: 2). Given that the manuscripts of the

Origo Gentis date from the tenth century and later (Waitz 1878: 1), we might wish to be cautious as to the original spelling of this name in this text, but Paul the Deacon's comment suggests that he did indeed know the name in a form spelt with <g>. Given that Latin *littera* could refer to a sound, not just the letter representing the sound, we might translate his comment either 'whom they called Godan with an added letter' or 'whom they called Godan with an added sound'. Whether Paul was thinking in terms of <g> as an added letter, or in terms of the addition of a sound to [w], however, it seems clear that this comment relates to the spelling of the name with initial <g>. That <g> spellings for the reflex of Proto-Germanic */w/ were in use in Lombard contexts in the later eighth century is also independently attested by a Lombard charter of 774 AD, in which we find the form *Galdilapus* (Brunetti 1806–1833: 1.632; Meyer 1877: 256), which Kaufmann (1965: 187) sees as containing the first element *Wald-* (although Meyer (1877: 287) sees the first element as *Geld-*). This is certainly consistent with the evidence of Paul the Deacon that spellings with initial <g> were in use among the Lombards in the eighth century if not before. In Frankish documents, however, it seems that the spelling <gu> is used little if at all before the ninth century (for an early instance of this spelling in a Frankish context see, e.g., the name form *Gualafridus* in a record relating to the late ninth century in Boretius and Krause 1883–1897: 2.369). We might tentatively propose, then, that <gu>, and its further development <g>, as a spelling for the reflex of Proto-Germanic */w/ developed first in Italy and spread north from there.

We will return shortly to the signficance of this chronology. It is clear, in any case, that a form in which the reflex of Proto-Germanic */w/ was represented by <gu> or <g> could easily have been misinterpreted by an English scribe as representing /g/, thus prompting the interpretation of the name as *Garmund* (a rare but attested Old English personal name; see *PASE*: s.v. *Garmund 1–2*) rather than *Waermund*. If we accept Lapidge's (2000: 16–20) point about confusion of <a> and <u> during the transmission process of *Beowulf*, due to the use of open-topped <a> in some early insular hands, then a continental form such as <guarmund> could readily have been interpreted as representing the name *Garmund*. In this sequence, misreading <u> as <a> in the first element yields <gaarmund>, which represents a plausible early Old English spelling of the name *Garmund*, since <aa> does, in fact, occur in some early Old English texts as a representation of /ɑː/ (see, e.g., the charter S 1171, edited in Hart 1953: 27–28, and forms such as *uaar* 'sea-weed', *faag* 'coloured, variegated' and *haam* 'garment' in the *Épinal Glossary*, edited by Pheifer 1974: 5 (l. 47), 6 (l. 61) and 14 (l. 244)), and it is this long sound that we would expect in the element *gar-*. Positing a continental stage in the development of the narrative materials of *Beowulf* – involving written transmission of at least some names from the Continent to England – might help explain an otherwise puzzling name form in *Beowulf*.

In the case of *Garmund*, however, another possible source for the spelling with initial <g> may be more likely than a continental source. The Anglian collection of English royal genealogies has been preserved in Old English forms, but also in forms influenced by Old Welsh. The manuscripts of the 'Harleian' recension of the *Historia Brittonum* include a collection of English royal genealogies that appears to derive from an older version of this collection than the one that is extant in Old English manuscripts (see Dumville 1976: 48), and in these manuscripts the name *Wærmund* appears in forms such as *guermund* and *guerdmund* (Dumville 1975: 1.241, 3.698). This reflects the Old Welsh use of <gu> as a representation of the velarised reflex of Proto-Celtic */w/. The development of the velarised reflex of */w/, and of the <gu> spelling for it, is discussed in some detail by Jackson (1953: 383–94), but this is not the place for a detailed rehearsal of these arguments. In relation to the name form *Garmund* in *Beowulf*, the Old Welsh phonological development and its associated spelling is of interest chiefly because it offers another way of understanding the different representation of /w/ in this name form as opposed to the form *Wonred*. The involvement of a Welsh scribe at some point in the transmission of the name *Waermund* into the narrative tradition of *Beowulf* could account for the form *Garmund* as well as a continental scribe. Since we know from the *Historia Brittonum*, moreover, that English royal genealogical materials circulated in Welsh circles, it does not seem particularly unlikely that this could account for the form *Garmund*. We might, then, ascribe this form not to the reception of narrative material from the Continent, but to the use of material in whose transmission a Welsh-speaking scribe had taken part. Given that spellings in <gu> and <g> among Germanic speakers (or in contexts of Romance-Germanic language contact) seem to have developed first in Italy around the seventh to eighth centuries and then spread north into Frankia in the ninth century, it seems, on balance, more likely that this form in *Beowulf* is the result of Welsh influence in the English royal genealogical tradition. After all, the spelling <gu> was already in use in Old Welsh when the *Surexit Memorandum* was penned in the eighth century (see Jenkins and Owen 1984: 91 and 101). This would fit with a dating of the production of *Beowulf* to around the eighth century, whereas the development of <gu> spellings on the Continent suggests that Frankish influence would be unlikely to produce such a spelling until the ninth century at the earliest. Lombard influence on the production of *Beowulf*, which could have produced such a spelling at an earlier date, seems less geographically plausible than Welsh influence. It would therefore seem more likely that the name form *Garmund* is the result of a stratum of Old Welsh influence in the transmission of the genealogy that the *Beowulf* poet used for this figure and his relatives.

This complex picture contrasts with the simplicity of understanding the name *Offa*. This name is clearly an Old English name, borne by, among others, the best known of the kings of Mercia. It is attested several times in the earliest strata of the *Durham Liber Vitae* (Rollason and Rollason 2007: 2.181), and *PASE* identifies around eight individual English bearers of this name, along with seven instances of the name in the *Domesday Book* (*PASE*: *Offa 1-Offa 11*). The figure of eight individual bearers discounts *Offa 1*, who is Offa of Angeln and therefore identical with the Offa under discussion here, and *Offa 5*, who appears to be the result of a scribal confusion. The name is also attested on the Continent (Förstemann 1900: s.v. *UB, UF*). In Scandinavia, however, this does not appear to be a native name, although Peterson (2007: s.v. *Uffi*) notes one instance of the use of the name *Uffi* in her Viking Age runic corpus, identifying this name as a loan from West Germanic. The existence of this name in Continental Germanic and English traditions is clearly consistent with Offa's place in the royal line of the continental Angles.

When we turn to Eomer, who appears to follow Offa in the line of succession as given in *Beowulf*, we find that his name is not actually attested in the *Beowulf* manuscript. The manuscript reading *geomor* has long been recognised as an error that must require emendation to some form of the name *Eomer*; Thorpe (1855: xii, 131) first proposed this emendation, and it has been widely accepted since (see Kelly 1982: 263 and Kelly 1983: 247). Neidorf (2017: 75–6) provides the most recent summary of the evidence that *geomor* is an erroneous form and the evidence for emending to *Eomer*, noting that line 1960 requires vowel alliteration, which *geomor* fails to provide, and that a figure called *Eomer* occurs in the Anglian royal genealogy. Oddly, Neidorf appears to be labouring under the misapprehension that the individual named *Eomer* appears as the son of Offa in the genealogy. Perhaps Neidorf was confused by the fact that Eomer is sometimes taken to be presented as Offa's son in *Beowulf* (see, e.g. Tolkien 1982: 177 n. 62; Leneghan 2009: 541), but in the Mercian royal genealogy he is, in fact, Offa's grandson, with a figure variously called *Angengeot, Angelgeot* or *Angelþeow* appearing as Offa's son and Eomer's father.

The apparent discrepancy between the lineage in *Beowulf* and that in all other sources requires some consideration. One possibility is that, as Leneghan (2009:

550–51) argues, *Beowulf* reflects an earlier tradition to which the figure *Angengeot/Angelgeot/Angelþeow* had not yet been added. It is also possible, however, to argue that the *Beowulf* poet knew this figure. At line 1960 of *Beowulf* the poet uses the phrase 'þonon Eomer woc' ('from whom Eomer arose') in reference to Offa. On the face of it, this could be taken as meaning that Eomer was the son of Offa, as noted above. When, however, the poet tells us 'þanon woc fela / geosceaftgasta; wæs þæra Grendel sum' (ll. 1265b–1266), this need not mean that Grendel's father was Cain. It seems that the poet could have used the verb *wæcnan* with *þonon* to indicate lineage rather than immediate parentage. That *wæcnan* could be used in this way also seems to be evidenced in *Genesis A*, where, alongside instances of use of the verb in relation to immediate parentage, we also find an explanation of the origins of the name *Hebrew*: 'an wæs eber haten, eafora semes. of þam eorle woc unrim þeoda þa nu æðelingas, ealle eorðbuend, ebrei hatað' ('one was called Eber, the son of Shem. From that warrior arose countless of the peoples whom noblemen, all earth-dwellers, call Hebrews'; Doane 1978: 159, ll. 1645–48). In this case, the verb is clearly used to indicate lineage, as it indicates how the Hebrews derive from a distant ancestor. Eomer could, then, be said to have arisen from Offa because he was of Offa's line, not because he was Offa's son. This allows for the possibility that the *Beowulf* poet, like the royal genealogies, knew Offa of Angeln as the grandfather of Eomer and the father of an individual called *Angengeot*, *Angelgeot* or *Angelþeow*.

It is even possible that the *Beowulf* poet referred to this figure in line 1968 when describing Hygelac as the 'bonan Ongenþeoes' ('killer of Ongenþeow'); while this is usually understood as a reference to the Swedish king Ongenþeow (see, e.g., Fulk, Bjork and Niles 2008: 227), at lines 2961–81 he is depicted being killed by the brothers Wulf and Eofor, which is perhaps incompatible with describing Hygelac as his killer. When set against the narrative of the Angle dynasty in the immediately preceding passage (lines 1931–62), we might see the reference to Hygelac as the killer of someone called *Ongenþeow* at line 1968 as a pointed allusion to a moment of conflict between the Geats and the Angles. The fact that the name here appears to be *Ongenþeow* rather than *Angengeot*, *Angelgeot* or *Angelþeow* may simply reflect confusion between these similar legendary names, or an attempt by a scribe to correct one of these forms based on knowledge of the Swedish Ongenþeow who figures much more prominently in the poem than this obscure king of the Angles. We cannot be sure that this is the case, and it is possible that line 1968 does indeed refer to the Swedish Ongenþeow, but this is an interesting possibility to which we should be open.

Leaving aside the problem of Eomer's relationship to Offa in *Beowulf*, we now turn to the origins of his name. The name *Eomer* is attested once on the Continent, according to Förstemann (1900: s.v. *AIVA*), and also occurs as a rare name in early medieval England; it is, for example, the name of the East Saxon assassin sent to kill King Edwin, who is mentioned in book 2, chapter 9 of Bede's *Historia Ecclesiastica* and in manuscript E of the *Anglo-Saxon Chronicle* (Plummer 1896: 98; Colgrave and Mynors 1969: 164; Irvine 2004: 24 s.a. 626 AD). Since the figure Eomer in the genealogies and in *Beowulf* forms part of the pre-migration royal house of the Angles, it is unsurprising to find that his name is one that is attested in early medieval England and on the Continent; there is no reason to expect that a legendary prince of the Angles should bear a Scandinavian name. It seems likely, then, that the name *Eomer* developed in England relatively early in the Old English period, and that *Beowulf* here reflects the poet's knowledge of English royal genealogical traditions.

The central royal line of the Angles thus appears consistent in its names with a Continental Germanic or Old English origin, but it is clearly derived from some version of the English royal genealogical tradition, and we can thus see it as deriving from English traditions of continental ancestry; it seems unlikely that the *Beowulf* poet made use of Continental Germanic materials for this. The name form *Garmund*, moreover, would appear to indicate a role for Welsh influence in the development of whatever form of the Anglian genealogy the *Beowulf* poet knew. It is odd, therefore, that the one other name that the poet provides for this royal house does not appear consonant with this general picture. Curiously, the name *Hemming*, which belongs to a kinsman of Offa (although the nature of that kinship is not specified) seems most readily explained as a Scandinavian name. Peterson (2004) does not include this name among her plausibly Proto-Scandinavian personal names in *Beowulf*, although this name is well attested in Viking Age Scandinavian runic inscriptions (Peterson 2007: s.v. *Hæmingr*). This Scandinavian name is also attested in a twelfth-century section of the *Durham Liber Vitae* (Rollason and Rollason 2007: 2, 225) and as the name of a ninth-century Danish king mentioned in the *Annales Lundenses* (Waitz 1892: 196). There can be little doubt, then, that this name formed part of Scandinavian naming traditions. The name is also attested on the Continent, where it usually appears with the root vowel represented as <a> (Förstemann 1900: s.v. *HAM*).

In England, the situation is a little less clear cut. *PASE* lists the Hemming who compiled Hemming's Cartulary as *Hemming 1*, and also lists a *Hemming 2* as a holder of a house in Worcester, but it would seem quite likely that these are one and the same individual, as the householder is named in Hemming's Cartulary. Under *Hemming 3*, *PASE* lists individuals in the *Domesday Book*, all of whom have name forms such as *Haming* and *Haiminc*; these spellings suggest that we have to do here with individuals bearing Continental Germanic forms of this name, or, in the case of the individual called *Haiminc*, a superficially similar name formed on a different root (for examples of comparable Continental Germanic forms, see Förstemann 1900: s.v. *HAM* and, for *Haiminc*, s.v. *HAIMI*). An alternative possibility is that *Domesday Book* scribes of continental origin were encountering an English name *Hemming* and recording it based on their perception of its similarity to Continental Germanic names with which they were familiar. Since the putative English name *Hemming* is only attested by one or perhaps two individual bearers in the eleventh century, however, we might reasonably wonder whether this name was not, in fact, borrowed from Scandinavian tradition during the Viking Age.

It is possible, then, that the name *Hemming* in *Beowulf* was created either in a Scandinavian or a continental context, or even potentially in England. Given the problematic evidence for an English name *Hemming*, creation in England seems the least likely of the three options. The fact that Continental Germanic forms of this name tend to represent the root vowel as <a> may also militate against an interpretation of this name as deriving from a continental milieu, although we cannot discount the possibility that a Continental Germanic form could have been altered in the course of the transmission of the poem due to the currency of a Scandinavian form *Hemingr* in Viking Age England. The absence of this figure from the genealogical tradition that otherwise reflects the same Angle dynasty also complicates the picture. Possibly this figure featured in the genealogy in some way that is now lost to us, or perhaps he represents an addition by the poet, possibly under Scandinavian influence.

The Goths

Turning to the characters associated with the cycle of narratives surrounding the early Gothic kings, we should note that the name *Eormenric* in *Beowulf* appears as the name of the historical Gothic king who features repeatedly in Germanic legendary history. He appears, for instance, in *Widsith* (see Malone 1962: 23 (l. 8) and 146–49) and *Deor* in Old English, and also in *Þiðreks saga* (Jónsson 1954: 1.22 *et passim*) in Old Norse and in the Middle High German Dietrich von Bern cycle (Lienert 2008: 90–93 (nos 109–10), 130–32 (no. 158); Lienert's enormous collection of textual references to Theoderic demonstrates the extraordinary vitality of narrative traditions concerning the early Gothic kings throughout the Middle Ages). This name, therefore, requires no particular analysis in terms of its geographical distribution although, as discussed above (see discussion of the name *Yrmenlaf* at pp. 98-100), the element *Eormen-* is a specifically Continental Germanic phenomenon.

Similarly, the name *Hama* requires little discussion given the clear association of the name with Continental Germanic narrative tradition. Although Dronke (1966-1969: 323-24) argues that Hama in *Beowulf* is a reflex of the Scandinavian god Heimdallr, the fact that Hama appears in *Beowulf* as part of an allusive narrative involving the Gothic king Eormenric indicates that he is, in all probability, a reflex of the figure known as *Heime* in Middle High German texts (see Lienert 2008: 104-5 (no. 128), 112-14 (no. 136), 127-28 (no. 153), 134-35 (no. 160)) and *Heimir* in *Þiðreks saga* (see Fulk, Bjork and Niles 2008: 193-94; Lienert 2008: 115-19 (no. 138)). The name *Hama*, moreover, is an exact cognate of Middle High German *Heime*. The fact that Hama can be identified with some confidence as a figure derived from Continental Germanic heroic tradition (which also informed the later Old Norse text *Þiðreks saga*) is of central importance to this discussion; we can be fairly sure that the narrative involving Hama made its way to England from the Continent, and thus demonstrates once again the use of continental narrative materials in *Beowulf*. This is perhaps why Peterson (2004) excludes *Hama* from her list of plausible Proto-Scandinavian personal names in *Beowulf*, despite identifying it as occurring in her data from early Scandinavian place-names (Peterson 2004: 26). Although this name can be identified as occurring in Scandinavia and also in England (*PASE*: s.v. *Hama 1*), we can be fairly certain that the *Beowulf* poet drew either directly or indirectly on Continental Germanic materials in alluding to the narrative surrounding Eormenric and Hama.

The Franks

Only one Frank (or Huga) is named in *Beowulf*, and this is Dæghrefn. As Kitson (2002: 113) points out, the name *Dæghrefn* is a characteristically Continental Germanic name form that is therefore appropriate as the name of a 'Huga cempan' ('champion of the Franks'; *Beowulf* l. 2502), as the *Beowulf* poet describes him. That this character should bear a Continental Germanic name rather than a Scandinavian or Old English name is, therefore, entirely appropriate to his ethnic affiliations. This could, as Kitson (2002: 112–13) suggests, reflect the Old English poet's knowledge of Continental Germanic naming practices. It is also worth asking, however, whether an Old English poet would necessarily have been concerned with onomastic verisimilitude of this kind. Perhaps they were, but perhaps we should also consider the possibility that Dæghrefn bears a Continental Germanic name not because an Old English poet made a conscious effort to achieve onomastic realism, but because this name was created on the Continent, as part of the development of the narrative materials that informed the creation of *Beowulf*. The lack of onomastic realism in the names of many of the Scandinavian characters in the poem discussed above tends to suggest that this may be the likelier explanation.

7

A glove in hood's clothing: Hondscio and the narrative tradition of *Beowulf*

The character named as *Hondscio* at *Beowulf* line 2076 receives, if the reader will pardon the pun, rather a raw deal. He is unceremoniously eaten by Grendel in the space of lines 740–45:

> ac he gefeng hraðe   forman siðe
> slæpendne rinc,   slat unwearnum,
> bat banlocan,   blod edrum dranc,
> synsnædum swealh;   sona hæfde
> unlyfigendes   eal gefeormod,
> fet ond folma.

> But he quickly seized for the first time a sleeping warrior, tore greedily, bit his joints, drank the blood from his veins, swallowed him in huge gobbets; immediately he had consumed all of the lifeless man, his feet and hands.

This splendidly gory description of Grendel's bad table manners is a favourite set translation for undergraduate courses, but many undergraduates who have been set this passage would probably be unable to put a name to Grendel's victim. This is scarcely surprising, as it is only over 1300 lines later that we finally learn his name, in Beowulf's own account of his fight with Grendel (lines 2076–80):

> Þær wæs Hondscio   hild onsæge,
> feorhbealu fægum;   he fyrmest læg,
> gyrded cempa;   him Grendel wearð,
> mærum maguþegne   to muðbonan,
> leofes mannes   lic eall forswealg.

> There battle was threatening Hondscio, a deadly evil for the doomed man; he, the belted warrior, was the first to lie dead; Grendel killed the famous warrior with his mouth, swallowed the dear man's body entirely.

One wonders how the early medieval audiences of *Beowulf* might have reacted to the revelation that Grendel's victim was called *Hondscio*. The name has always seemed to the present author to have the potential for more than a touch of grim humour. It is readily identified with Modern German *Handschuh* 'glove', and there is a neat symmetry in Grendel's destruction of Beowulf's 'glove' being followed by Beowulf himself tearing off Grendel's arm. The possibilities of such a reading were not lost on Rosier (1963), who explored this idea at some length, focusing also on the extraordinary range of vocabulary referring to the hand in the poem. The first description of the fight is replete with references to the hand, fingers and arm: we see Grendel's *handa* (l. 746), *folme* (l. 748) and *earm* (l. 749), followed by Beowulf's *mundgripe* (l. 753), then Grendel's fingers (ll. 760 and 764) and his hand (*honda*) again (l. 814), before finally 'hildedeor hond alegde, / earm ond eaxle' ('the battle-beast [i.e. Grendel] laid down his hand, his arm and shoulder'; ll. 834–35). No one can be left in any doubt that this is hand-to-hand combat in the most literal sense, and to reach line 2076 and find that Grendel ate Beowulf's glove before Beowulf rendered him armless is to feel that a long-delayed punchline has arrived. In case we miss the symmetry, the naming of Hondscio is closely followed by another of Beowulf's revelations in his account of the fight: at line 2085 we discover that Grendel is in possession of a *glof* 'glove', into which he wanted to put Beowulf (ll. 2089–90). Where Grendel has devoured Beowulf's 'glove', Beowulf shows more sense in ignoring Grendel's glove and taking his hand instead.

Did the Old English poet intend, or did their audience apprehend, this grim irony? Rosier clearly thought so. While Old English seems to have lacked the Continental Germanic term *Handschuh* 'glove', the form *Hondscio* was probably readily analysable by an Old English-speaking audience as *hand* 'hand' + *scoh* 'shoe', and it does not take any great leap of imagination to interpret 'hand-shoe' as 'glove'. In selecting and shaping the traditional materials that informed *Beowulf*, the poet could have developed this grim jest, along with the name *Hondscio* itself, and we should not be hastily dismissive of the possibility of such humour in the poem. Nor, indeed, can we rule out the possibility that this symmetry between Beowulf's companion and his adversary existed in one of the earlier traditional narratives. The possibilities of reading *Hondscio* as a name developed in order to carry symbolic weight in the poem have, moreover, been explored by a number of scholars since Rosier. Harris (1982: 415–17) reads the name *Hondscio* as encoding an emphasis on physical strength as a feature of heroism, contrasting with a reference to wisdom as a heroic quality encoded in the discovery of the head of Grendel's other named victim, Æschere. Weil

(1989: 99) treats this name as part of a pattern of thematisation of hands in the poem. Hill (2007: 245–48) reads Beowulf's fight with Grendel in the light of Týr's loss of his hand in Old Norse mythology, suggesting that Hondscio's name relates to his role as a pledge equivalent to Týr's hand. Pakis (2008: 105–8) accepts Rosier's treatment of the name *Hondscio*.

The discussions presented above, however, have demonstrated that the great majority of the personal names of *Beowulf* are drawn from the ordinary onomasticon. They may (or may not) have been interpreted symbolically by poet or audience, but they were derived from ordinary naming practices and patterns. *Hondscio* differs in that it is not formed using the variation principle that is common to most Germanic two-element names. The words *hand* 'hand' and *scoh* 'shoe' are not regular variation elements in the onomasticon in England or elsewhere in the Germanic-speaking world. We have to reckon, therefore, not only the possibility that this name was propagated by the *Beowulf* narrative itself, but also that the name was created as part of the development of the narrative. We must also consider the possibility that this is not a personal name, but a noun meaning 'glove', corresponding to the identical Old High German compound *hantscuoh*. In order to make sense of *Hondscio*, therefore, we must first look at the question of whether it can safely be identified as the name of a character in *Beowulf*, before addressing the other evidence for a personal name *Hondscio*.

Is Hondscio a personal name in *Beowulf*?

Skeat (1886: 126–27) argued that the word *hondscio* at *Beowulf* line 2076a is not a personal name, but rather a noun cognate with Modern German *Handschuh*, meaning 'glove'. Skeat's interpretation turns around the meaning of the word *onsæge* in line 2076. This he relates to the verb *sīgan* 'to sink, descend', suggesting the meanings '"ready to descend", or "impending"' (Skeat 1886: 127). The word appears twice in *Beowulf*, first in Beowulf's account of his fight with Grendel, the passage which Skeat discusses (lines 2076–2079):

> Þær wæs Hondscio   hild onsæge,
> feorhbealu fægum;   he fyrmest læg,
> gyrded cempa;   him Grendel wearð,
> mærum maguþegne   to muðbonan,

In this passage, the fact that both *hondscio* and the manuscript reading *hilde* appear to be dative forms has created some problems. Fulk, Bjork and Niles

(2008: 70) emend *hilde* to *hild* (an emendation previously adopted by, among others, Sedgefield 1913: 64; Wyatt and Chambers 1925: 103; Wrenn 1953: 149; Dobbie 1953: 64; Swanton 1978: 132; Jack 1994: 149), thus creating a nominative form and allowing the interpretation 'there was for *hondscio* the battle *onsæge*, a deadly evil for the fated man [...]'. Skeat (1886: 127) does not discuss the problem, simply leaving the manuscript reading *hilde* to stand and assuming that *hondscio* can be read as a nominative form, so that he can interpret the passage 'there was the glove, i.e. paw, ready to descend in conflict, a life-bale [was it] to the doomed man [...]'. This is a readily defensible reading of the grammar of *hondscio*, as forms lacking final <h> appear a few times in the DOEC in contexts where they unmistakeably represent the accusative singular, which, like the nominative singular, should appear with final <h> (Hogg and Fulk 2011: 2.80 §3.25); consider, for example, 'man sohte þone sco swyðe geornlice' ('they sought very carefully for the shoe'; Skeat 1881–1900: 1.450–51 (l. 128)), 'þone sco genam & þan halge gebrohte' ('he took the shoe and brought it to the saint'; Warner 1917: 131 (l. 14–15)) and 'þone sco of his bosme ateah' ('he took the shoe from his breast'; Hecht 1900: 18 (col. 2, l. 25–26)). It seems perfectly plausible, then, that the form *hondscio* in the *Beowulf* manuscript is a nominative singular form, although we are equally unable to rule out the possibility that it is a dative singular form. Skeat's reading of this passage is, then, grammatically feasible, although it is not the only feasible grammatical reading of the manuscript text. If we read *hondscio* as dative, it does not follow that we must emend *hilde* to avoid another dative; a translation such as 'there was a deadly evil *onsæge* in battle for *hondscio*, for the fated man [...]' also seems possible.

The grammar of *hondscio* is inconclusive, and we must therefore return to the word *onsæge* for further clues. The second occurrence of this term in *Beowulf* comes in Beowulf's account of the death of Hæðcyn in battle against the Swedes (lines 2482b–2483b):

> Hæðcynne wearð
> Geata dryhtne guð onsæge
> Battle became *onsæge* for Hæðcyn, lord of the Geats

Fulk, Bjork and Niles (2008: 233; see also Wyatt and Chambers 1925: 103) take this as a parallel for the earlier passage, demonstrating that *hilde* should be emended to *hild* and taken as a nominative agreeing with *onsæge*. On the other hand, if we do not emend *hilde* to *hild*, the parallel is somewhat weakened. Line 2483b could be taken to represent a formula (albeit not a frequently attested one) BATTLE + *onsæge*, with the term for 'battle' in the nominative, forming part of a larger formulaic phrase NAME (dative) + *beon/weorðan* + BATTLE + *onsæge* ('battle was/became *onsæge* for NAME'). The two phrases are very similar if the term for 'battle' in each case occurs in the nominative, but the parallel is weakened if one is dative and one nominative. The emendation of *hilde* to *hild* is not a huge leap, and it is therefore tempting to accept the view that these two passages both contain the same formulaic phrase in which a word for 'battle' (*hild* and *guð* in these cases) appears in the nominative as the thing which is *onsæge* for the character named in the dative. This would militate against Skeat's reading, since *hondscio* would have to be the name in the dative that this formulaic phrase seems to require.

Leaving aside for a moment the argument for a formulaic phrase, we must consider the precise meaning of the term *onsæge*. Skeat argues that his gloss of *onsæge* as 'ready to descend' or 'impending' is as applicable in the passage relating to Hæðcyn's death as in the earlier passage (p. 127). The alternative gloss 'fatal' makes Hæðcyn's death very explicit, whereas Skeat's gloss would involve an interpretation of this passage as alluding, in a non-explicit way, to his death presenting it merely in terms of battle impending. Both readings seem possible, and it is therefore useful to consider the other occurrences of the term *onsæge* in Old English. There are four in all: one occurs in Wulfstan's *Sermo Lupi ad Anglos* (Bethurum 1957: 257 (line 50), 262 (line 62) and 269 (line 54)); two appear in anonymous homilies that draw on Wulfstan's work, the homily 'To eallum folce' commonly termed Napier 27 (Napier 1883: 128–30) and the homily 'Larspel and scriftboc' commonly termed Napier 47 (Napier 1883: 242–45); and one is to be found in a letter purportedly sent by St Dunstan to King Æthelræd (Napier and Stevenson 1895: 18–19).

In Napier 27, the author writes that 'is þisse ðeode fela hearma onsæge' ('many harms are *onsæge* to this nation'; Napier 1883: 128)). In this instance, it is certainly possible that *fela hearma* 'many harms' are fatal to the nation, and this is based on Wulfstan's phrase 'we ær þysan oftor bræcan þonne we bettan, & þy is þysse þeode fela onsæge' ('before this we more often broke [God's commands] than we made amends, and therefore many things are *onsæge* to this nation'; Bethurum 1957: 269 (lines 53–54)), in which the possibility of fatal effects on the nation as a result of sin has also to be reckoned with. In Napier 47, it seems less plausible to argue for the meaning 'fatal'. Here, a catalogue of misfortunes are identified as being *onsæge*: 'is onsæge oft, næs æne, here and hunger, bryne and blodgyte, unwæstm and unweder, stalu and steorfa and fela ungelimpa' ('often, not just once, there is *onsæge* army and hunger, fire and bloodshed, crop failure and adverse weather, theft and pestilence and many evil occurrences'; Napier 1883: 243). Most of the afflictions mentioned, such as armies (*here*), hunger and fire (*bryne*), can be fatal, but *stalu* 'theft' ordinarily cannot (this list of afflictions is closely modelled on that which follows the use of *onsæge* in the *Sermo Lupi* and which, as Bethurum (1957: 360) notes, can be taken to define the 'many things' that Wulfstan sees as *onsæge*; Wulfstan's version of this list also includes *stalu* (Bethurum 1957: 269 (line 57))). One could, however, stretch a point and argue that theft could have fatal consequences if one's means of subsistence were stolen. In the case of Dunstan's letter, on the other hand, it seems impossible to treat *onsæge* as meaning 'fatal'. The letter refers back to an earlier time when 'lariowas [...] gewitun of angla lande . for þære geleafleste þe him þa onsæge gewearþ' ('teachers [...] departed from England because of the unbelief that then became *onsæge* for them'; Napier and Stevenson 1895: 19). It is clearly possible for unbelief to prove fatal to Christian teachers, but it is not possible (barring a miracle) for teachers to depart because of unbelief which has already proved fatal to them; as a rule, dead teachers stay put. Alternatively, if we follow the translation by Napier and Stevenson (1895: 106), the unbelief can be read as *onsæge* for England, but the fact that England was evidently still in existence at the time of Dunstan's writing also precludes an interpretation of *onsæge* as 'fatal' when we read the passage in this way. It is natural to understand *onsæge* in this passage as meaning something like 'threatening' or 'assailing' (as, indeed, Napier and Stevenson (1895: 106) do), and it is perfectly possible to treat it as having the same sense in the other passages as well. There seems little reason to accept the gloss 'fatal', and we should therefore be reluctant to accept this gloss in *Beowulf*. A sense within the spectrum of 'impending, threatening, assailing' is perfectly acceptable for both cases in *Beowulf* if we treat them as referring to the threat of imminent death that befalls both Beowulf's retainer and Hæðcyn. In arguing for this meaning, Skeat was undoubtedly right.

To summarise the argument so far, we are presented here with a number of possibilities for interpreting the passage containing the form *hondscio*. To begin with, we can either emend the manuscript reading *hilde* to *hild*, or we can attempt to make sense of it as it stands. If we attempt to make sense of the manuscript reading 'þær wæs hondscio hilde onsæge / feorhbealu fægum' as it stands, we are presented with two possibilities; we can read *hondscio* as a nominative form, as Skeat does, or as a dative form. If we follow Skeat's reading, we must translate along the lines 'there was *hondscio* threatening in battle, a deadly evil for the fated man'. If, however, we treat *hondscio* as a dative form, then we would translate along the lines 'there was a deadly evil threatening in battle for *hondscio*, the fated man'. In the former case, it is difficult to read *hondscio* other than as a noun, presumably meaning 'glove', while in the latter case, a reading of *hondscio* as a personal name seems more probable. If we emend *hilde* to *hild*, then we strengthen the parallel with the passage on the death of Hæðcyn, and we would certainly read *hondscio* as a personal name.

It is difficult to decide between these interpretations. Skeat's reading is attractive insofar as it avoids emending the manuscript reading, but the manuscript text of *Beowulf* clearly contains a not insignificant number of scribal errors (see Lapidge 2000, Neidorf 2018b), so the emendation of *hilde* to *hild* is not a particularly implausible editorial decision. Grammatically, moreover, the manuscript reading remains compatible with treating *hondscio* as a personal name in the dative, although the parallel with the passage on the death of Hæðcyn would be weakened in such a reading, and this parallel has, probably rightly, carried some weight with recent editors of the poem. This leaves us at something of an impasse, with a number of plausible readings, including Skeat's reading, in which *hondscio* is not a personal name, and others in which *hondscio* must represent a personal name. We have not, however, considered the metrical implications of these different readings.

Bliss (1958: 153) treats the verse 2076a as belonging to his type d1b, that is, two unstressed syllables followed by a long, stressed syllable, followed by two unstressed syllables. He evidently understands *hondscio* to represent a personal name, and his scansion therefore accords with his view that the second elements of two-element personal names carry only tertiary stress, which is, in practice, often equivalent to a lack of stress (pp. 25–26). In scanning the verse as type d1b, Bliss clearly treats the second element as disyllabic, despite the manuscript form; this implies that he understands *hondscio* to be a later representation of an archaic dative form *hondscohe. Fulk is less certain of this interpretation, treating the verse as ambiguous; in Fulk's view, the verse could also be scanned as type a1b, treating the second element of *hondscio* as a single unstressed syllable. Verses of type a1b are, however, very rare in *Beowulf*, with Bliss identifying only seven lines as belonging to this type:

ēow hēt secgan (391a)
ic þæt hogode (632a)
ðē wē ealle (941a)
mē man sægde (1175a)
on him gladiað (2036a)
þæt se mǣra (2587a)
lēt se hearda (2977a)

It is notable that none of these verses involves a personal name carrying the single lift in the verse, whereas lines of type d1b, which are very common in the text, include several in which a personal name is used in this way. For example:

þā wæs Hrōðgāre (64a and 1399a)
þæt hīo Bēowulfe (623a)
ðǣr wæs Bēowulfes (856b)
ond ðā Bēowulfe (1043a)
fore Healfdenes (1064a)
ofer Hrōðgāres (1899a)
þǣr wæs Æschere (2122b)
þæt wæs Hrōðgār(e) (2129a; accepting the highly probable emendation)
þā wæs Bīowulfe (2324a)

If *hondscio* represents a personal name with a contracted dative form, then verse 2076a is highly unusual. It seems preferable, therefore, to understand *hondscio* as an updated form of an earlier uncontracted **hondscohe*. If, however, we suppose that *hondscio* is a compound noun with the sense 'glove', then it seems to the present author that it is likely to be one of those analysable compounds that Bliss (1958: 25) treats as bearing secondary stress on the root syllable of their second elements. If we treat *hondscio* as a nominative form, as Skeat suggests, and as an analysable compound, then we must treat the verse as having a metrical pattern consisting of two unstressed syllables, followed by a syllable carrying primary stress and then a syllable carrying secondary stress. This is a pattern that never occurs in *Beowulf*, according to Bliss; this would be classified in Bliss's system of notation as type a2b, which is lacking from his tabulation of verse in *Beowulf* (Bliss 1958: 124). This fact seems to weigh very heavily against treating *hondscio* as a nominative form of an ordinary noun. On these grounds, therefore, we must reject Skeat's ingenious suggestion that *hondscio* in *Beowulf* is a noun, rather than a personal name.

Other possible attestations of the personal name *Hondscio*

Having established that *Hondscio* is indeed intended as a personal name in *Beowulf*, we must now consider whether there is any other evidence for such a personal name in the Germanic onomasticon. The only absolutely certain attestation of this name is in *Beowulf* itself, but it has been plausibly claimed that the personal name also appears in a number of place-names. The place-name *Andscohesham* appears in a charter (S 27) preserved in the *Textus Roffensis*

(Rochester, Cathedral Library, A. 3. 5., fols 119v–120v), whose rubric identifies the name as an older name for Stoke, in Hoo Hundred in Kent (Sawyer 1957–1962; Campbell 1973: 4; Wallenberg 1931: 36–37; see Figure 7.1). Grimm (1842: 794) also notes Handschuhsheim, Heidelberg, another place with the same name in Alsace, which must be Handschuheim near Strasbourg, and Henschleben near Erfurt; about the form *Hantscôhasheim* that he reports in a Fulda charter (in fact, the form in this charter of 788 AD is *Hantscohashaim*; see Schannat (1724: 42 no. 84) and Stengel (1913–1958: 2.269–70, no. 176)), he expresses uncertainty as to whether it is Handschuhsheim, Handschuheim or a third, lost place with this name, but Stengel (1913–1958: 2.269, n. 2) identifies the name very plausibly with Handschuheim near Strasbourg. As Stengel (1913–1958: 2.269) notes, the names of many of the places in this charter can be identified with place-names in the region around Strasbourg, a situation that is summarised in Map 7.1. We can therefore be confident that Stengel is right to identify the name in the charter with this place-name and, to the best of the current author's knowledge, there are therefore only two instances of this place-name on the Continent, along with *Henschleben*, in which the final element of the name differs.

We should not just consider the Continent, however, in looking for attestations of this possible personal name. There is a place in Denmark called *Handske* (Bregninge parish, island of Tåsinge), although Pedersen and Wohlert (1970: 239) identify the name with the common noun *hanske* 'glove', suggesting that the name derives from the shape of the area. Sweden also boasts a place called

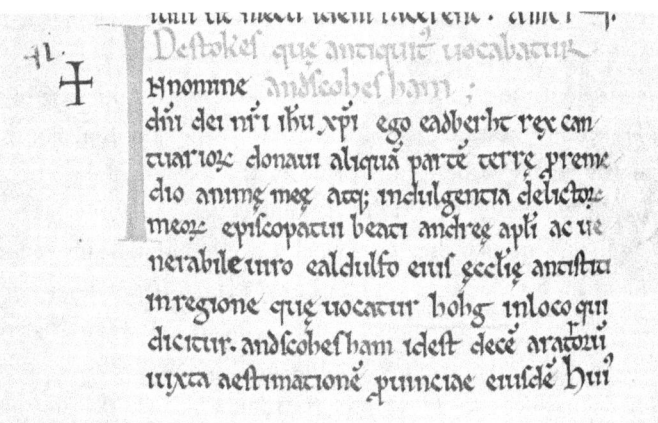

Figure 7.1 Detail of Rochester, Cathedral Library, A. 3. 5. (*Textus Roffensis*), fol. 119v (reproduced by permission of Rochester Cathedral), showing the place-name form *andscohesham* and the rubric identifying it with Stoke, Hoo Hundred, Kent.

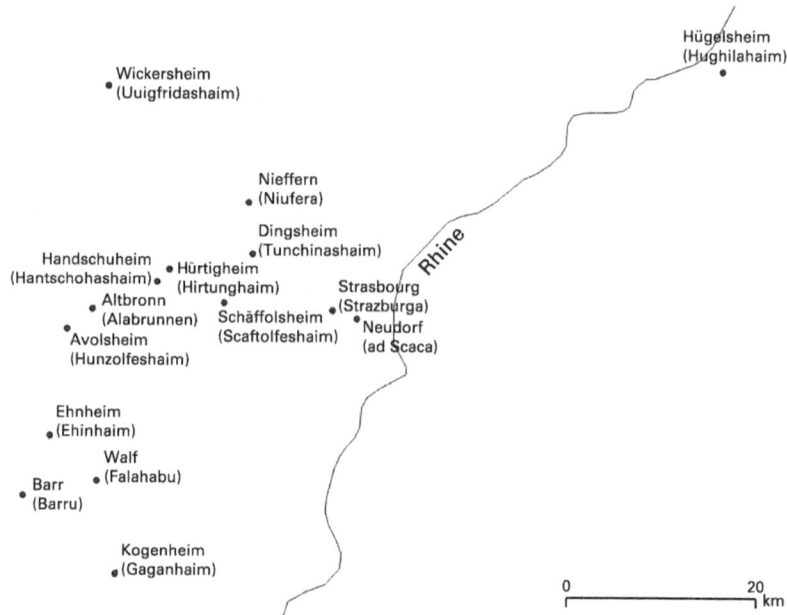

Map 7.1 Map depicting places in the Fulda charter of 788 AD mentioning *Hantscohashaim* that can be identified with extant place-names, following the identifications by Stengel (1913-1958: 2.269).

Hanaskog, which looks superficially similar, but the *Svenskt Ortsnamnslexikon* is certainly correct to interpret this as *hane* 'male bird' plus *skog* 'wood[land]' (Wahlberg 2003: s.v. *Hanaskog*). The Old Norse cognate of Old English *scoh* 'shoe' was *skór* 'shoe', and the <g> that survives in the spelling of *Hanaskog* through to the present day demonstrates that the second element cannot be Old Norse *skór* but must rather be *skógr* 'wood[land]'. In the case of *Handske*, the form appears to be essentially identical with the common noun meaning 'glove', which appears to be a borrowing of the Continental Germanic term *Handschuh*; the fact that the Scandinavian languages have forms such as *hanske* for this noun suggests that they borrowed it in the phonetically reduced form that is evident in, for example, Middle Low German *hantsche* or *hantzke* (De Vries 1962: s.v. *hanzki*). Such a reduced form appears to have in existence by the early twelfth century, when it appears as one of the earliest recorded forms of the place-name Henschleben, *Hanscisleve* (Grimm 1842: 794). The place-name *Handske*, however, is unlikely to contain – as *Henschleben* may – a personal name *Handschuh*. A place is unlikely to be named after a person without some sort of generic to specify what sort of place it is. In the case of the name

Handschuhsheim, for instance, it is at least plausible that a place might have been called 'the settlement of a man called *Handschuh*', whereas to call a place 'a man called *Handschuh*' makes little sense. Whether or not the area called *Handske* in Denmark is, or was once, glove-shaped, is unknown to the present author, but that the name does not consist of a personal name, but rather originally meant 'glove' (whatever that might mean for the relationship between the name and the locality named) seems clear.

The question of whether the continental place-names contain a personal name or the noun meaning 'glove', however, is more complex. Scholars of place-names have come to be very cautious about uncritical identification of personal names in place-names (for a brief outline of the issues and debate, see Clark 1992: 468, 476). Where an element occurs repeatedly in place-names, and especially where it appears repeatedly in combination with the same generic element, the probability that it is a personal name is clearly reduced, leading to a preference for explaining elements that occur in multiple place-names as deriving from the ordinary lexicon, not from personal names (Clark 1992: 468). We should perhaps temper this slightly with the observation that there are some cases of the same name occurring in more than one place in a given area, perhaps because of the impact of a particularly important landholder (see, e.g. the names *Rutland* and nearby *Ratby* (Leicestershire), both with the personal name *Rōta* as a first element; Ekwall 1960: s.v. *Ratby Le* suggests that the bearer of this name 'must have been a great land-owner'). Nevertheless, the observation that any given personal name will tend not to recur frequently in place-names seems a sound one, that should be given due weight in attempting to elucidate their origins.

This observation seems relevant, moreover, in the case of the *Handschuh* names on the Continent. The two instances compounding *Handschuh* with *-heim* lie within 100 miles of one another as the crow flies. They are, moreover, both situated along the Rhine corridor between Heidelberg and Strasbourg (see Map 7.2). The occurrence of two place-names formed of exactly the same elements relatively close to one another must raise suspicions that the first element of this place-name may not be a personal name, but rather the word meaning 'glove'. It is worth asking, therefore, what the word 'glove' might mean in the context of these place-names. Grimm (1842: 794) suggested that these places were either settlements laid out with five roads, mimicking the fingers of a glove, or may have been the sites of markets which were advertised using the glove as the sign for the market. Why Grimm thought a glove might have been used in this way is not entirely clear, but the suggestion does not immediately

Map 7.2 Continental place-names formed with *Handschuh* 'glove' as a first element (Strasbourg and Heidelberg included for location).

recommend itself as a plausible possibility. The hypothesis of road layouts resembling a glove is perhaps more plausible, but short of some remarkable and extensive archaeological excavations in these places, this cannot be tested. Another possibility, of course, is that these were places where gloves were made, but again, short of some very remarkable archaeological finds, this is a hypothesis that would be extremely difficult to test.

There is, however, one hypothesis that we can test. The work of Margaret Gelling and Anne Cole has demonstrated in the case of English place-names that the Old English vocabulary referring to physical features of the landscape was very rich and precise. For example, there are numerous words in Old English that can be (and often are) loosely glossed as 'hill', but Gelling and Cole have shown, by close examination of place-names containing these words and of the landscapes in which they are found, that each of these words refers to a hill of a particular shape, with quite clearly defined characteristics. To give an example, Gelling and Cole (2000: 145–52) show with numerous examples that the Old English word *beorg* refers specifically to a 'rounded hill' or a 'tumulus', whereas Old English *hlið* denotes a 'concave hillside' (182–85).

In the light of Gelling and Cole's work, we might ask whether in some Continental Germanic dialects that word *Handschuh* 'glove' could have been used as a way of referring to some sort of landscape feature. The English evidence that Gelling and Cole examine demonstrates that landscape could be thought of partially in terms of shapes from the human body, such as *bæc* 'back', referring to a ridge (Gelling and Cole 2000: 144), and *hoh* 'heel', referring to a hill spur shaped like a human heel (Gelling and Cole 2000: 186–90). It would not be very surprising, then, if a distinctively shaped item of human clothing such as a glove could also be deployed as a metaphor for landscape features that share some aspect of their shape.

In the case of Handschuhsheim near Heidelberg, there is an obvious possibility for reading the landscape as resembling an item of clothing for the human hand. Handschuhsheim lies immediately below a connected pair of hill spurs that resemble a mittened hand reaching towards the site of the settlement. In the aerial view of Heidelberg and its suburbs in Figure 7.2, these hill spurs can be

Figure 7.2 Aerial view of Heidelberg and its suburbs with highlight indicating approximate centre of Handschuhsheim (photo by Christos Vittoratos). Available at: https://upload.wikimedia.org/wikipedia/commons/9/91/Heidelberg-luftbild-aerial-photograph.jpg (accessed 10 June 2018). Used under a Creative Commons Attribution-ShareAlike 3.0 Unported licence. Available at: https://creativecommons.org/licenses/by-sa/3.0/> (accessed 10 June 2018); highlight added by the author.

seen immediately above Handschuhsheim (on the ground they lie immediately to the east of Handschuhsheim). In Modern German, the term *Handschuh* refers to both gloves and mittens, with the more specific terms *Fingerhandschuh* ('glove', literally 'finger-*Handschuh*') and *Fausthandschuh* ('mitten', literally 'fist-*Handschuh*') distinguishing between these different forms of hand wear. It is harder to determine with certainty whether Old High German *hantscuoh* could similarly refer to both types of hand wear, but it seems plausible that it could have done. It is tempting, then, to suppose that Handschuhsheim derived its name from the resemblance of its landscape to a mitten.

In the case of Handschuheim near Strasbourg, on the other hand, the surrounding landscape is fairly flat, raising questions about whether a hill form resembling a glove or mitten is likely to be apparent. There is, nevertheless, a slight rise to the west of Handschuheim that is divided into a longer northern ridge and a shorter southern ridge, somewhat resembling a hand viewed from the side. Map 7.3 shows the location of Handschuheim in relation to this hill feature. The highest points, shaded in black and white, show the hand-shaped hill form, with the opening between thumb and fingers oriented towards

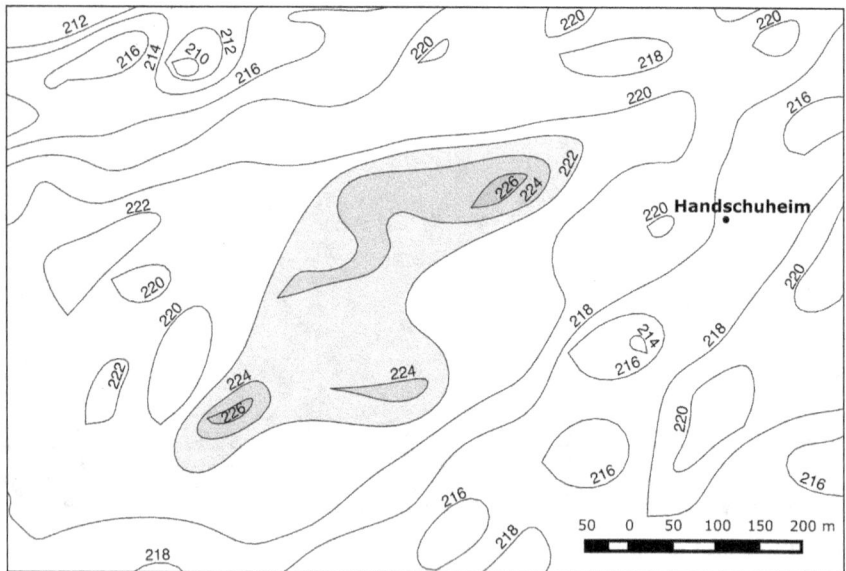

Map 7.3 Map of Handschuheim near Strasbourg and its immediate surroundings, with 2m contour lines. This map was created with data from Digital Elevation Model over Europe (EU-DEM). Available at: https://data.europa.eu/euodp/en/data/dataset/data_eu-dem (accessed 4 October 2013), processed in QGIS by the author.

Handschuheim to the east. This is a less obvious feature than the hill form lying to the west of Handschuhsheim near Heidelberg, but it is not impossible that this feature lies behind the origin of the name Handschuheim.

The site of Henschleben also lies in comparatively flat country, but, as with Handschuhsheim, the current settlement is situated close to a rise in the ground that forms two prongs. In Map 7.4, the main ridge line can be seen running approximately southwest to northeast, ending in two prongs at the northeast end, just to the east of Henschleben. The more northerly of these prongs is a good deal smaller in area than the more southerly one, suggesting the thumb of a mitten, while the larger, southerly prong suggests the larger compartment for the fingers. The slopes involved here are a little more pronounced than those in the case of Handschuheim, and the ground rises fairly steeply from the site of Henschleben up onto the ridge line in question. That this feature of the landscape would have been quite apparent to early medieval inhabitants of the area is therefore plausible.

The site of Upper Stoke in Kent, once known as *Andscohesham*, is also quite low-lying. As with Handschuheim and Henschleben, however, it is also possible

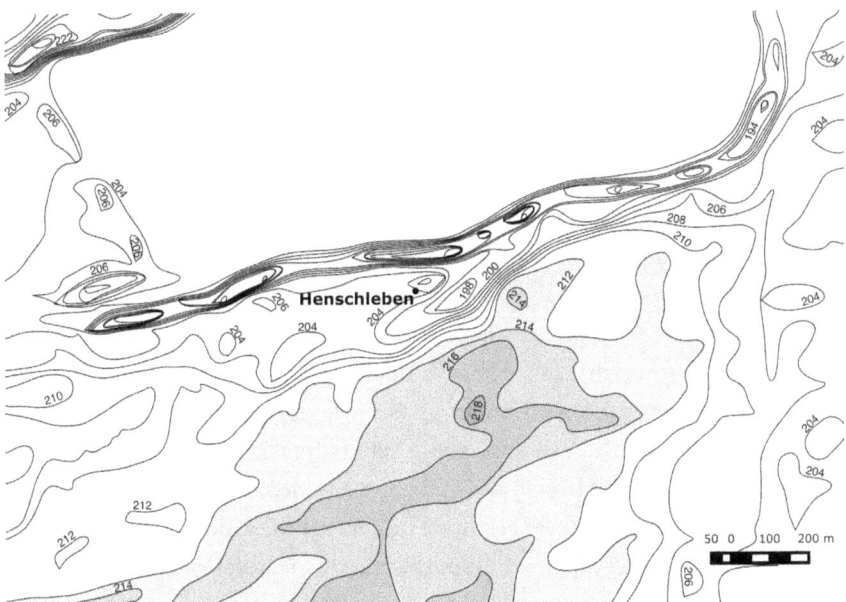

Map 7.4 Map of Henschleben and its immediate surroundings, with 2m contour lines. This map was created with data from Digital Elevation Model over Europe (EU-DEM). Available at: https://data.europa.eu/euodp/en/data/dataset/data_eu-dem (accessed 4 October 2013), processed in QGIS by the author.

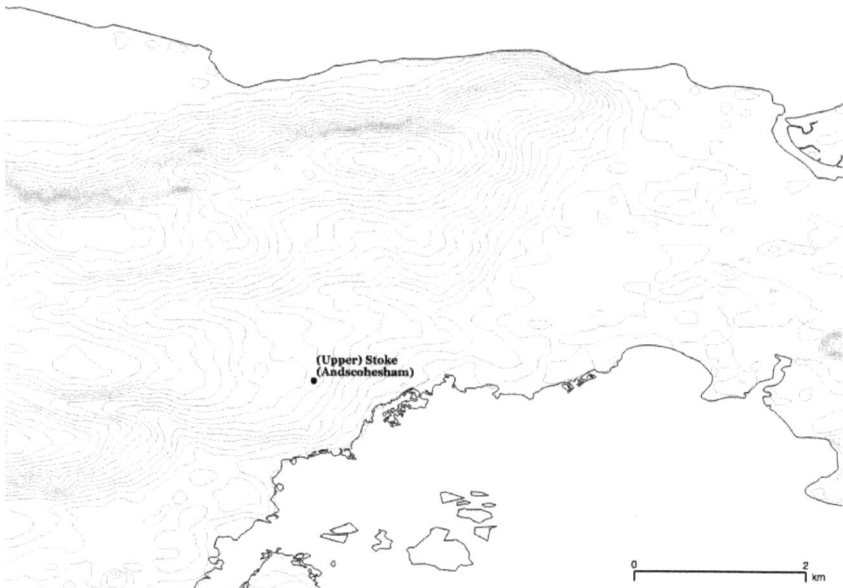

Map 7.5 Map of Stoke (previously *Andscohesham*) and its surroundings, with 2m contour lines. This map was created with data from Digital Elevation Model over Europe (EU-DEM). Available at: https://data.europa.eu/euodp/en/data/dataset/data_eu-dem (accessed 4 October 2013). Processed in QGIS by the author.

to observe a two-pronged rise in the ground near this settlement. Map 7.5 shows the current site of Upper Stoke on the end slope of the shorter hill spur, with the longer spur lying to the north of the settlement. The slopes of these spurs are, however, quite shallow, and the spurs themselves cover substantial areas. This raises questions about the extent to which this hill formation would have been perceptible to early medieval inhabitants of the area.

This examination of places whose names contain forms of *Handschuh* as a first element is somewhat inconclusive. In all of these places, two-pronged hill spurs can be observed, which might be taken to appear similar to a mittened hand. However, while the hill spurs above Handschuhsheim are steep and would be very readily apparent from the vicinity of the settlement, the landscapes in all of the other three places are far less dramatic. We are therefore left with questions as to the visual impact of these hill spurs for early medieval inhabitants of these areas. At the same time, we might also wonder why place-names of this type are not more common, since two-pronged hill spurs are probably to be found much more widely across the Germanic-speaking world. The question must therefore remain open whether the name *Hondscio* in *Beowulf* could derive from a rare personal name that is otherwise attested only in place-names, or from the place-names themselves. If the place-names do indeed reflect use of a term for 'mitten' or 'glove' to refer to a landscape feature, then it is possible that *Hondscio* could represent a back formation from a place-name, misinterpreting the first element as a personal name.

Whether we accept that the etymon of Modern German *Handschuh* was used as a landscape term in some Continental Germanic place-names, or argue that it was used as a personal name that appears in place-names, the place-name evidence discussed above is clearly relevant to our understanding of the name *Hondscio* in *Beowulf*. If this word were in wider use as a personal name, it is possible that it simply entered the narrative tradition of *Beowulf* at some point from the stock of personal names. However, if it were not a personal name before it became one in the *Beowulf* tradition, how and why was it developed into one in this tradition? At this point, it may be useful to try to understand more about the place of the character who in *Beowulf* is called *Hondscio* in the narrative tradition from which *Beowulf* draws. This necessitates that we consider whether there are any characters analogous to Hondscio in the analogues of *Beowulf*.

A glove in hood's clothing?

While one hesitates to add anything to the roaring debate over the relatedness (or otherwise) of *Beowulf* to Scandinavian traditions reflected in saga narratives, it is interesting in relation to Hondscio that in *Hrólfs saga kraka*, Bǫðvarr Bjarki has a companion – who is initially rather pathetic but ultimately becomes a heroic warrior – called *Hǫttr* ('hood'). It has long been noted that Beowulf and Bǫðvarr share a number of similarities (see, e.g., Olson 1916; Chambers 1921: 55–61; Rosenberg 1969: 54–55; Earl 2010: 300; Abram 2017: 406–7), and perhaps we should add to these their companions. Although hoods and gloves are quite different items of clothing, the fact that these two dragon fighters, who both do battle on behalf of Scylding kings (albeit Beowulf serves the uncle, Hroðgar, and Bǫðvarr the nephew, Hrólfr, who appears in *Beowulf* as Hroðulf) both have companions whose names are words for items of clothing, seems worthy of exploration.

At first glance, there is little similarity between Hondscio and Hǫttr. Hondscio is eaten the moment he is mentioned in the narrative of *Beowulf*, whereas Hǫttr is rescued by Bǫðvarr from his ignominious abode in a heap of bones (Jónsson 1904: 65; Slay 1960: 74) and reinvented as a more-or-less heroic figure by means of a staged dragon fight (Jónsson 1904: 69–71; Slay 1960: 80–82). There is, however, a puzzling detail in the narrative of Hǫttr's rescue from the bone heap that recalls *Beowulf*. When Bǫðvarr comes across Hǫttr, his first glimpse of him consists of his terribly dirty hand projecting from the heap of bones. Bǫðvarr grabs this disembodied hand and pulls Hǫttr out. The similarity with *Beowulf* is obviously slight, but there is a similarity; in both cases, we have heroes who grapple with a hand in a hall, though with very different outcomes.

In considering the similarities between Beowulf and Bǫðvarr, we might note that Bǫðvarr only fights one monster to Beowulf's three, and that Bǫðvarr's monster seems to be more like a dragon than a humanoid ogre. On this view, if Bǫðvarr springs in some way from the same traditional figure as Beowulf, then he has lost some of his monsters along the way, although Olrik (1919: 249) argues that none of Beowulf's three main monster fights closely resembles Bǫðvarr's fight. A reconsideration of Bǫðvarr's introduction to Hǫttr, however, suggests that the monsters may not have disappeared entirely. We have noted above that Hǫttr's black hand might stand in for Grendel's hand, and, if so, we can potentially see Hǫttr in this episode as a comic inversion of the traditional monstrous figure whose reflex in *Beowulf* is Grendel. If we consider the whole narrative of Bǫðvarr's meeting with Hǫttr and his dragon fight as a potential comic inversion of something like the narrative of Beowulf's monster fights, some interesting possibilities emerge.

Having pulled Hǫttr out of the bone pile in which he has been hiding, Bǫðvarr immediately carries him off to a nearby lake and washes him (Jónsson 1904: 66; Slay 1960: 75). Where Grendel flees to a lake and Beowulf (later) pursues him, Hǫttr has to be forcibly taken to the lake by Bǫðvarr. At the lake, Bǫðvarr does not encounter Hǫttr's mother, as Beowulf does Grendel's, because Bǫðvarr has already met her earlier in the narrative, when he stumbles across her house in the pouring rain (Jónsson 1904: 63–65; Slay 1960: 72–74). This watery female, unlike Grendel's mother, is both harmless and hospitable, and tells Bǫðvarr about her son's high-spirited trip to King Hrólfr's hall that has led to his predicament in the bone pile. Like Grendel, Hǫttr is an outsider who has travelled to the hall of the Danish king, but whereas Grendel proves more than a match for all the Danish warriors, Hǫttr is quite the opposite, and is victimised by them.

When Bǫðvarr returns from the lake with Hǫttr, he sits down in the hall with him. As the Danish warriors enter the hall, Hǫttr evinces a strong desire to flee (Jónsson 1904: 66; Slay 1960: 75), just as Grendel does when Beowulf holds him fast. Bǫðvarr, for his part, plays Beowulf's role here by keeping hold of Hǫttr and preventing his flight. Since Hǫttr's mother is clearly unlikely to avenge her son on the Danish warriors, it is Bǫðvarr himself who fulfils this role, killing one of Hrólfr's retainers with the bone that the man had himself thrown (Jónsson 1904: 67; Slay 1960: 76). Even the bones themselves, which pile up in a corner of the hall and fill the air during feasting, appear to mirror with comical exaggeration the arm of Grendel, solemnly displayed in isolation as a trophy of battle. In *Hrólfs saga kraka*, it seems that the two humanoid monsters represented by Grendel and his mother in *Beowulf* may have been humorously refigured as Hǫttr and Bǫðvarr themselves. The dragon-like monster that Bǫðvarr goes on to fight can be seen as a counterpart to the dragon of *Beowulf*, and the ways in which this fight inverts the version represented in *Beowulf* are quite readily apparent. Where Beowulf receives stalwart aid from Wiglaf, Bǫðvarr receives no help at all from Hǫttr, throwing him into some moss when he starts screaming on catching sight of the monster (Jónsson 1904: 69; Slay 1960: 78–79). Finally, the narrative achieves one of its most comical effects in presenting the hero's companion not as food for a monster, but as feeding off a monster; whereas Hondscio is eaten by Grendel, Hǫttr instead eats part of the winged monster that Bǫðvarr defeats (Jónsson 1904: 69; Slay 1960: 79).

We need not doubt that the account of Bǫðvarr in *Hrólfs saga kraka* and *Beowulf* drew on some of the same narrative traditions. If nothing else, the historical backdrop of the Scylding court, whether under the rule of Hroðgar or his nephew Hroðulf/Hrólfr, links these two narratives of monster slayers (Earl (2010: 300), however, accepts a strong link between Hroðulf in *Beowulf* and Hrólfr, yet expresses doubts about the relatedness of Bǫðvarr). It seems possible, moreover, that we have not fully appreciated the extent to which the saga mirrors narrative elements that are also present in *Beowulf*. The apparent absence of two out of three monsters may, in fact, be the result of a humorous re-working of the traditional material in which the hero and his companion undertake comical versions of the actions that the monsters perform in other reflexes of the narrative. In light of this possibility, it is worth re-opening the question of a possible relationship between the names *Hondscio* and *Hǫttr*. Panzer (1910–1912: 1.383) suggested that the name *Hǫttr* could derive from *hanzki* as a reflex of a HAND-SHOE form. This was quite rightly rejected by Björkman (1920b: 67), as *hanzki* is clearly a loanword into Scandinavian – and probably a fairly late loan at that – from the Continental Germanic forms of *Handschuh*. An alternative possibility that Panzer (1910–1912: 1.383) appears to raise is that the name *Hǫttr* is the result of a scribal error for *Vǫttr*, a name that appears as that of another of Hrólfr's champions in the saga. Since Old

Norse *vǫttr* means 'glove', this would create a correspondence between the meanings of the names of Beowulf's and Bǫðvarr's companions. One is always reluctant to emend readings that are satisfactory on their own terms, so perhaps we should not be too quick to replace *Hǫttr* 'hood' with *Vǫttr* 'glove'. In the light of the symmetries between Hǫttr and Hondscio, however, it is certainly tempting do so.

Hondscio and the narrative tradition of *Beowulf*

The name *Hondscio* in *Beowulf* is a significant anomaly in the naming of characters within the poem. While the other human characters all bear names formed according to the usual patterns of name formation in the Germanic languages, the name *Hondscio* appears to be an exception to this rule. It is possible that this word referring to a mitten had developed into a personal name (perhaps at first as a by-name) on the Continent, appearing in place-names as a personal name, but it is also possible that the place-name evidence points towards the use of the word with the sense 'mitten' as a topographical term describing landscape features that resemble mittens. The name *Hondscio* in *Beowulf*, then, is an anomaly not only within the text itself, but also in relation to Germanic naming practices. We do not find evidence for use of the name outside *Beowulf*, even as a response to *Beowulf* (which may account for some uses of the name *Beowulf* itself). The closest parallel we possess for this name in the Germanic languages is, in fact, the name *Vǫttr* 'glove', applied to a character in *Hrólfs saga kraka*. It seems possible, moreover, that this was originally the name of the character *Hǫttr*, whose role in *Hrólfs saga* corresponds to that of *Hondscio* in *Beowulf*.

We are therefore left with questions as to whether the Scandinavian or the English tradition has priority in relation to the naming of this character. Was the hero's sidekick originally a character in a Scandinavian narrative who was called *Vǫttr*, and whose name was subsequently translated into Continental Germanic as *Hondscio*? Or did this character originate in a Continental Germanic narrative as *Hondscio*, later undergoing translation into Old Norse as *Vǫttr*? The place-name evidence from the Continent would seem to suggest a plausible solution to this problem. One notable feature of various medieval historiographical texts is their interest in providing explanations of the origins of place-names in their areas of interest. The Brut tradition, beginning with Geoffrey of Monmouth and continuing through Wace's *Roman de Brut*, Layamon's *Brut* and beyond, yields numerous examples; constraints of space allow only for the specimen example here of the explanation of the name *Leicester* with reference to King Lear (Wright 1985: 19; Arnold 1938–1940: 1.91; Brook and Leslie 1963–1978: 1.74). Closer to *Beowulf* chronologically and culturally, the *Anglo-Saxon Chronicle* also makes efforts to tie the English landscape to its legendary past, as in the case of the settler Port who supposedly gives his name to Portsmouth (Irvine 2004: 18 s.a. 501). The two instances of *Handschuhsheim*-type place-names on the Continent could very easily have been reinterpreted as having originally had the sense 'settlement of a man named *Handschuh*', in line with the numerous names in *-heim* in the region in which the first element is a personal name. This would provide a plausible mechanism for the development of a character called *Hondscio*, and it would appear to be related to a region on the Continent in which the personal name *Beowulf* appears to have been in use, as evidenced by the place-name Biécourt and the Bishop of Strasbourg bearing this name. While this falls short of cast iron proof, it seems plausible that the narrative that gave rise to *Beowulf* and (with major comic modifications) the episode of Bǫðvarr's monster-slaying in *Hrólfs saga kraka*, entered the Germanic heroic tradition through a version that developed in this region.

This order of precedence fits with the chronology of *Beowulf* and *Hrólfs saga kraka*, and it also provides a satisfactory explanation for the otherwise anomalous names *Hondscio* and *Vǫttr*. It does not, of course, explain why the hero's sidekick is actually called *Hǫttr* in *Hrólfs saga*, and the name *Vǫttr* has been transferred to another character. Such a transfer between two very similar names, however, does not seem terribly surprising. The name *Hondscio* in *Beowulf*, it turns out, fits with the evidence discussed above for the continental origins of the narrative materials of *Beowulf*, but it takes us further in suggesting a possible region in which onomastic evidence suggests that these materials may have taken shape.

This discussion obviously raises questions about the nature of the central narrative of *Beowulf*. It has certainly been remarked before that it shares characteristics with folktales (see, for instance, Chambers 1921: 62–68; Scowcroft 1999: 22–29), and its relationship with *Hrólfs saga kraka* is difficult – if not impossible – to explain in terms of literary transmission. Indeed, while the overarching similarities in the narratives can be detected, the rearrangement of narrative elements and the entirely different tone of the two narratives suggests that we should not even think in terms of a shared heroic narrative tradition here, but rather in terms of two representatives of a very malleable folk tradition. The overarching lines of this tradition involve a hero who, with a companion, confronts a monster on his home territory. He then pursues the wounded monster to its den, defeating it definitively (possibly along with an associated monster). The hero then goes on to defeat a dragon.

The name *Hondscio* thus sheds light on the kind of narrative tradition that ultimately informs both *Beowulf* and *Hrólfs saga kraka*. Both texts can be seen as deriving at some point from a folktale tradition that has been treated in very different ways in these two heroic narratives. *Beowulf* reshapes the tradition to form the overarching narrative of an epic that brings together various parts of the heroic narrative traditions of the Germanic-speaking world. In doing so, one might suggest that it undertakes in a much subtler fashion the same sort of work of anthologising the heroic past as *Widsith*. By contrast, *Hrólfs saga* develops the tradition into a comic interlude within a heroic narrative centring on a scion of the Scylding dynasty. Yet both texts agree in situating the narrative in relation to the Scylding dynasty, suggesting some sort of point prior to the creation of either text at which a loose relationship between the folk tradition and the Scyldings developed. In some ways, the situation in *Hrólfs saga*, where the folktale is a narrative framed within the heroic, dynastic narrative, seems the more likely pattern for the origins of such an association. Similar insertions of apparently folkloric material into the backdrop of a heroic, royal court are to be found in some of the narratives set in Camelot in later medieval texts such as *Sir Gawain and the Green Knight* and 'The Wife of Bath's Tale' (see Andrew and Waldron 1987: 207–300; Benson 1987: 116–22). The name *Hondscio*, taken together with the name *Beowulf*, moreover, seems to point towards a possible place of origin for the combination of the folktale with heroic tradition in the region lying along the Rhine between Strasbourg and Heidelberg.

Conclusion

Out of the sixty-nine personal names of human figures in *Beowulf*, around twenty are most readily explained as Continental Germanic names, while another twenty or so could have arisen anywhere in the Germanic-speaking world, around eighteen could be Scandinavian in origin and around ten Old English, although seven of these ten could as easily be Continental Germanic as Old English. Within the names that could be Scandinavian, moreover, there are more than ten that could also derive from the Continent. These are very striking findings in a poem written in Old English and depicting for the most part events taking place in Scandinavia and involving characters who are identified as Scandinavian. It is surprising to discover how small the Old English contribution to the names of the poem could be, and the Scandinavian component is also potentially quite small. One possible explanation for this situation is that the personal names of *Beowulf* reflect an older period of Germanic personal naming in which these names existed either in Scandinavia, England, or both, before falling out of use in these areas. While we cannot rule this out entirely, it is unlikely that the loss of names would have been as skewed towards Scandinavia and England as the pattern we see here suggests. Moreover, the evidence for written transmission of some of these names from the Continent (see discussions of *Eadgils*, *Scef* and *Unferð* above at pp. 106–8, 54–59 and 92–95) supports the view that the personal names of some – perhaps many – of the figures in the poem were of Continental Germanic origin. On balance, then, it seems that we should not ascribe the preponderance of apparently Continental Germanic personal names in the poem simply to loss of personal names in Scandinavian and English onomastic traditions. It is also interesting to note that the names that appear to be most probably Old English in origin belong to the English royal genealogical tradition (*Beow*, *Hengest*) and to Beowulf's helper in his dragon fight, Wiglaf, and his father. The use of English genealogical tradition in the poem is unsurprising. The fact that Wiglaf and his father appear more likely than not to have come into being in England, however, might suggest that these figures – who are otherwise unknown to heroic tradition – were created by the Old English poet simply to provide Beowulf with a companion in his final fight. This might prompt us to consider further the ways in which the origins of characters' names may reveal how they were developed.

Certain characters within *Beowulf* are historically attested individuals, whose names simply reflect their actual origins; for example, the name *Eormenric*, applied to the Gothic king Ermanaric in *Beowulf*, is simply an Anglicised form of this individual's name, and it is unsurprising to find that his name is one native not to England or Scandinavia, but to the Continental Germanic dialects. In most cases, however, we have no evidence for the historical existence of the characters of the poem, and the origins of their names can be seen as evidence for the ways in which the heroic traditions that fed into *Beowulf* developed. In order to explore this evidence more fully, it is helpful to consider these names within their tribal and familial groupings, and the analysis presented above has therefore grouped names in this way. Figure 8.1 summarises this work, showing the names arranged as far as possible in family trees and according to their tribal groupings. Obviously this represents a simplification of a complex situation, since some of the family relationships are not entirely clear (e.g. Swerting could be Hygelac's grandfather or his uncle, given the ambiguity of the Old English word *nefa* at line 1203, and Hemming is described only as the *mæg* 'kinsman' of Offa and Eomer at lines 1944 and 1961). The tribal groupings are not always straightforward; for example, Wulfgar appears here among the Scylding courtiers, but he is described as *Wendla leod* 'a man of the *Wendlas*' at line 348 and is therefore perhaps not a Dane, while Hengest in the Finnsburh episode has been classified in this diagram as a Dane based on his role in the episode, although if he is to be identified with Hengest the English ancestor figure, he might have been understood by an English audience to be a Jute. This diagram is also problematic in that it presents a picture of apparently clear-cut distinctions between names with different geographical distributions, although the analysis presented in this book has shown that, in some cases, it is difficult to arrive at clear conclusions on the distribution of a particular name. Although we must allow for these difficulties in presenting a diagrammatic summary of this sort, this nevertheless remains a helpful way to view the overall situation.

When we consider Figure 8.1, it becomes apparent how little the dynasties depicted in *Beowulf* owe to Scandinavian tradition. Very few names in the poem can only be explained satisfactorily as names of Scandinavian origin. Healfdene and his descendants present the clearest case of Scandinavian origins, but they are presented within the poem with courtiers and in-laws whose names point

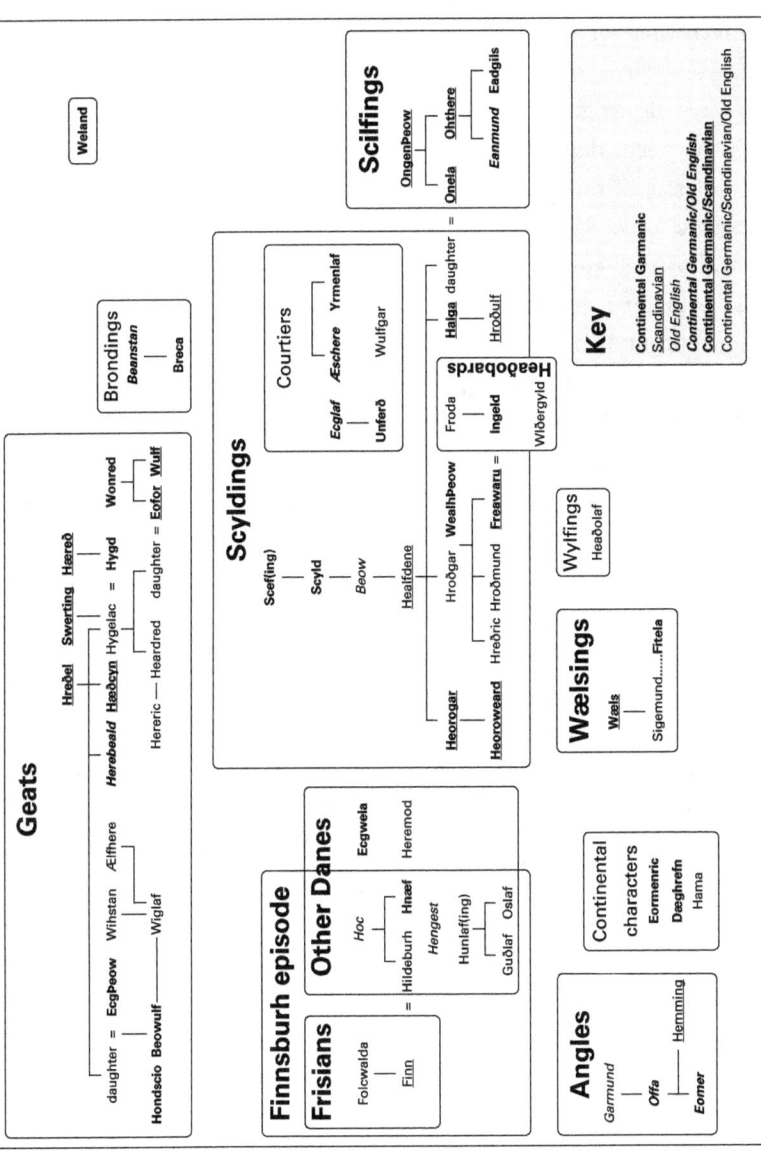

Figure 8.1 The characters of *Beowulf* shown in tribal groupings and family relations, visually coded for the probable origins of their names.

towards the Continent, and with royal ancestors whose names reflect English royal genealogical tradition but also indicate the role of the Continent in the development of that tradition. This suggests that the part of the Scylding dynasty from Healfdene onwards probably developed as a Scandinavian tradition, which is very much what we might expect. The figures peripheral to this dynasty, in contrast, show signs of being developed on the Continent before making their way into *Beowulf*. This could indicate that the Scylding backdrop to the events of the poem derives from Scandinavian traditions about the Scylding dynasty, filtered through a Continental Germanic narrative in which the courtiers and other peripheral figures developed. The generations above Healfdene, however, consisting of names of English and continental origin that also feature in English royal genealogies, could represent either an English transference from this genealogical tradition, or a Continental Germanic element in the narrative deriving from a version of the English genealogical tradition known on the Continent. If we accept the suggestion that the name *Scef* in the genealogical tradition in fact derives from an Old High German form of the word *ship*, however, this would tend to suggest that the English royal genealogical tradition has been influenced by something like the narrative presented in *Beowulf*, and that this existed in some form on the Continent before passing into *Beowulf* itself.

The other major royal houses of the poem, those of the Geats and the Swedes, in contrast, do not contain any names that have to have developed in Scandinavia. It is possible that with these dynasties we also have to reckon with a Scandinavian dynastic core that has been augmented with figures created in a Continental Germanic context. The main Geatish line of descent, from Hreðel to Hygelac to Heardred, consists of figures with names that could have developed in Scandinavia, while some more peripheral figures in the dynasty, such as Hygelac's wife Hygd, or his in-laws Wonred, and Ecgþeow and his nephew Beowulf, have names that are highly likely to have developed on the Continent. Similarly, the Swedish royal figures Ongenþeow, Onela and Ohthere could be of Scandinavian origin, although Ohthere's sons are more readily explicable as deriving from the Continent or, in the case of Eanmund, perhaps from England. It is certainly tempting to read these dynasties as instances of reception and augmentation of Scandinavian tradition on the Continent and in England. We should, however, consider an alternative possibility, which is perhaps even a better explanation of the picture presented here; perhaps both of these dynasties originated on the Continent as narratives about the Scandinavian homeland to which some Continental Germanic tribes ascribed their origins. In the case of the Geats, there is little evidence that these traditions were then adopted in Scandinavia, with the possible exception of some narrative similar to the central narrative of *Beowulf* influencing *Hrólfs saga kraka*, but in the case of the Scilfings, *Ynglingatal* provides evidence for relatively early adoption of part of this dynastic tradition in Scandinavia.

When we turn to the other groups that feature in *Beowulf*, besides the main three Scandinavian dynasties and their courts, we find almost no evidence of Scandinavian origins for names. The Frisian *Finn* and Angle *Hemming* are exceptions, but the Brondings, the Heathobards and the Wælsings all appear to belong to Continental Germanic narrative traditions, to judge from their personal names. Since the Brondings, Heathobards and Wælsings are not clearly tied to a specific part of the Germanic-speaking world, however, we might hypothesise that these were all Continental Germanic tribes and that traditions about them therefore contain Continental Germanic names. However, such a hypothesis, could not account for the fact that the Danes who appear in the Finnsburh episode, and the obscure Danish royal figure Ecgwela, have names that also point towards continental origins. Clearly, the names of these figures suggest that they came into being as part of Continental Germanic narrative traditions concerning Scandinavia and did not arise as Scandinavian narrative traditions. The Angles are the odd one out among the minor groupings of *Beowulf*; unlike the Brondings, Danes outside the Scylding tradition, Heathobards and Wælsings, the Angles bear names such as *Offa* and *Eomer* that are consistent with Old English origins, and the name form *Garmund*, which may suggest Welsh influence in the spelling of early English royal genealogical materials. That the Angle dynasty should show signs of originating in early medieval England is, however, very much to be expected; here we see the interplay between *Beowulf* and English royal genealogies in relation to a continental tribal group who were identified as a key ancestor group of the English.

In summary, the evidence presented and analysed here suggests that *Beowulf* is in part the imaginative work of an Old English poet who created some figures such as Wiglaf and also incorporated English royal genealogical tradition into the poem – but this accounts for only small parts of the narrative. The main narrative of the poem, depicting Beowulf against the backdrop of the Scylding, Scilfing and Geatish dynasties, as well as many of the significant digressions, were drawn by the poet from some Continental Germanic source or sources. It is probable, moreover, that some of this narrative material was transmitted from the Continent to England in written form. The Continental Germanic source(s), moreover, combine figures who must have been created in a Continental

Germanic context with figures who appear to have formed part of Scandinavian heroic tradition. This poem is not simply an Old English poem, nor yet just an English treatment of Scandinavian traditional material; in order to appreciate the poem within its context of production, we need to acknowledge that it owes a very great deal to Continental Germanic heroic narrative tradition.

This also raises questions about the Continental Germanic narrative traditions underlying the poem and their transmission to England. That there were Continental Germanic heroic narrative traditions, and that they came to be recorded in written form, is evidenced by a few surviving texts such as the *Hildebrandslied* and the *Waltharius*, as well as by Einhard's explicit statement that Charlemagne had such texts recorded in writing (Pertz and Waitz 1911: 33 (chapter 29)). The original extent of these narrative traditions is not recoverable, but if we consider Old English heroic poetry in the light of the evidence presented here, we might wonder if it does not owe a great deal to the Continent. Leaving aside clearly later and originally Old English compositions in the heroic mode, such as *The Battle of Maldon* and *The Battle of Brunanburh*, we can relate the Old English *Waldere* very directly to the Continental Germanic *Waltharius*, while *Deor* centres around Weland (whose name, as we have seen, may place his origins in the Continental Germanic area) and the heroic tradition stemming from the Gothic kings Theoderic and Ermanaric. The evidence presented above suggests that *Beowulf* and *The Fight at Finnsburh* may derive in large part from Continental Germanic narrative traditions, while *Widsith* presents a geographically wide-ranging treatment of ethnological knowledge with a largely continental centre of balance. The relative paucity of continental textual representatives of such heroic narratives in comparison to the Old English tradition may be to a considerable extent an accident of preservation of material in England and loss of material on the Continent. Even in England, the extant texts are few, rendering it difficult to draw firm conclusions about how much there once was and how much we have lost, either in England or on the Continent.

It is also worth remarking on the Scandinavian setting of *Beowulf* in relation to its continental narrative materials. The English origin myths, like the origin myths of some Continental Germanic tribes, looked to a seaborne migration, but they differ from their Continental Germanic counterparts in identifying that migration as a crossing of the North Sea rather than the Baltic. The English identified their ancestors as tribal groups from the Continent and the southern shores of the Baltic, whereas Continental Germanic tribes such as the Goths and Lombards traced their origins to migrants from Scandinavia. When considered in relation to this key difference in traditions of migratory ethnogenesis, the Scandinavian backdrop against which Beowulf is seen perhaps makes more sense as a Continental Germanic vision of the imagined Scandinavian homeland than it does as an English representation of a Scandinavian past. This is not to suggest that Scandinavia held no interest for the English, but rather to note that some Continental Germanic groups particularly looked to Scandinavia as a homeland and setting for the heroic traditions of their past. Understanding *Beowulf* as drawing on Continental Germanic narrative materials allows us to set it within this cultural context.

We might ask, then, how and why these narrative materials made their way to early medieval England. While no definitive answer can be given to this question, we should note that there are some hints in the evidence discussed above that point to written transmission, at least in part, and this should prompt us to consider the possibility that ecclesiastical personnel were involved. Moreover, Alcuin's famous rhetorical question 'Quid Hinieldus cum Christo?' (on which, see the discussion of the name *Ingeld* at pp. 81–86 above) was addressed to an individual he calls *Speratus*, whom Bullough (1993) has very plausibly identified with bishop Unwona of Leicester – an individual who himself bears a Continental Germanic personal name. That a number of Continental Germanic ecclesiastics made their way to England in the late sixth to eighth centuries is not to be doubted (consider, for instance, Liudhard, chaplain to the Frankish princess Bertha in late sixth-century Kent, or Agilbert, bishop of the West Saxons in the later seventh century), although it would be difficult to quantify the level of mobility. Alcuin's complaint suggests that some such continental personnel brought with them to England their taste for heroic narrative – and the narratives themselves. The songs of Ingeld apparently enjoyed by Unwona may not have been Old English heroic verse at all, but rather Continental Germanic material that formed the guilty pleasure of ecclesiastical migrants from the Continent. Alcuin, after all, as an Englishman on the Continent, was well placed to observe the tastes of Continental Germanic ecclesiastics, and may have written his letter to a Continental Germanic bishop in England with these tastes in mind.

We might also wish to consider the geographical distribution on the Continent of the evidence for the Continental Germanic personal names in *Beowulf*. Some of the names involved are particularly attested in the southerly regions, Alamannia and Bavaria. The name *Beowulf* is best attested in the neighbourhood of Strasbourg (with the other continental attestation in Bavaria), while his companion Hondscio might also be related to the area around Strasbourg and Heidelberg. The name *Scyld* also seems to be attested particularly in Alamannia and Bavaria, and if we accept the identification of his putative father *Scef* as a form of the Old High German word *skef* 'ship', then this would also be consistent with an origin in this broad area. This could suggest that we should look to this region for the origins of some of the narrative materials of the poem, and perhaps particularly for the central narrative concerning Beowulf himself. This in some ways fits with the case made by Hammer (2005) for the currency of names present in *Beowulf* in Bavaria and Alamannia around the eighth century, although the present author does not agree with Hammer in seeing this as a product of transmission of names from Scandinavia to this region around this time. However, the evidence here is clearly very limited, and it could certainly be the case that *Beowulf* and *Scyld* were simply rare names that happen to be attested only in these areas by chance. The possible derivation of *Hondscio* from a place-name such as *Hantscohashaim*, however, is perhaps slightly harder to dismiss, given that the three names formed with these exact elements occur around Strasbourg, Heidelberg and in Kent; this is certainly suggestive of a connection between this area on the Continent and Kent, which is consistent with the general evidence for close contacts between Kent and Frankia, and also consistent with the importance of the region around Strasbourg/Heidelberg within the Frankish realm and its religious life. One cannot push this too far, however. We might hypothesise that the region around Strasbourg and Heidelberg is a plausible place to seek the origins of some of the Continental Germanic narrative materials that informed the production of *Beowulf*, but this remains a hypothesis rather than any sort of conclusion.

It might be suggested that some of the arguments presented here amount to a return to the *Liedertheorie* of the composition of *Beowulf*. This is not what is proposed here, however; the unity of the poem as it has survived to us is not challenged by observing that it had a pre-history in the form of different narrative traditions that were synthesised and drawn together by the *Beowulf* poet into a unified (if complex) poem. The recent application of lexomic methods to the poem by Drout et al. (2016) has, similarly, suggested the possibility that the poet used a number of different sources. At the same time, the new interpretation of the relationship between *Beowulf* and *Hrólfs saga kraka* presented here makes the case for a folk narrative structured around three monster fights that has been developed in *Beowulf* into the overarching narrative for the entire poem. When Rauer (2000: 31) observed that 'no surviving *Beowulf* analogue seems to present precisely the same distinctive sequence of two monster fights set in Denmark, fought in the hero's younger days, and a dragon-fight in Geatland, involving an old and dying hero', she could not have known that the structure of two monster fights followed by a dragon fight was very probably a legacy from the folkloric part of the poem's origins. The locations in Denmark and Geatland, and the different chronological placements within the hero's life, are more probably innovations that serve to create plausible contexts for the insertion of the figure of Beowulf into the legendary dynastic traditions of the Scyldings and the Geats. This setting of Beowulf against a Scandinavian backdrop may, however, as we have already noted, derive from Continental Germanic materials on which the *Beowulf* poet drew.

The dating of the composition of *Beowulf* is very much a live debate in Old English studies, and this book is not intended primarily as a contribution to that debate, although it is worth noting that the arguments presented here are consistent with a broadly early dating of the poem, perhaps to around the eighth century. That we should also seek to read the poem within its later English contexts of reception is also not in doubt. This book, however, should prompt us to reconsider our understanding of the centre of gravity of Germanic heroic narrative traditions, and of the place of *Beowulf* in the Old English poetic tradition. In terms of the great bulk of Old English poetry, *Beowulf* is something of an anomaly, part of a very small group of texts recording early heroic traditions and contrasting with the much larger body of verse on Christian themes. Of course, that Christian verse does make use of poetic conventions and tropes that seem to belong to a heroic tradition, but that does not alter the fact that *Beowulf* appears to draw heavily on material from the Continent, and this should prompt us to question our sense of how the written corpus of Old English verse that survives to this day developed. The story of Cædmon, recounted by Bede in book 4, chapter 24 of his *Historia Ecclesiastica* (Plummer 1896: 258–61; Colgrave and Mynors 1969: 414–18), points to a moment of origination for the written tradition of Old English verse in which fresh composition for Christian purposes sprang out of the existing oral tradition and was transferred into a Christian, literate context. This is a legend, and not to be taken at face value, but it is suggestive. The early medieval English no doubt had heroic narrative traditions that circulated in oral form prior to their Christianisation, and may have continued to circulate in this form after Christianisation as well; but it does not therefore follow that the adoption of Old English verse in literate contexts in the earlier part of the period involved the recording in writing of such heroic narratives. Instead, this adoption of Old English verse may have been essentially a Christian enterprise that co-opted the verse forms and tropes for representing Christian narratives. The heroic poetry in written form from early medieval England may owe its existence, then, to the tastes of Continental Germanic ecclesiastics in England, who opened up the possibility of recording such material in written form.

Notes

2 The Scyldings, Heathobards and Helmings

1 It is worth noting that this tradition may not have been limited to the Kentish royal house but may reflect a wider tradition in the upper echelons of the early Kentish and East Saxon kingdoms. The name element *Eorcen-*, which is very common on the Continent (Förstemann 1900: s.v. *ERCAN*), occurs in England only in the Kentish royal house, as the name of a seventh-century bishop of the East Saxons (*PASE*: s.v. *Eorcenwald 1*) and in names of moneyers (*PASE*: s.v. *Ercanher 1, Ercanmund 1, Ercenbald 1*) and in the *Domesday Book* (*PASE*: s.v. *Erchenbrand 1*). Similarly, the element *Swæf-*, which is moderately common on the Continent (Förstemann 1900: s.v. *SVABA*), occurs only in the Kentish royal house, in the name of Swæfred, king of the East Saxons around the end of the seventh century (*PASE*: s.v. *Swæfred 1*), in the names of moneyers (*PASE*: s.v. *Swefheard 1-6*) and in the name form *Suaefgild* in the *Calendar of St Willibrord* (*PASE*: s.v..*Swæfgild 1*). It should perhaps not surprise us that Kent and the East Saxons, immediately facing the Franks across the English Channel, show signs of close cultural and political influence during the Merovingian period from the Frankish sphere (on which, see Wood 1994: 176–79).

Bibliography

Manuscripts

Cambridge, Corpus Christi College, MS 41
London, British Library, Cotton Augustus ii.55
London, British Library, Cotton Nero D. i
London, British Library, Cotton Vespasian B. vi
London, British Library, Harley 208
London, British Library, Harley 3859
Munich, Bayerisches Hauptstaatsarchiv, HL Freising 3a
Rochester, Cathedral Library, A. 3. 5.
St Gall, Stiftsbibliothek, Cod. Sang. 56
Vatican, Reginae Christinae 272
Würzburg, Staatsarchiv, Mainzer Bücher verschiedenen Inhalts 72
Zürich, Zentralbibliothek, MS Rh. hist. 27

Primary

Althof, H., ed. (1899–1905), *Waltharii Poesis: Das Waltharilied Ekkehards I. von St. Gallen*, 2 vols, Leipzig: Dieterich.
Althoff, G., and J. Wollasch, eds (1983), *Die Totenbücher von Merseburg, Magdeburg und Lüneburg*, MGH: Libri memoriales et Necrologia n.s. 2, Hannover: Hahn.
Andrew, M., and R. Waldron, eds (1987), *The Poems of the Pearl Manuscript*, Exeter: University of Exeter Press.
Arnold, T., ed. (1882–1885), *Symeonis Monachi Opera Omnia*, Rolls Series 75, 2 vols, London: Longman.
Arnold, I., ed. (1938–1940), *Le Roman de Brut de Wace*, 2 vols, Paris: Société des Anciens Textes Français.
Baker, P. S., ed. (2000), *The Anglo-Saxon Chronicle: A Collaborative Edition: Volume 8 MS F*, Cambridge: Brewer.
Bately, J., ed. (1980), *The Old English Orosius*, EETS s.s. 6, Oxford: Oxford University Press.
Bately, J. M., ed. (1986), *The Anglo-Saxon Chronicle: A Collaborative Edition: Volume 3 MS A*, Cambridge: Brewer.
Baumann, F. L., ed. (1888), *Necrologia Germaniae I: Dioeceses Augustensis, Constantiensis, Curiensis*, MGH: Necrologia Germaniae 1, Berlin: Weidmann.

Benediktsson, J., ed. (1968), *Íslendingabók; Landnámabók*, ÍF 1, 2 vols, Reykjavík: Íslenzka Fornritafélag.

Benson, L. D., ed. (1987), *The Riverside Chaucer*, 3rd edn, Oxford: Oxford University Press.

Bethurum, D., ed. (1957), *The Homilies of Wulfstan*, Oxford: Clarendon Press.

Bitterauf, T., ed. (1905–1909), *Die Traditionen des Hochstifts Freising*, 2 vols, Munich: Rieger.

Bloch, H., P. Wentzcke, A. Hessel and M. Krebs, eds (1908–1928), *Regesten der Bischöfe von Strassburg*, 2 vols, Innsbruck: Wagner.

Boretius, A., and V. Krause, eds (1883–1897), *Capitularia regum Francorum*, MGH: Leges, 2 vols, Hannover: Hahn.

Brook, G. L., and R. F. Leslie, eds (1963–1978), *Laȝamon: Brut*, EETS 250, 277, Oxford: Oxford University Press.

Bruckner, A., and R. Marichal, eds (1954), *Chartae Latinae Antiquiores I: Switzerland: Basle-St. Gall*, Olten: Graf.

Bruckner, A., and R. Marichal, eds (1956), *Chartae Latinae Antiquiores II: Switzerland: St. Gall-Zurich*, Olten: Graf.

Brunetti, F., ed. (1806–1833), *Codice Diplomatico Toscano*, 2 vols, Florence: Pagani.

Campbell, A., ed. (1962), *The Chronicle of Æthelweard*, London: Nelson.

Campbell, A., ed. (1973), *Charters of Rochester*, Anglo-Saxon Charters 1, London: British Academy.

Chambers, R. W. (1912), *Widsith: A Study in Old English Heroic Legend*, Cambridge: Cambridge University Press.

Colgrave, B., ed. and trans. (1927), *The Life of Bishop Wilfrid by Eddius Stephanus*, Cambridge: Cambridge University Press.

Colgrave, B., and R. A. B. Mynors, eds and trans. (1969), *Bede's Ecclesiastical History of the English People*, Oxford: Clarendon Press.

Cubbin, G. P., ed. (1996), *The Anglo-Saxon Chronicle: A Collaborative Edition: Volume 6 MS D*, Cambridge: Brewer.

Darlington, R. R., and P. McGurk, eds (1995), *The Chronicle of John of Worcester: Volume II: The Annals from 450 to 1066*, Oxford: Clarendon Press.

Diplomata Imperatorum Authentica (1831), Monumenta Boica 29, Augsburg: Cotta.

Doane, A. N., ed. (1978), *Genesis A: A New Edition*, Madison, WI: University of Wisconsin Press.

Dobbie, E. V. K., ed. (1942), *The Anglo-Saxon Minor Poems*, ASPR 6, New York: Columbia University Press.

Dobbie, E. V. K., ed. (1953), *Beowulf and Judith*, ASPR 4, London: Routledge.

Domesday Book = *Domesday Book or The Great Survey of England of William the Conqueror: Fac-Simile of the Part Relating to Dorsetshire* (1862), Southampton: Ordnance Survey.

Dronke, E. F. J., ed. (1850), *Codex Diplomaticus Fuldensis*, Kassel: Fischer.

Dronke, U., ed. and trans. (1969–2011), *The Poetic Edda*, 3 vols, Oxford: Clarendon Press.

Duemmler, E., ed. (1895), *Epistolae Karolini Aevi: 2*, MGH: Epistolae, Berlin: Weidmann.

Dumville, D. N., ed. (1975), 'The Textual History of the Welsh-Latin *Historia Brittonum*', PhD thesis, 3 vols, University of Edinburgh, Edinburgh.

Dumville, D. N. (1976), 'The Anglian Collection of Royal Genealogies and Regnal Lists', *Anglo-Saxon England*, 5: 23–50.

Dumville, D. N., ed. (1985), *The Historia Brittonum: 3 The 'Vatican' Recension*, Cambridge: Brewer.

Electronic Sawyer = Sawyer, P. H., S. Keynes, S. Kelly, S. Miller, R. Rushforth, E. Connolly, R. Naismith, D. Pelteret, L. Roach and D. Woodman (eds), *Electronic Sawyer*. Available online: https://esawyer.lib.cam.ac.uk/searchfiles/index.html (accessed 31 October 2019).

Faulkes, A., ed. (1988), *Snorri Sturluson: Edda: Prologue and Gylfaginning*, London: Viking Society for Northern Research.

Faulkes, A., ed. (1998), *Snorri Sturluson: Edda: Skáldskaparmál*, 2 vols, London: Viking Society for Northern Research.

Fisher, P., trans., and H. Ellis Davidson, ed. (1979–1980), *Saxo Grammaticus: The History of the Danes: Books I–IX*, 2 vols, Cambridge: Brewer.

Friis-Jensen, K., ed., and P. Fisher, trans. (2015), *Saxo Grammaticus: Gesta Danorum*, 2 vols, Oxford: Clarendon Press.

Fulk, R. D., R. E. Bjork and J. D. Niles, eds (2008), *Klaeber's Beowulf and the Fight at Finnsburg*, Toronto: University of Toronto Press.

Fulk, R. D., ed. and trans. (2012), 'Hákonarmál', in D. Whaley (ed.), *Poetry from the Kings' Sagas 1: Part 1*, SPSMA 1, 171–95, Turnhout: Brepols.

Garmonsway, G. N., and J. Simpson, trans. (1968), *Beowulf and its Analogues*, London: Dent.

Glöckner, K., ed. (1929–1936), *Codex Laureshamensis*, 3 vols, Darmstadt: Verlag des historischen Vereins für Hessen.

Grendon, F., ed. (1909), 'The Anglo-Saxon Charms', *Journal of American Folk-Lore*, 22: 105–237.

Guðnason, B., ed. (1982), *Danakonunga sǫgur: Skjǫldunga saga, Knýtlinga saga, Ágrip af sǫgu Danakonunga*, ÍF 35, Reykjavík: Hið Íslenzka Fornritafélag.

Hart, C., ed. and trans. (1953), *The Early Charters of Barking Abbey*, Colchester: Benham.

Haury, J., ed. (1905–1913), *Procopii Caesariensis Opera Omnia*, 3 vols, Leipzig: Teubner.

Hearne, T., ed. (1723), *Hemingi Chartularium Ecclesiæ Wigorniensis*, 2 vols, Oxford: Sheldonian.

Hecht, H., ed. (1900), *Bischofs Wærferth von Worcester Übersetzung der Dialoge Gregors des Grossen*, Bibliothek der angelsächsischen Prosa 5, Leipzig: Wigand.

Hlawitschka, E., K. Schmid and G. Tellenbach, eds (1970), *Liber Memorialis von Remiremont*, MGH: Antiquitates, Libri Memoriales 1, 2 vols, Zürich: Weidmann.

Irvine, S., ed. (2004), *The Anglo-Saxon Chronicle: A Collaborative Edition: Volume 7 MS E*, Cambridge: Brewer.

Jack, G., ed. (1994), *Beowulf: A Student Edition*, Oxford: Clarendon Press.
Jónsson, F., ed. (1904), *Hrólfs saga kraka og Bjarkarímur*, Copenhagen: Møller.
Jónsson, G., ed. (1954), *Þiðreks saga af Bern*, 2 vols, Reykjavík: Íslendingasagnaútgáfan.
Jónsson, G., ed. (1959), *Fornaldar sögur Norðurlanda*, 4 vols, Reykjavík: Íslendingasagnaútgáfan.
Keydell, R., ed. (1967), *Agathiae Myrinaei Historiarum Libri Quinque*, Corpus Fontium Historiae Byzantinae 2, Berlin: de Gruyter.
Keynes, S., ed. (1996), *The Liber Vitae of the New Minster and Hyde Abbey Winchester*, EEMF 26, Copenhagen: Rosenkilde and Bagger.
Knott, E., ed. (1936), *Togail Bruidne Da Derga*, Dublin: Stationery Office.
Kölzer, T., ed. (2001), *Die Urkunden der Merowinger*, MGH: Diplomata regum Francorum e stirpe Merovingica 1, Hannover: Hahn.
Kristjánsson, J., and V. Ólason, eds (2014), *Eddukvæði*, 2 vols, Reykjavík: Hið Íslenzka Fornritafélag.
Krusch, B., ed. (1896), *Passiones Vitaeque Sanctorum Aevi Merovingici et Antiquiorum Aliquot*, MGH: SrM 3, Hannover: Hahn.
Krusch, B., and W. Levison, eds (1913), *Passiones Vitaeque Sanctorum Aevi Merovingici*, MGH: SrM 6, Hannover: Hahn.
Krusch, B., and W. Levison, eds (1920), *Passiones Vitaeque Sanctorum Aevi Merovingici*, MGH: SrM 7, Hannover: Hahn.
Krusch, B., and W. Levison, eds (1951), *Gregorii Episcopi Turonensis Libri Historiarum X*, MGH: SrM 1.1, Hannover: Hahn.
Kurze, F., ed. (1895), *Annales regni Francorum inde ab a. 741 usque ad a. 829, qui dicuntur Annales Laurissenses maiores et Einhardi*, MGH: SrG 6, Hannover: Hahn.
LangScape = *LangScape: The Language of Landscape: Reading the Anglo-Saxon Countryside*. Available online: http://langscape.org.uk, version 0.9 (accessed 10 July 2018).
Lienert, E., ed. (2008), *Dietrich-Testimonien des 6. bis 16. Jahrhunderts*, Tübingen: Niemeyer.
Loewenfeld, S., ed. (1886), *Gesta Abbatum Fontanellensium*, MGH: SrG 28, Hannover: Hahn.
Malone, K., ed. (1962), *Widsith*, Copenhagen: Rosenkilde and Bagger.
Marold, E., ed. (2012), 'Ynglingatal', in D. Whaley (ed.), *Poetry from the Kings' Sagas 1: Part 1*, SPSMA 1, 3–60, Turnhout: Brepols.
Meyer, C. (1877), *Sprache und Sprachdenkmäler der Langobarden*, Paderborn: Schöningh.
Miller, C. H., trans. (2007), 'Fragments of Danish History', *ANQ*, 20(3): 9–22.
Mommsen, T., ed. (1898), *Chronica Minora Saec. IV. V. VI. VII: Volume 3*, MGH: Auctores Antiquissimi 13, Berlin: Weidmann.
Munby, J., ed. (1982), *Domesday Book 4: Hampshire*, Chichester: Phillimore.
Mynors, R. A. B., R. M. Thomson and M. Winterbottom, eds and trans. (1998–1999), *William of Malmesbury: Gesta Regum Anglorum*, 2 vols, Oxford: Clarendon Press.

Napier, A., ed. (1883), *Wulfstan: Sammlung der ihm zugeschriebenen Homilien nebst Untersuchungen über ihre Echtheit*, Berlin: Weidmann.

Napier, A. S., and W. H. Stevenson, eds and trans. (1895), *The Crawford Collection of Early Charters and Documents*, Oxford: Clarendon Press.

O'Brien O'Keeffe, K., ed. (2001), *The Anglo-Saxon Chronicle: A Collaborative Edition: Volume 5 MS C*, Cambridge: Brewer.

Pertz, G. H., and G. Waitz, eds (1911), *Einhardi Vita Karoli Magni*, MGH: SrG 25, Hannover: Hahn.

Pheifer, J. D., ed. (1974), *Old English Glosses in the Épinal-Erfurt Glossary*, Oxford: Clarendon Press.

Piper, P., ed. (1884), *Libri Confraternitatum Sancti Galli, Augiensis, Fabariensis*, MGH: Antiquitates, Necrologia Germaniae, Supplement, Berlin: Weidmann.

Plummer, C., ed. (1896), *Venerabilis Baedae Historiam Ecclesiasticam Gentis Anglorum: Historiam Abbatum: Epistolam ad Ecgberctum una cum Historia Abbatum Auctore Anonymo*, 2 vols, Oxford: Clarendon Press.

Ried, T., ed. (1816), *Codex Chronologico-Diplomaticus Episcopatus Ratisbonensis*, 2 vols, Regensburg: Schaupp.

Ring, A., ed. and trans. (2016), *Waltharius*, Leuven: Peeters.

Rollason, D., and L. Rollason, eds (2007), *The Durham Liber Vitae: London, British Library, MS Cotton Domitian A.vii*, 3 vols, London: British Library.

Rumble, A., ed. (1983), *Domesday Book: Essex*, Domesday Book: A Survey of the Counties of England 32, Chichester: Phillimore.

Rumble, A., ed. (1986), *Domesday Book: Suffolk*, Domesday Book: A Survey of the Counties of England 34, 2 vols, Chichester: Phillimore.

Sawyer, P., ed. (1957-1962), *Textus Roffensis: Rochester Cathedral Library A. 3. 5.*, EEMF 7-8, Copenhagen: Rosenkilde and Bagger.

Sawyer, P. H., ed. (1979), *Charters of Burton Abbey*, Oxford: Oxford University Press.

Schannat, J. F., ed. (1724), *Corpus Traditionum Fuldensium*, Leipzig: Weidmann.

Schmid, K. (1986), 'Versuch einer Rekonstruktion der St. Galler Verbrüderungsbücher des 9. Jahrhunderts', in M. Borgolte, D. Geuenich and K. Schmid (eds), *Materialien und Untersuchungen zu den Verbrüderungsbüchern und zu den älteren Urkunden des Stiftsarchivs St. Gallen*, St. Galler Kultur und Geschichte 16, Subsidia Sangallensia 1, 81-283, St Gall: Staatsarchiv.

Sedgefield, W. J., ed. (1913), *Beowulf*, 2nd edn, Manchester: Manchester University Press.

Seyfarth, W., ed. (1978), *Ammiani Marcellini Rerum Gestarum Libri qui Supersunt*, 2 vols, Stuttgart: Teubner.

Sickel, T., ed. (1879-1884), *Diplomatum Regum et Imperatorum Germaniae 1: Conradi I. Heinrici I. et Ottonis I. Diplomata*, MGH: Diplomata, Hannover: Hahn.

Sievers, E., ed. (1960), *Tatian: Lateinisch und altdeutsch mit ausführlichem Glossar*, Paderborn: Schöningh.

Skeat, W. W., ed. and trans. (1881-1900), *Ælfric's Lives of Saints*, EETS o.s. 76, 82, 94, 114, 2 vols, London: Trübner.

Slay, D., ed. (1960), *Hrólfs saga kraka*, Copenhagen: Munksgaard.
Steinmeyer, E. v., ed. (1916), *Die kleineren althochdeutschen Sprachdenkmäler*, Berlin: Weidmann.
Stengel, E. E., ed. (1913–1958), *Urkundenbuch des Klosters Fulda*, 3 vols, Marburg: Elwert.
Strecker, K., ed. (1937), *Poetae Latini Medii Aevi 5: Die Ottonenzeit 1*. MGH: Antiquitates, Leipzig: Hiersemann.
Strecker, K., and P. Vossen, eds and trans. (1947), *Waltharius*, Berlin: Weidmann.
Swanton, M., ed. and trans. (1978), *Beowulf*, Manchester: Manchester University Press.
Taylor, S., ed. (1983), *The Anglo-Saxon Chronicle: A Collaborative Edition: Volume 4 MS B*, Cambridge: Brewer.
Thorpe, B., ed. (1855), *The Anglo-Saxon Poems of Beowulf, The Scôp or Gleeman's Tale, and The Fight at Finnesburg*, Oxford: Wright.
Tremp, E., ed. (1995), *Thegan: Die Taten Kaiser Ludwigs; Astronomus: Das Leben Kaiser Ludwigs*, MGH: SrG 64, Hannover: Hahn.
Turville-Petre, G., ed. ([1956] 2014), *Hervarar saga ok Heiðreks*, London: Viking Society for Northern Research.
Vigfússon, G., and C. R. Unger, eds (1860–1868), *Flateyjarbok: En Samling af Norske Konge-Sagaer*, 3 vols, Christiania: Malling.
von Arx, I., ed. (1829), *Scriptores Rerum Sangallensium: Annales, Chronica et Historiae Aevi Carolini*, MGH: SS 2, Hannover: Hahn.
Waitz, G., ed. (1878), *Scriptores Rerum Langobardicarum et Italicarum Saec. VI-IX*, MGH: Scriptores, Hannover: Hahn.
Waitz, G., ed. (1887), 'Translatio et Miracula SS. Marcellini et Petri auctore Einhardo', in *Supplementa Tomorum I-XII, Pars III*, MGH: SS 15.1, 238–64, Hannover: Hahn.
Waitz, G., ed. (1892), *Ex Rerum Danicarum Scriptoribus Saec. XII. et XIII*, MGH: SS 29, Hannover: Hahn.
Warner, R. D.-N., ed. (1917), *Early English Homilies from the Twelfth Century MS. Vesp. D. xiv*, EETS o.s. 152, London: Kegan Paul, Trench, Trübner.
Wartmann, H., ed. (1863–1866), *Urkundenbuch der Abtei Sanct Gallen*, 2 vols, Zürich: Höhr.
Whitelock, D., ed. and trans. (1930), *Anglo-Saxon Wills*, Cambridge: Cambridge University Press.
Wigand, P., ed. (1843), *Traditiones Corbeienses*, Leipzig: Brockhaus.
Williams, A., and G. H. Martin, eds (1991), *The Dorset Domesday*, London: Alecto.
Wilmanns, G., ed. (1881), *Inscriptiones Mauretaniarum*, CIL 8: Inscriptiones Africae Latinae 2, Berlin: Reimer.
Winterbottom, M., and M. Lapidge, eds and trans. (2012), *The Early Lives of Saint Dunstan*, Oxford: Clarendon Press.
Winterbottom, M., and R. M. Thomson, eds and trans (2002), *William of Malmesbury: Saints' Lives: Lives of Ss. Wulfstan, Dunstan, Patrick, Benignus and Indract*, Oxford: Clarendon Press.

Wrenn, C. L., ed. (1953), *Beowulf with the Finnesburg Fragment*, London: Harrap.
Wright, N., ed. (1985), *The Historia Regum Britannie of Geoffrey of Monmouth, I: Bern, Burgerbibliothek, MS. 568*, Cambridge: Brewer.
Wyatt, A. J., and R. W. Chambers, eds (1925), *Beowulf with the Finnsburg Fragment*, Cambridge: Cambridge University Press.
Zangemeister, C., ed. (1905), *Inscriptiones Germaniae Superioris*, CIL 13: Inscriptiones Trium Galliarum et Germaniarum Latinae 2.1, Berlin: Reimer.

Secondary

Abram, C. (2017), 'Bee-Wolf and the Hand of Victory: Identifying the Heroes of *Beowulf* and *Vǫlsunga Saga*', *Journal of English and Germanic Philology*, 116: 387–414.
Andersen, H. (1973), 'Svarteborg-medaljonens runeindskrift endnu en gang', *Arkiv för Nordisk Filologi*, 88: 111–17.
Antonsen, E. H. (1975), *A Concise Grammar of the Older Runic Inscriptions*, Tübingen: Niemeyer.
Arcamone, M. G. (1997), 'Die langobardischen Personennamen in Italien: *nomen* und *gens* aus der Sicht der linguistischen Analyse', in D. Geuenich, W. Haubrichs, and J. Jarnut (eds), *Nomen et Gens: Zur historischen Aussagekraft frühmittelalterlicher Personennamen*, ERGA 16, 157–75, Berlin: de Gruyter.
Armstrong, A. M., A. Mawer, F. M. Stenton and B. Dickins (1950–1952), *The Place-Names of Cumberland*, EPNS 20–22, 3 vols, Cambridge: Cambridge University Press.
Bazelmans, J. (2009), 'The Early-medieval Use of Ethnic Names from Classical Antiquity: The Case of the Frisians', in T. Derks and N. Roymans (eds), *Ethnic Constructs in Antiquity: The Role of Power and Tradition*, 321–38, Amsterdam: Amsterdam University Press.
Biggs, F. M. (2014), 'History and Fiction in the Frisian Raid', in L. Neidorf (ed.), *The Dating of Beowulf: A Reassessment*, 138–56, Cambridge: Brewer.
Björkman, E. (1919), 'Zu einigen Namen im Beowulf', *Beiblatt zur Anglia*, 30: 170–80.
Björkman, E. (1920a), 'Hæðcyn und Hákon', *Englische Studien*, 54: 24–34.
Björkman, E. (1920b), *Studien über die Eigennamen im Beowulf*, Studien zur englischen Philologie 58, Halle a. S.: Niemeyer.
Bliss, A. J. (1958), *The Metre of Beowulf*, Oxford: Blackwell.
Bloomfield, M. W. (1949), 'Beowulf and Christian Allegory: An Interpretation of Unferth', *Traditio*, 7: 410–15.
Bosworth and Toller = Bosworth, J., and T. N. Toller, eds (1898), *An Anglo-Saxon Dictionary*, London: Oxford University Press; Toller, T. N., ed. (1921), *An Anglo-Saxon Dictionary: Supplement*, London: Oxford University Press.
Braune, W., and H. Eggers (1975), *Althochdeutsche Grammatik*, 13th edn, Tübingen: Niemeyer.

Braune, W., and F. Heidermanns (2018), *Althochdeutsche Grammatik*, 16th edn, Berlin: de Gruyter.
Breen, N. A. (2009), '*Beowulf*'s Wealhtheow and the *Ðeowwealh*: A Legal Source for the Queen's Name', *ANQ*, 22 (2): 2–4.
Briggs, E. (1987), 'Religion, Society, and Politics, and the *Liber Vitae* of Durham', PhD thesis, 2 vols, University of Leeds, Leeds.
Brooks, N. (1992), 'The Career of St Dunstan', in N. Ramsay, M. Sparks and T. Tatton-Brown (eds), *St Dunstan: His Life, Times and Cult*, 1–23, Woodbridge: Boydell.
Bruce, A. M. (2002), *Scyld and Scef: Expanding the Analogues*, London: Routledge.
Bullough, D. A. (1993), 'What has Ingeld to do with Lindisfarne?', *Anglo-Saxon England*, 22: 93–125.
Cameron, K. (1959), *The Place-Names of Derbyshire*, EPNS 27–29, 3 vols, Cambridge: Cambridge University Press.
Chambers, R. W. (1921), *Beowulf: An Introduction to the Study of the Poem with a Discussion of the Stories of Offa and Finn*, Cambridge: Cambridge University Press.
Christensen, A. S. (2005), 'Beowulf, Hygelac og Chlochilaichus: Om beretningskronologien i *Beowulf*, *Historisk Tidsskrift*, 105: 40–79.
Clark, C. (1992), 'Onomastics', in Hogg, R. M. (ed.), *The Cambridge History of the English Language: Volume 1: The Beginnings to 1066*, 452–89, Cambridge: Cambridge University Press.
Clark, G. (2009), 'The Date of *Beowulf* and the Arundel Psalter Gloss', *Modern Philology*, 106: 677–85.
Cleasby, R., G. Vigfússon and W. A. Craigie (1957), *An Icelandic-English Dictionary*, 2nd edn, Oxford: Clarendon Press.
Clover, C. J. (1980), 'The Germanic Context of the Unferþ Episode', *Speculum*, 55: 444–68.
Davis, C. R. (1992), 'Cultural Assimilation in the Anglo-Saxon Royal Genealogies', *Anglo-Saxon England*, 21: 23–36.
de Planhol, X., and P. Claval (1994), *An Historical Geography of France*, trans. J. Lloyd, Cambridge: Cambridge University Press.
De Vries, J. (1962), *Altnordisches etymologisches Wörterbuch*, 2nd edn, Leiden: Brill.
DOE = Cameron, A., A. Crandell Amos, A. diPaolo Healey and R. Liuzza, eds (2016), *Dictionary of Old English: A to H Online*, Toronto: Dictionary of Old English Project.
DOEC = diPaolo Healey, A., with J. Price Wilkin and X. Xiang (2009), *Dictionary of Old English Web Corpus*, Toronto: Dictionary of Old English Project.
Dronke, U. (1989), 'The Scope of the *Corpvs Poeticvm Boreale*', in R. McTurk and A. Wawn (eds), *Úr Dölum til Dala: Guðbrandur Vigfússon Centenary Essays*, Leeds Texts and Monographs n.s. 11, Leeds: University of Leeds.
Drout, M. D. C., Y. Kisor, L. Smith, A. Dennett and N. Piirainen (2016), *Beowulf Unlocked: New Evidence from Lexomic Analysis*, London: Palgrave Macmillan.
Dumville, D. N. (1974), 'Some Aspects of the Chronology of the *Historia Brittonum*', *Bulletin of the Board of Celtic Studies*, 25: 439–45.

Dumville, D. N. (1994), 'English Square Minuscule Script: The Mid-century Phases', *Anglo-Saxon England*, 23: 133–64.
Earl, J. W. (2010), 'The Forbidden *Beowulf*: Haunted by Incest', *PMLA*, 125: 289–305.
Ekwall, E. (1960), *The Concise Oxford Dictionary of English Place-Names*, 4th edn, Oxford: Clarendon Press.
Eliason, N. E. (1963), 'The Þyle and Scop in *Beowulf*', *Speculum*, 38: 267–84.
Felder, E. (2003), *Die Personennamen auf den merowingischen Münzen der Bibliothèque nationale de France*, Munich: Bayerische Akademie der Wissenschaften.
Forssner, T. (1916), *Continental-Germanic Personal Names in England in Old and Middle English Times*, Uppsala: Appelberg.
Förstemann, E. (1900), *Altdeutsches Namenbuch: Erster Band, Personennamen*, 2nd edn, Bonn: Hanstein.
Förstemann, E. (1913–1916), *Altdeutsches Namenbuch: Zweiter Band, Orts- und sonstige geographische Namen*, 2 vols, 3rd edn, Bonn: Hanstein.
Frank, R. (1991), 'Germanic Legend in Old English Literature', in Malcolm Godden and Michael Lapidge (eds), *The Cambridge Companion to Old English Literature*, 88–106, Cambridge: Cambridge University Press.
Frank, R. (2007), 'Terminally Hip and Incredibly Cool: Carol, Vikings, and Anglo-Scandinavian England', *Representations*, 100: 23–33.
Fulk, R. D. (1987), 'Unferth and His Name', *Modern Philology*, 85: 113–27.
Fulk, R. D. (1989), 'An Eddic Analogue to the Scyld Scefing Story', *Review of English Studies*, 40: 313–22.
Fulk, R. D. (2007), 'The Etymology and Significance of Beowulf's Name', *Anglo-Saxon*, 1: 109–36.
Gelling, M., and A. Cole (2000), *The Landscape of Place-Names*, Stamford: Shaun Tyas.
Godiveau, H. (1988), 'Peuplement et Christianisation entre Pays de France et Beauce', *Médiévales*, 15: 9–16.
Goldast, M. H. (1730), *Rerum Alamannicarum Scriptores*, 3 vols, Frankfurt: Fleischer.
Gordon, E. V. (1935), '*Wealhþeow* and Related Names', *Medium Ævum*, 4: 169–75.
Graff, E. G. (1834–1842), *Althochdeutscher Sprachschatz*, 6 vols, Berlin, Nicolaische Buchhandlung.
Grimm, J. (1842), '*Rectitudines Singularum Personarum*' (review), *Jahrbücher für wissenschaftliche Kritik*, 99–100: 791–97.
Gwara, S. (2008), 'The Foreign Beowulf and the "Fight at Finnsburg"', *Traditio*, 63: 185–233.
Hammer, C. I. (2005), 'Hoc and Hnaef in Bavaria? Early-Medieval Prosopography and Heroic Poetry', *Medieval Prosopography*, 26: 13–50.
Harris, A. L. (1982), 'Hands, Helms, and Heroes: The Role of Proper Names in *Beowulf*', *Neuphilologische Mitteilungen*, 83: 414–21.
Harris, S. J. (2001), 'The Alfredian *World History* and Anglo-Saxon Identity', *Journal of English and Germanic Philology*, 100: 482–510.

Henning, R. (1874), *Über die sanctgallischen Sprachdenkmäler bis zum Tode Karls des grossen*, Strassburg: Trübner.

Henry, P. L. (1966), *The Early English and Celtic Lyric*, London: George Allen & Unwin.

Hill, T. D. (1990), '"Wealhtheow" as a Foreign Slave: Some Continental Analogues', *Philological Quarterly*, 69: 106-12.

Hill, J. M. (2007), 'Gods at the Borders: Northern Myth and Anglo-Saxon Heroic Story', in S. O. Glosecki (ed.), *Myth in Early Northwest Europe*, 241-56, Tempe, AZ: Arizona Center for Medieval and Renaissance Studies.

Hogg, R. M., and R. D. Fulk (2011), *A Grammar of Old English*, 2 vols, Chichester: Wiley-Blackwell.

Horovitz, D. (2003), *A Survey and Analysis of the Place-Names of Staffordshire*, PhD thesis, 2 vols, University of Nottingham, Nottingham.

Hulbert, J. R. (1951), 'Surmises Concerning the *Beowulf* Poet's Source', *Journal of English and Germanic Philology*, 50: 11-18.

Jackson, K. (1953), *Language and History in Early Britain: A Chronological Survey of the Brittonic Languages, First to Twelfth Century A.D.*, Edinburgh: Edinburgh University Press.

Jänichen, H. (1976), 'Die alemannischen Fürsten Nebi und Berthold und ihre Beziehungen zu den Klöstern St. Gallen und Reichenau', *Blätter für deutsche Landesgeschichte*, 112: 30-40.

Jenkins, D., and M. E. Owen (1984), 'The Welsh Marginalia in the Lichfield Gospels Part II: The 'Surexit' Memorandum', *Cambridge Medieval Celtic Studies*, 7: 91-120.

Jones, A. H. M., P. Grierson and J. A. Crook (1957), 'The Authenticity of the "Testamentum S. Remigii"', *Revue belge de philologie et d'histoire*, 35: 356-73.

Jónsson, F., and E. Jørgensen (1923), 'Nordiske Pilegrimsnavne i Broderskabsbogen fra Reichenau', *Aarbøger for nordisk Oldkyndighed og Historie*, series 3, 13: 1-36.

Jurasinski, S. (2007), 'The Feminine Name *Wealhtheow* and the Problem of *Beowulf*ian Anthroponymy', *Neophilologus*, 91: 701-15.

Kaufmann, H. (1965), *Untersuchungen zu altdeutschen Rufnamen*, Munich: Fink.

Kaufmann, H. (1968), *Altdeutsche Personennamen: Ergänzungsband*, Munich: Fink.

Kelly, B. (1982), 'The Formative Stages of *Beowulf* Textual Scholarship: Part I', *Anglo-Saxon England*, 11: 247-74.

Kelly, B. (1983), 'The Formative Stages of *Beowulf* Textual Scholarship: Part II', *Anglo-Saxon England*, 12: 239-75.

Kitson, P. R. (2002), 'How Anglo-Saxon Personal Names Work', *Nomina*, 25: 91-121.

Krause, W. (1966), *Die Runeninschriften im älteren Futhark*, 2 vols, Göttingen: Vandenhoeck & Ruprecht.

Krusch, B. (1895), 'Reimser Remigius-Fälschungen', *Neues Archiv der Gesellschaft für ältere deutsche Geschichtskunde*, 20: 509-68.

Lapidge, M. (2000), 'The Archetype of *Beowulf*', *Anglo-Saxon England*, 29: 5-41.

Lapidge, M. (2004), 'Dunstan [St Dunstan] (d. 988), archbishop of Canterbury', *Oxford Dictionary of National Biography*. Available online: www.oxforddnb.com/

view/10.1093/ref:odnb/9780198614128.001.0001/odnb-9780198614128-e-8288 (accessed 20 February 2019).
Leneghan, F. (2009), 'The Poetic Purpose of the Offa-Digression in *Beowulf*', *Review of English Studies*, 60 (246): 538-60.
Lind, E. H. (1905-1915), *Norsk-Isländska Dopnamn ock Fingerade Namn från Medeltiden*, 9 vols, Uppsala: Almqvist & Wiksell.
Malone, K. (1930), 'Ingeld', *Modern Philology*, 27: 257-76.
Malone, K. (1932), 'Notes on *Beowulf*', *Anglia*, 56: 436-37.
Malone, K. (1941), 'Hygd', *Modern Language Notes*, 56: 356-58.
Malone, K. (1953), 'Royal Names in Old English Poetry', *Names*, 1: 153-62.
Mawer, A., and F. M. Stenton (1925), *The Place-Names of Buckinghamshire*, EPNS 2, Cambridge: Cambridge University Press.
McKinnell, J. (1990-1993), 'The Context of *Vǫlundarkviða*', *Saga-Book of the Viking Society*, 23: 1-27.
McKinnell, J. (2005), *Meeting the Other in Norse Myth and Legend*, Woodbridge: Brewer.
Melefors, E. (1993), 'Namnet *Hákon*', in L. Peterson (ed.), *Personnamn i nordiska och andra germanska fornspråk*, 61-79, Uppsala: NORNA.
Melefors, E. (2002), 'The development of Old Nordic personal names', in: Bandle, O., and K. Braunmüller, E. H. Jahr, A. Karker, H.-P. Naumann and U. Teleman (eds), (2002-2005), *The Nordic Languages: An International Handbook of the History of the North Germanic Languages*, 2 vols, 1.963-71, Berlin: de Gruyter.
Müllenhoff, K. (1865), 'Zeugnisse und Excurse zur deutschen Heldensage', *Zeitschrift für deutsches Alterthum*, 12: 253-386.
Müllenhoff, K. (1889), *Beovulf: Untersuchungen über das angelsächsische Epos und die älteste Geschichte der germanischen Seevölker*, Berlin: Weidmann.
Müller, R. (1901), *Untersuchungen über die Namen des nordhumbrischen Liber Vitae*, Palaestra 9, Berlin: Mayer & Müller.
Neidorf, L. (2013a), 'Beowulf before *Beowulf*: Anglo-Saxon Anthroponymy and Heroic Legend', *Review of English Studies*, n.s. 64: 553-73.
Neidorf, L. (2013b), 'Scribal Errors of Proper Names in the *Beowulf* Manuscript', *Anglo-Saxon England*, 42: 249-69.
Neidorf, L. (2015), 'Cain, Cam, Jutes, Giants, and the Textual Criticism of *Beowulf*', *Studies in Philology*, 112: 599-632.
Neidorf, L. (2017), *The Transmission of Beowulf: Language, Culture and Scribal Behavior*, Ithaca: Cornell University Press.
Neidorf, L. (2018a), 'Wealhtheow and Her Name: Etymology, Characterization, and Textual Criticism', *Neophilologus*, 102: 75-89.
Neidorf, L. (2018b), 'The Archetype of *Beowulf*', *English Studies*, 99: 229-42.
Neuß, E. (2008), '*Hûn-* in zweigliedrigen germanischen Personennamen und das Ethnonym *Hunne(n)*', in L. Uwe and T. Schilp (eds), *Nomen et Fraternitas: Festschrift für Dieter Geuenich zum 65. Geburtstag*, ERGA 62, 39-52, Berlin: de Gruyter.

Niles, J. D. (1994), 'Editing *Beowulf*: What Can Study of the Ballads Tell Us?', *Oral Tradition*, 9: 440–67.
Niles, J. D. (1999), '*Widsith* and the Anthropology of the Past', *Philological Quarterly*, 78: 171–213.
North, R. (2006), *The Origins of Beowulf: From Vergil to Wiglaf*, Oxford: Oxford University Press.
O'Donoghue, H. (2003), 'What has Baldr to do with Lamech? The Lethal Shot of a Blind Man in Old Norse Myth and Jewish Exegetical Traditions', *Medium Ævum*, 71: 82–107.
Ogilvy, J. D. A. (1964), 'Unferth: Foil to Beowulf?', *PMLA*, 79: 370–75.
Okasha, E. (1971), *Hand-List of Anglo-Saxon Non-Runic Inscriptions*, Cambridge: Cambridge University Press.
Okasha, E. (1992), 'A Second Supplement to *Hand-List of Anglo-Saxon Non-Runic Inscriptions*', *Anglo-Saxon England*, 21: 37–85.
Olrik, A. (1919), *The Heroic Legends of Denmark*, trans. L. M. Hollander, New York: American-Scandinavian Foundation.
Olson, O. L. (1916), 'The Relation of the *Hrólfs saga kraka* and the *Bjarkarímur* to *Beowulf*', *Publications of the Society for the Advancement of Scandinavian Study*, 3: 1–104.
Orel, V. (2003), *A Handbook of Germanic Etymology*, Leiden: Brill.
Orton, P. (1985), 'An Approach to *Wulf and Eadwacer*', *Proceedings of the Royal Irish Academy. Section C: Archaeology, Celtic Studies, History, Linguistics, Literature*, 85C: 223–58.
Owen-Crocker, G. R. (2000), *The Four Funerals in Beowulf and the Structure of the Poem*, Manchester: Manchester University Press.
Owen-Crocker, G. R. (2007), 'Beast Men: Eofor and Wulf and the Mythic Significance of Names in Beowulf', in S. O. Glosecki (ed.), *Myth in Early Northwest Europe*, 257–80, Tempe, AZ: Arizona Center for Medieval and Renaissance Studies.
Pakis, V. A. (2008), 'The Meaning of Æschere's Name in Beowulf', *Anglia*, 126: 104–13.
Panzer, F. (1910–1912), *Studien zur germanischen Sagengeschichte*, 2 vols, Munich: Beck.
Parsons, D. N., and T. Styles (2000), *The Vocabulary of English Place-Names (BRACE-CÆSTER)*, Nottingham: Centre for English Name-Studies.
PASE = Prosopography of Anglo-Saxon England. Available online: www.pase.ac.uk (accessed 12 August 2019).
Pedersen, B. H., and I. Wohlert, eds (1970), *Svendborg Amts Naturnavne I: Sunds Herred*, Danmarks Stednavne 15, Copenhagen: Akademisk Forlag.
Peterson, L. (2004), *Lexikon över urnordiska personnamn*, Uppsala: Institutet för språk och folkminnen. Available at: www.sofi.se/images/NA/pdf/urnord.pdf (accessed 16 March 2018).
Peterson, L. (2007), *Nordiskt runnamnslexikon*, 5th edn, Uppsala: Institutet för språk och folkminnen.
Rauer, C. (2000), *Beowulf and the Dragon: Parallels and Analogues*, Cambridge: Brewer.

Reichert, H. (2009), 'Sprache und Namen der Wandalen in Afrika', in A. Greule and M. Springer (eds), *Namen des Frühmittelalters als sprachliche Zeugnisse und als Geschichtsquellen*, ERGA 66, 43–120, Berlin: de Gruyter.

Rembold, I. (2018), *Conquest and Christianization: Saxony and the Carolingian World, 772–888*, Cambridge: Cambridge University Press.

Rix, R. W. (2015), *The Barbarian North in the Medieval Imagination: Ethnicity, Legend, and Literature*, New York: Routledge.

Robinson, F. C. (1964), 'Is Wealhþeow a Prince's Daughter?', *English Studies*, 45: 36–39.

Robinson, F. C. (1968), 'The Significance of Names in Old English Literature', *Anglia*, 86: 14–58.

Rosenberg, B. A. (1969), 'The Necessity of Unferth', *Journal of the Folklore Institute*, 6: 50–60.

Rosenfeld, H. (1969), 'Der Name Wieland', *Beiträge zur Namenforschung*, N.F. 4: 53–62.

Rosier, J. L. (1963), 'The Uses of Association: Hands and Feasts in *Beowulf*', *PMLA*, 78: 8–14.

Rumble, A. R. (1984), 'The Status of Written Sources in English Onomastics', *Nomina*, 8: 41–56.

Salberger, E. (1987), 'Två mansnamn i urnordiskan', *Namn och Bygd*, 75: 5–22.

Sayers, W. (2016), '*Skírnismál*, *Byggvir*, and *John Barleycorn*', *Arkiv för nordisk filologi*, 131: 21–46.

Schlaug, W. (1962), *Die altsächsischen Personennamen vor dem Jahre 1000*, Lund: Gleerup.

Schramm, G. (1957), *Namenschatz und Dichtersprache: Studien zu den zweigliedrigen Personennamen der Germanen*, Ergänzungshefte zur Zeitschrift für vergleichende Sprachforschung auf dem Gebiet der indogermanischen Sprachen 15, Göttingen: Vandenhoeck & Ruprecht.

Scowcroft, R. M. (1999), 'The Irish Analogues to *Beowulf*', *Speculum*, 74: 22–64.

Shaw, P. A. (2002), 'Uses of Wodan: The Development of his Cult and of Medieval Literary Responses to It', PhD thesis, University of Leeds, Leeds.

Shaw, P. A. (2011a), 'The Role of Gender in Some Viking-Age Innovations in Personal Naming', *Viking and Medieval Scandinavia*, 7: 151–70.

Shaw, P. A. (2011b), *Pagan Goddesses in the Early Germanic World: Eostre, Hreda and the Cult of Matrons*, London: Bristol Classical Press.

Shaw, P. A. (2013a), 'Adapting the Roman Alphabet for Writing Old English: Evidence from Coin Epigraphy and Single-sheet Charters', *Early Medieval Europe*, 21: 115–39.

Shaw, P. A. (2013b), 'Personal Names from Ethnonyms? Scandinavia and Elsewhere', *Nomina*, 36: 53–73.

Shippey, T. (2014), 'Names in *Beowulf* and Anglo-Saxon England', in L. Neidorf (ed.), *The Dating of Beowulf: A Reassessment*, 58–78, Cambridge: Brewer.

Skeat, W. W. (1886), 'On the Signification of the Monster Grendel in the Poem of *Beowulf*; with a Discussion of Lines 2076–2100', *The Journal of Philology*, 15: 120–31.

Smart, V. (1986), 'Scandinavians, Celts, and Germans in Anglo-Saxon England: The Evidence of Moneyers' Names', in M. A. S. Blackburn (ed.), *Anglo-Saxon Monetary History: Essays in Memory of Michael Dolley*, 171–84, Leicester: Leicester University Press.

Stanley, E. G. (1990), '"Hengestes Heap", *Beowulf* 1091', in A. Bammesberger and A. Wollmann (eds), *Britain 400–600: Language and History*, Heidelberg: Winter.

Stanley, E. G. (2002), 'Paleographical and Textual Deep Waters: <a> for <u> and <u> for <a>, <d> for <ð> and <ð> for <d> in Old English', *ANQ*, 15: 64–72.

Terrien, M.-P. (2007), *La Christianisation de la Région Rhénane due IVe au milieu du VIIIe siècle*, Besançon: Presses universitaires de Franche-Comté.

Tolkien, J. R. R. (1982), *Finn and Hengest: The Fragment and the Episode*, ed. A. Bliss, London: Allen & Unwin.

Tolley, C. (1996), 'Beowulf's Scyld Scefing Episode: Some Norse and Finnish Analogues', *Arv*, 52: 7–48.

Townend, M. (2002), *Language and History in Viking Age England: Linguistic Relations between Speakers of Old Norse and Old English*, Turnhout: Brepols.

Vickrey, J. F. (2009), *Beowulf and the Illusion of History*, Bethlehem: Lehigh University Press.

von Feilitzen, O. (1937), *The Pre-Conquest Personal Names of Domesday Book*, Uppsala: Almqvist & Wiksell.

Voyles, J. B. (1992), *Early Germanic Grammar: Pre-, Proto-, and Post-Germanic Languages*, San Diego: Academic Press.

Wagner, A. (1876), *Über die deutschen Namen der ältesten Freisinger Urkunden*, Erlangen: Jacob.

Wagner, N. (2009), 'Zum *ssigaduʀ* des Svarteborg-Medaillons', *Beiträge zur Namenforschung*, n.s. 44: 209-11.

Wahlberg, M., ed. (2003), *Svenskt ortnamnslexikon*, Uppsala: Språk- och folkminnesinstitutet.

Wallenberg, J. K. (1931), *Kentish Place-Names: A Topographical and Etymological Study of the Place-Name Material in Kentish Charters Dated before the Conquest*, Uppsala: Lundquist.

Wessén, E. (1927), *Nordiska Namnstudier*, Uppsala Universitets Årsskrift: Filosofi, Språkvetenskap och Historiska Vetenskaper 3, Uppsala: Lundequist.

Weil, S. (1989), 'Grace Under Pressure: "Hand-Words," *Wyrd*, and Free Will in *Beowulf*', *Pacific Coast Philology*, 24: 94–104.

Weiskott, E. (2011), 'Three *Beowulf* Cruces: *Healgamen, Fremu, Sigemunde*', *Notes and Queries*, 58: 3–7.

Weyhe, H. (1908), 'König Ongentheows Fall', *Englische Studien*, 39: 14–39.

Wood, I. (1994), *The Merovingian Kingdoms 450–751*, London: Longman.

Wormald, P. (2006), '*Beowulf*: The Redating Reassessed', in P. Wormald, *The Times of Bede: Studies in Early English Christian Society and its Historian*, ed. S. Baxter, 71–105, Malden, MA: Blackwell.

Indices

In these indices, thorn <þ> and eth <ð> are alphabetised as if they were <th> and æsc <æ> is alphabetised as if it were <ae>. Letter forms with diacritic markings such as <é>, <ø> and <ǫ> are treated as the base letter for purposes of alphabetisation.

Index of Personal Names

This index records personal name forms discussed, and thus contains both normalised name forms and attested forms. It functions as an index to discussions of name forms and of the literary figures bearing those names (well-known historical individuals are indexed addditionally within the subject index). Differing forms of the same name have been grouped together where possible, but in some cases they are listed separately where a reader might be expected to look up any one of the different forms.

Aculf 70
Ælfgar 75
Ælfgeat 109
Ælfhere 15, 36, 97
Ælfric 76
Ælfstan 37
Ælfwald 120
Ælfwaru 80
Æschere 7, 53, 92, 96–8, 152, 158
Æthelgar 75
Æthelgeat 109
Æthelm 107
Æthelric 76
Æthelstan 37
Æthelwald 120
Æthelwalh 91
Ætheric 107
Æthred 107
Æthulf 107
Æthwine 107
Agabert 96
Agebald 96
Agmundr 26, 112
Agni 26
Agviðr 26
Aleifus 128
Alfarr 36
Álfgeirr 101
Áli see Onela
Anganberto 108
Angandeo 110–11
Anganhilda 108
Anganricho 108
Anganterus/Anganturus 111
Angantýr/*Anganþér 109–11

Anganulfus 108
Angelgeot 108, 145–6
Angelþeow 27, 109, 1456
Angengeat/Angengeot/Angengiot 108–9, 145–6
Angenþeow 109
Anila/Anilo/Anulo see Onela
Anna 104
Ansgar 97
Arnchetil 65
Arngeirr 101
Arngrímr 31
Arnulf 100
Ásbjǫrn 126
Ásborg 126
Ásbrandr 126
Ásdís 126
Ásgautr 126
Ásgeirr 101, 126
Ásgerðr 126
Ásgrímr 126
Áshildr 126
Áskell 126
Áslæifr 126
Áslákr 126
Ásleif 126
Ásleikr 126
Ásmundr 112, 126
Ásólfr 126
Ásrøðr 126
Ásvaldr 126
Ásvǫr 126
Aðils/Aðisl/Athisl/Athislus/Atislus see Eadgils
Athulf 107
Aunemund/Aunimund 112

Baldr/Balderus 15, 21, 22, 24, 25, 51, 196
Beanstan/*Beonstan 7, 47–51
Beccel 104
Beorhthæth 24
Beorhtlaf 47, 126
Beorhtric 76
Beorhtwald 120
Beorhtwaru 80
Beornhæth 24
Beornlaf 47
Beornstan 49–51 (*see also* Beanstan/*Beonstan)
Beowa 62
Beowulf 15–16, 26, 27–8, 29–35, 36, 38, 46, 51–2, 62, 87, 92, 98, 100–1, 103, 114, 115, 151–6, 158, 167–71, 173–4, 176, 177–80
Berthold 116
Beulf[us] 33 (*see also* Beowulf)
Biǫrnkarl 50
Biǫrnmundr 50
Biǫrnúlfr 50
Biulfus/Biulfi 33–4 (*see also* Beowulf)
Bjólfr 33 (*see also* Beowulf)
Boisil 104
Brand/Brond 48
Breca/Breoca 7, 47–8, 51
Brecho 47–8
Brecosind 47
Brica 48
Bricco/Bricho 48
Burlaf 47
Byrhtwynne 72 (*see also* Brihtwyn, mother of Wynflæd)

Catualda 120
Cenlaf 47
Cenwealh 91
Ceollaf 47
Chariovalda 120
Chrodulf *see* Hroðulf
Cunlaf 47
Cuðgar 75
Cynegar 75
Cynelaf 47
Cynewaru 80

Dæghrefn 149–50
Dæglaf 47

Deorlaf 47
Dunwalh 91
Durchil 64

Eadgar 75
Eadgils 103, 106–8, 111, 114
Eadlaf 47
Eadric 76
Eadwald 120
Eadweard 72
Ealhswaru 80
Ealhwaru 80
Eanberht/Eandberht/EONBERECH[T] 112
Eanfric 112
Eanmund 103–4, 111–14, 176
Eardulfes 70
Earmentruth 100
Earngeat 109
Ebroin 4 (*see also* Eferwine)
Ecgbald 26
Ecgbeorht 26
Ecgburg 26
Ecgheard 26
Ecglaf 26, 47, 92–3, 95–6
Ecgmund 26
Ecgþeow 15, 26–9, 35, 38, 46, 95, 109, 129, 176
Ecgwela 7, 128–32, 176
Ecgwine 26
Ecgwulf 26
Eckileip/Eggileib 96
Eferwine 4 (*see also* Ebroin)
Eggibald 96
Eggibert 96
Eggideo 96
Eggþér/Egtherum/Egtherus 26, 28–9, 110
Ekkeburg 96
Engelbald 109
Engelbert 109
Engeler 109
Engelric 109
Eoferheard 42
Eofermund 42
Eoferwulf 42
Eofor 15, 31, 38, 41–3, 146
Eomer 27, 108, 122, 141, 145–7, 175, 177
Eorcenberht 99–100

Index of Personal Names

Eorcengota 100
Eorcenwald 183
Eormenburg 98–9
Eormengyth 98–9
Eormenhild 98–9
Eormenred 98–9
Eormenric 98–9, 141, 148–9, 174, 178
Eormenthryth 98–100
Ercanher 183
Ercanmund 183
Ercenbald 183
Erchanwela/Erchanwola 130–1
Erchenbrand 183
Erlenteo 110
Ermenfrid/Ermenfridus 98
Eymundr 111–12

Fesselo/Fezzilo/Fizzilo 136–7
Filwola 131
Finn/Fin 115, 116, 119–23, 128, 141, 176, 192, 198
Finni 120
Fitela 133, 136–7, 139
Fiðr 120
Folcard 123
Folcrad 123
Folcwalda/Folcwald/Fodepald/Folcpald/Folcuald/Foleguald 115, 119, 120–3
Folkaðr 123
Folkbiǫrn 123
Folkgæirr 123
Folkgærðr 123
Folkmarr 123
Folkstæinn 123
Fólkungr 123
Fólkvarðr 123
Folkvī 123
Folkviðr 123
Frealaf 79–80
Freawaru 7, 74, 79–80, 81, 89
Frehelm/*Freðohelm 80
Freothomund 112
Freowinus 80
Freuuin(us) 80
Friðleifr 47, 126, 127
Friðmundr 112
Frithumund 112
Froda/Fróði/Frothi 7, 85, 86, 89

Galdilapus 143
Galter 142
Garmund 141–5, 147, 177
Geirleifr 47, 126
Geirleifus 128
Geirmundr 112
Godestio 110
Godwulf 122
Gotascilt/Gotasilt 60–1
Gualafridus 143
Gundlaf 73
Gunnleifus 128
Guðheard 126
Guðlac 126
Guðlaf 95, 125–8
Guðlafr 125
Guðleifr 47, 126–7
Guðmund 11, 126

Hadacuan 23
Hæreð 16, 26, 39, 43–6
Hærrøðr 44
Haeðberct 22
Hæðcyn 15, 21–5, 35, 51–2, 154–7
Hæðred 22
Haiminc 148
Hákon 22–3
Hálfdanr/Halfdan 64, 80
Halga 7, 53, 65–6, 80
Hallgeirr 101
Haming 148
Haret 44
Haruþs 44
Hathobald 47
Hathoberht 47
Hathored 47
Hathowald 47
Hathowulf 47
Hathufrith 47
Hathulac 47
Heahred 19, 44
Healfdene 53, 63–7, 74–5, 79, 80, 89, 91–2, 103, 128, 158, 175
Heardred 15, 16, 18–19, 176
Heared 19, 44
Heaðolaf 27, 28, 46–7, 90, 95
Heaþoric 109
Heaðucyn 23
Heathuwulf 47

Heime 149
Heimir 149
Heiðrekr 109
Helgi/Hælgi 65, 80
Heming/Hæmingr 147–8
Hemming 110, 141, 142, 147–8, 175, 176
Hengest 88, 115, 118, 120–5, 173, 175
Hengist 124
*Heorlaf 69–71 (see also Hjǫrleifr)
Heorogar/Heregar 53, 66–7, 74
Heoroweard 53, 66–7, 74, 80
Heorstan/Heorstanus/Heorstanum/*Heorustan 72–4
*Heorulf/*Heoruwulf 67, 70–2
Herebald 23
Herebeald/Herebald 15, 21–5, 35, 51–2, 130
Heregar see Heorogar/Heregar
Heremod 7, 128–32
Hereric 16, 19
Herestan 72–3
Herleifus 128
Hermenild 98
Hermóðr/Hærmōðr 131–2
Herred/Herrid 44
Heruuald 67
Hialmar 116
Hildeburh/Hildeburg/Hildiburg 7, 115–19, 125
Hildewine 73
Hiltburg 116 (see also Hildeburh/Hildeburg/Hildiburg)
Hinieldus/Himeldus 82–3, 85, 178 (see also Ingeld)
Hjálmþér 110
Hjǫrleifr 47, 71, 126
Hjǫrvarðr/Hiǫrvarðr 66, 80
Hliþe 109 (see also Hlǫðr)
Hloðhere 99
Hlǫðr 109
Hnabi see Hnæf
Hnæf 115–19, 125–8
Hnefi see Hnæf
Hoc/Hooc 115, 117–19
Hocca see Hoc
Hoccho see Hoc
Hömothus 111–12
Hondscio 7, 8, 151–72, 179
Horsa 88, 121–4

Hǫrðr 44 (see also Hæreð)
Hǫðr/Hotherus 15, 21–5, 51
Hǫttr 167–71
Hrafnkell 31
Hreiðarr 17
Hreiðmarr 17
Hreiðúlfr 17
Hreiðunna 17
Hreiðunnr 17
Hreðel/Hrædlan/Hrædles/Hreðles/Hreþles 15–17, 21, 25–7, 35, 75, 129–30, 176
Hreðric 53, 74, 76–9
Hrodulf see Hroðulf
Hrólfr see Hroðulf
Hrolleifr 47, 126
Hrómundr 112
Hrørikr 78
Hroðberht/HROETHBERH[TE] 77
Hroðgar 27–8, 35, 53, 74–6, 79, 90–2, 96, 98, 100–1, 115, 129, 158, 167, 169
Hróðgeirr 75, 78, 101
Hroðmund 53, 74, 75–6
Hroðmund 76
Hrothuin 77
Hroðulf 53, 65–6, 77, 79, 80, 167–69
Hroðwaru 77, 80
Hroðweard 77
Hroðwulf see Hroðulf
Hrotulf see Hroðulf
Hrotuuari see Hroðwaru
Hruodolf see Hroðulf
Hrut 80
Hubertus/Hubetho/Hubezo 45–6
Hugaldr 17, 45
Hugbiǫrn 17, 45
Hugizo 45–6
Hunbert 93
Húnbogi 127
Hunferð see Unferð
Hunfrið 95
Húngerðr 127
Hunlaf 47, 125–8
Hunleif/Hunleifus 128
Húnrøðr 127
Hūnviðr 127
Hunwald 93
Huoching 116, 118–19

Huohhi 118
Hygd 7, 16, 26, 39, 43, 45–6, 176
Hygebald 24, 45, 84
Hygeberht 45
Hygelac 8–10, 13, 15–19, 25, 26, 34, 38–9, 43, 45, 146, 175, 176
Hyglac 18

Incgenþeow 109 (see also Ongenþeow)
Infrith 81
Ingcél 85
Ingeld/Ingellus/Ingialdr/Ingialldus/Ingjaldr 80–6, 89, 92, 178–9
Ingimundr 112
Ingwald/Ingweald/Inuald 81
Ingweard/Inuard 81
Inwine 82
Iǫrmunrekr 98 (see also Eormenric)
Ísleifr 47, 126
Iurminburg see Eormenburg

Jólgeirr 101

Lantscild 60–1
Leofgar 75
Leofgeat 109
Leofric 76
Leofstan 37
Leofwaru 80
Liudhard/Liudhardo 4, 179
Lobaheri 31
Lobahilt 31
Lopolf 31

Merewalh 91
Mergeat 109
Modþryð 141

nafa see Hnæf
Nebe/Nebi see Hnæf
nfa see Hnæf

Oddgeirr 101
Oddleifr 47, 126, 127
Oddleifus 128
Offa 27, 108, 141, 145–7, 175, 177
Ohtcarius 106
Ohthere/Ohter/Ohtere/Ohteri/Ohtor 103–8, 111–13, 176

Óleifr 47, 126, 127
Onela 103–4, 108, 113, 176
Ongendus 110–11
Ongenþeow 27, 103–4, 108, 110–11, 114, 129, 146, 176
Ordgar 75
Ordlaf 47, 125–8
Ordulf 70–1
Ormr 124
Orso 124
Osgar 97
Osgeat 109
Oslaf 47, 95, 125–8
Oswald 120
Oswaru 80
Óttarr see Ohthere/Ohter/Ohtere/Ohteri/Ohtor

Pæogthath 24
Paginolf 50
Penwealh 91
Petrus 74
Pichil 104
Piholf 33 (see also Beowulf)
Port 171

Ræthhun 17
Ringwaru 80
Rørik see Hrørikr
Rōta 161
Rotbertus 115

Sægeat 109
Sælaf 47
Sæmundr 112
Sæwaru 80
Sceaf/Sceafa/Scef 54–9, 60, 62, 138, 173, 175–6, 179
Scealdwa/Sceldwa 62
Scefing see Sceaf/Sceafa/Scef
Sceua 54
Scilto 60–1
Sciltolf 60–1
Sciltung 60–1
Sculd 60–1
Sculdung 60
Scyld 48, 53–64, 92, 129, 132, 179
Seaxlaf 47
Seskef 54, 138 (see also Sceaf/Sceafa/Scef)

Sifka/Sifecan 109
sigaduz/siğahaduz 105
Sigemund/Sigmund 13, 112, 133, 136–7, 139
Sigewaru 80
Siggeot 109
Sigmundr 29, 112, 136 (*see also* Sigemund/Sigmund)
Sigurðr 136
Sinfjǫtli 136–8 (*see also* Fitela)
Sintarfizilo 137–8 (*see also* Fitela)
Skeifi/Skeifr 54
Skjǫldr 63 (*see also* Scyld)
Suaefgild 183
Suein 64 (*see also* Swegen)
Svartkell 19
Svertingr/Sværtingr 19–20 (*see also* Swerting)
swabaharjaz 36
Swæfheard 100
Swæfred 183
Swefheard 183
Swegen 88 (*see also* Suein)
Swerting 16, 19–20, 174

Þored 88
Þorgeirr 101
Þorleifr 47, 126
Thryth 7
Þurgysl 88
Ðurhild 88
Toca 88
Toki 65
Toui 88
Trasmund 112

Uddr 127
Ufegeat 109
Uffi 145 (*see also* Offa)
Uitta 88
Úlfarr 101
Ulfgæirr 101
Úlfljótr 101
Úlfr 42, 124
Unbert 93–4
Unferð 7–8, 53, 84, 90, 92–6, 173
Untancus 94
Unwald 93–4
Unwona 84, 178–9

Urso *see* Orso
Uuelisung/Uuelisuug 138–9
Uuenoðus 40

Vandráðr 39–41
VELANDV 134 (*see also* Weland)
Véleifr 47, 126
Vémundr 112
Vermundr 142
Vésteinn 37
Vīstæinn *see* Wihstan
Viðarr/Vuithar/Wither 88–9
Vitrodorus 88
Vlf *see* Úlfr
Vǫlsi *see* Wæls
Vǫlsungr 136, 138
vǫttr 169–71

Wæls 129, 133, 136, 138–9
Wærlaf 47
Wærmund/Waermund/Guerdmund/Guermund 142–5 (*see also* Garmund)
Waland 135
Walateo 110
Walbert 91
Waltere 73
Wanbald 39
Wanburg 39
Wanfrid 39
Wanhard 39
Wanheri 39
Wanibert 39
Wanmund 39
Wanrad 40–1
Wanrat 39
Wanulf 39
Wealhberht 91
Wealheard 91
Wealhheard 91
Wealhhere 91
Wealhhun 91
Wealhþeow 7, 8, 46, 90, 91, 129
Weland/Welant/Wieland/Wielandia/Wielant 133–5, 177
Welisinch/Welisunc 138–9
Welland 134
Welnoð 135
Wenoth *see* Uuenoðus

Weohstan *see* Wihstan
Weoðogeot/Weoðulgeot/Weoþolgiot 109
Wicga 63
Widerolf 87
Widragasius 87
Widrebold 87
Wiglaf 7, 15, 36-8, 47, 51, 95, 111, 113-14, 169, 173, 177
Wihstan 15, 36-8, 51, 113
Wihtgar 75
Wihtlaf 47
Wine 82
Wiohstan 38
Wiðergyld/Widargelt 86-9
Witheric 88

Wlf *see* Úlfr
Wonred 15, 26, 38-41, 84, 144, 176
Wulfberht 31
Wulfgar 75, 92, 100-1, 175
Wulfgeat 109
Wulfhath 24
Wulflaf 47, 126
Wulfric 68-9, 72
Wulfstan 31, 37
Wulfwaru 80
Wurgeat 109
Wyrmhere 31
Wyðburh 88

Yrmenlaf 92, 96, 98-100, 149

Word Index

Gothic
wens 40

Latin
usque 82

Old English
ban 50
beaw 62–3
beo 30
beon 155
beor 49
beorg 162
beow 62
brecan 47
breost 130
Bretwalda 116
budda 63

eafera/eafora 129–30
ealdemoder 69
earm 152
ecg 96
eofor 4, 31, 41

faag 143
folm 152
fremu 141

geomor 122, 145
geweorc 133
glof 152

haam 143
haca 117
hama 7
hand 152–3
hlaford 69
hlið 162
hoc 117
hoh 163

hors 124
hræð 17
hygd 46

leof 69

mæg 175
moder 69
mundgrip 152

nefa 19, 137, 175

onsæge 151, 153–6

reafian 130

sceaða 40
sceaf 57, 59
scield 58
scipu 59
scoh 152–4, 160
scop 115
se 54, 138
sīgan 153
sigewif 32
sin 137–8
stan 49
stanbreca 7

ðeowwealh 7, 192
þanon/þonon 146

uaar 143
unþanc 94

wæcnan 146
wan 39
wansped 39
wēn 40
weorðan 155
wicga 63

Old High German
ebur 41
ekke 96

hantscuoh 153, 164
hros 124

lantwalto 121

neuo 137

pihal 35

sigiwalto 121
sin 137–8
skef/schef 59, 179

wān 39–40
widar 87

Old Norse
fólkvaldi 121–2

gýgr 29

haki 117
hirðir 29
hross 124

jǫfurr 41

skógr 160
skór 160

ván 40
viðr 89
vǫlr 138

Subject Index

Æthelheard, Archbishop of Canterbury, 13
Æthelræd, King ("the Unready"), 40, 155
Æthelstan, Ætheling, 68–72
Æthelstan, King, 72–3
Æthelthryth, Saint, 88
Æthelweard's *Chronicon*, 27, 54–8, 88, 100
Æthelwulf, Bishop, 49
Æthelwulf, King of Wessex, 55–6
Agathias, 44
Agilbert, bishop of the West Saxons, 179
Alamannia, 60–1, 116, 118, 130, 179
Alcuin, 82–6, 110, 178–9
Alfred the Great, 55, 100 (*see also* Old English *Orosius*)
Alfred, minister of King Æthelstan, 73
Alfredian *Orosius*, *see* Old English *Orosius*
alliterative metre, *see* metre, alliterative
Alsace, 61–2, 159
Ammianus Marcellinus, 88
Anglo-Saxon Chronicle, 27, 44, 54–6, 62, 64, 105, 109, 132, 147, 171
Annales Lundenses, 147
Annales regni Francorum, 110–11
Annals, Tacitus, 120–1
Arnulf I, Count of Flanders, 100
Arundel Psalter gloss, 10

B, see *Vita Sancti Dunstani*, B
Baldr, 15, 21–5, 51
Baldwin II, Count of Flanders, 100
Battle of Brunanburh, The, 177
Battle of Maldon, The, 177
Bavaria, 6, 33–4, 61–2, 137, 179, 193
bears, 29, 30–2
Bede, *see Historia Ecclesiastica Gentis Anglorum*, Bede
Beornstan, Bishop of Winchester, 49
Bertha, Frankish princess, 179
Berthold, Alamannic prince, 116
Biulfus, Archbishop of Strasbourg, 33–4
Bjarmaland, 26

Bǫðvarr Bjarki, 30–1, 167–71
borrowings, *see* loaned names *and* loanwords
Brihtwyn, mother of Wynflæd, 72 (*see also* Wynflæd)
Byggvir, 30–2

Cædmon, 181
Cain, 146
Calendar of St Willibrord, 183
Charlemagne, 177
charms, 32
charters, 38, 40, 48, 70–1, 84, 88, 99, 116, 118, 131, 137, 158–60 (*see also* land grants)
bounds, 62, 81–2
handwriting and scribal practice, 11, 60–1, 94, 143
by Sawyer number
8, 99
14, 99
27, 158–9
29, 63
37, 82
68, 91
111, 82
114, 81–2
123, 84
128, 84
139, 84
153, 84
155, 84
268, 82
359, 49
360, 49, 71
365, 49
366, 49, 71
369, 49
370, 49
380, 49
407, 49, 64
416, 62

Subject Index

422, 71
423, 49
425, 22, 64
428, 64
447, 71
453, 71
479, 71
526, 71
529, 71
535, 71
542, 70
607, 70
657, 70
673, 70
679, 64
842, 70
862, 40
883, 70
887, 70
894, 48
911, 88
922, 88
952, 64
958, 88
1038, 40
1171, 118, 143
1182, 82
1184, 38, 84
1186a, 84
1205, 49
1206, 38
1246, 118
1248, 118
1259, 11–12
1417, 72–4
1429, 77
1431b, 19, 44
1443, 49
1503, 70–2, 88
1532, 42–3
1536, 71
1539, 72–3
  scribal errors, 69–70
  spurious, 112, 142
  witnesses, 22, 49, 60–1, 64, 72, 99
Chaucer, 186
church councils, 84
  Clofesho 803 AD, 44
Cnut the Great, 64

coins, *see* moneyers
confraternity book
  of Hornbach, 61
  of Reichenau, 5, 64–5, 138–9
  of St Gall, 61, 130–1
  of Surbourg, 61
Cozroh Codex, *see* Munich, Bayerisches
    Hauptstaatsarchiv, HL Freising
    3a *under* manuscripts

Decem Libri Historiarum, Gregory of
    Tours, 9, 18
Deor, 148, 177
Destruction of Da Derga's Hostel, The, see
    Togail Bruidne Da Derga
Domesday Book, 5, 20, 33, 37, 42, 44, 54,
    64, 67, 68, 76, 80, 88, 97, 109,
    134, 145, 148, 183
Dunstan, Saint, 72–4, 155–6
Durham Liber Vitae, 5, 18, 19, 20, 22, 30,
    32, 33, 37, 42, 45, 47, 60, 64, 65,
    67, 75, 76, 77, 81, 98, 99, 100,
    109, 115, 117, 118, 123, 124,
    127, 131, 134, 136, 145, 147

Ebroin, mayor of the palace, 4
eddaic poems, see *Poetic Edda*
Eddius Stephanus, see *Vita Sancti Wilfridi*,
    Eddius Stephanus
Edward the Elder, 49, 72–3
Edwin, King of Northumbria, 147
Einhard, *see Vita Karoli Magni*, Einhard
Eorcenberht, King of Kent, 99–100
Eorcenwald, Bishop of the East Saxons,
    183
Eormenric, Gothic king, 98, 141, 148–9,
    174, 178
Épinal Glossary, 143
Ermanaric, Gothic king, *see* Eormenric
ethnogenesis, 125, 178
euhemerisation, 22, 25

Fight at Finnsburh, The, see Finnsburh
    episode
Finni enn draumspaki, 120
Finnr enn auðgi Halldórsson, 120
Finnr enn skjálgi, 120
Finnr Hallsson, 120
Finnr Otkelsson, 120

Finnsburh episode, 115–28, 175, 176, 178
Flanders, 100
folk etymology, 59
folktales, 7, 30, 34–5, 171–2, 180

genealogies, *see* royal genealogies
Geoffrey of Monmouth, *see* Historia
   Regum Britannie, Geoffrey of
   Monmouth
Gesta Danorum, Saxo Grammaticus, 21,
   25, 26, 28–9, 85–6, 106, 111
Gesta Regum Anglorum, William of
   Malmesbury, 57–8
Getica, Jordanes, 32, 57
giants, 27–9, 38, 168
Godan, *see* Wodan
Gregory of Tours, *see* Decem Libri
   Historiarum, Gregory of Tours
Grendel, 7–8, 130, 146, 151–3, 168–9
Grendel's mother, 98, 130, 168–9

Hákonarmál, 132
Hedeby, Denmark, 57
Heidelberg, Germany, 159, 161–3, 165,
   172, 179–80
Heimdallr, 149
Heiðreks saga, 109–10
Hel, 29
Helgakviða Hundingsbana I, 136
Hemming, King of the Danes, 110
Hereðaland, *see* Hordaland, Norway
Hildebrandslied, 177
Hincmar of Reims, *see* Vita Sancti Remigii,
   Hincmar of Reims
Historia Brittonum, 20, 109, 121–2, 144
Historia Ecclesiastica Gentis Anglorum,
   Bede, 4, 23, 88, 147, 181
Historia Langobardorum, Paul the Deacon,
   142–3
Historia Norwegiae, 106
Historia Regum Britannie, Geoffrey of
   Monmouth, 170–1
Historia Regum, Symeon of Durham, 80
Hloðhere, King of Kent, 99
hostages, 60
Hǫðr, 15, 21–5, 51
Hordaland, Norway, 44
Hroðweard, Archbishop of York, 77
Hrólfs saga kraka, 106, 167–72, 176, 180

Hygebald, Bishop of Lindisfarne, 84
Hyndluljóð, 132
hypercorrection, 11–12
hypocorism, 35, 45

Ine, King of Wessex, 7
inscriptions
   roman alphabet
      Ebersheim near Mainz, memorial
         inscription, 134
      Falstone, Northumberland, sundial,
         77
      Flixborough, Lincolnshire, lead
         plate, 112–13
   runic
      Baconsthorpe, Norfolk, tweezer-
         like object, 63
      Rö stone, 36
      Rök stone, 44
      Svarteborg medallion, 104–5
insects, 31–2, 62–3
insular minuscule, 11–12, 49, 143

Jordanes, *see* Getica, Jordanes

Kálfsvísa, 37
kennings, 7, 29–30, 32, 129

land grants, 47, 72–3, 106, 111, 124
   Biécourt or Biocourt, Vosges, 33–4
   Ham, Wiltshire, 62
   Palzing, Bavaria, 33
   Stoke, Hoo Hundred, Kent, 158–9
   Thanet, Kent, 99
   Wylye, River, Wiltshire, land near, 49
Landnámabók, 33, 42, 44, 47, 54, 64, 65,
   75, 81, 86, 100–1, 112, 117, 120,
   125, 126, 127, 136
landscape, 162–7
'Larspel and scriftboc', 155–6
law-codes, 7
Layamon's *Brut*, 170–1
Lear, legendary king, 171
Liber Historiae Francorum, 18
Liber Memorialis of the Abbey of
   Remiremont, 33–4
Liber Monstrorum, 18
litotes, 56
Liudhard, Bishop, 4, 179

Subject Index

loaned names, 4, 34, 81, 85, 98, 99–100, 110, 116–17, 135, 145, 148
loanwords, 160, 169
Lokasenna, 32
Lull, Archbishop of Mainz, 77

manuscripts
    Cambridge, Corpus Christi College, MS 41, 32
    London, British Library, Cotton Augustus ii.55, 11–12
    London, British Library, Cotton Nero D. i, 42
    London, British Library, Cotton Vespasian B. vi, 88
    London, British Library, Harley 208, 82
    London, British Library, Harley 3859, 121
    Munich, Bayerisches Hauptstaatsarchiv, HL Freising 3a, 33, 60–1
    Rochester, Cathedral Library, A. 3. 5. 158–9
    St Gall, Stiftsbibliothek, Cod. Sang. 56, 59
    Vatican, Reginae Christinae 272, 82
    Würzburg, Staatsarchiv, Mainzer Bücher verschiedenen Inhalts 72, 131
    Zürich, Zentralbibliothek, MS Rh. hist. 27, 138–9
metaphor, 29, 32, 163
metre, alliterative, 24, 93, 157–8
moneyers, 6, 20, 23, 42, 75–7, 96, 127, 131, 183
Movierung, 79, 91, 126
mythology, 15, 21–5, 26, 29, 35, 40, 44, 51–2, 133, 153, 178

Napier 27, *see* 'To eallum folce'
Napier 47, *see* 'Larspel and scriftboc'
New Minster Liber Vitae, 88, 117
nicknames, 59, 90
Noah, 55–6

Offa, King of Mercia, 145
Offlow Hundred, Staffordshire, 68
ogres, *see* giants
Ohtcarius, Bishop of Chur, 106

Old English *Orosius*, 105
Old High German *Physiologus*, 59
Old High German *Tatian*, 59
Origo Gentis Langobardorum, 142–3
Örvar-Odds saga, 116

patronymics, 20, 59–60, 121, 138–9
Paul the Deacon, *see Historia Langobardorum*, Paul the Deacon
Physiologus, Old High German, *see* Old High German *Physiologus*
Poetic Edda, 21, 32, 132, 136
Procopius, 44
Prose Edda, Snorri Sturluson, 21, 54, 116, 132, 138

Quadi, 88

Ræthhun, Abbot of Abingdon, 17
Ræthhun, Bishop of Leicester, 17
Remigius, Saint, 87
Roman de Brut, Wace, 170–1
royal genealogies
    Anglian collection, 20, 76, 108–9, 142, 144, 145, 147
    Deira, 20
rune-stones, *see* inscriptions, runic

Saxo Grammaticus, *see Gesta Danorum*, Saxo Grammaticus
scribal corrections, 49, 93, 95, 121–2, 146
scribal errors, 10–13, 40–1, 49–51, 69–70, 72–3, 74, 80, 82–3, 121, 130–1, 142–3, 145, 157, 169
Sermo Lupi ad Anglos, Wulfstan, 155–6
shortened names, *see* hypocorism
Sir Gawain and the Green Knight, 172
skaldic poems, 37, 85–6, 103–8, 132, 176
Skírnismál, 122
Skjoldunga saga, Arngrim's epitome of, 85, 128
Snorri Sturluson, *see Prose Edda*, Snorri Sturluson
sound changes
    affrication, Old English, 83
    back mutation, Old English, 23, 48
    devoicing, Old High German, 106
    gemination, West Germanic, 96

i-mutation
  Continental Germanic, 138–9
  Old English, 16, 46, 60–1, 77–8, 138–9
  Old Norse, 77–8
monophthongisation, Continental Germanic, 4
phonetic reduction
  Middle Low German, 160
  Old English, 68, 71–2
  Old Norse, 89, 107
syncopation, Old Norse, 139
u-mutation, Old Norse, 139
velarisation, Medieval Welsh, 144
Speratus, 82, 84, 178
Starkather, 86
Strasbourg, France, 33–4, 61, 159, 161–2, 164, 171–2, 179–80
Surbourg, France, 61
Surexit Memorandum, 144
Swæfheard, King of Kent, 100
Symeon of Durham, *see Historia Regum*, Symeon of Durham

Tacitus, *see Annals*, Tacitus
Tatian, Old High German, *see* Old High German *Tatian*
textual transmission
  oral, 2, 13, 18, 59, 95, 131, 138, 181
  written, 2, 59, 95, 122, 131, 138, 144, 173, 177–8
Textus Roffensis, *see* Rochester, Cathedral Library, A. 3. 5. *under* manuscripts
Thegan, 116
Theoderic, Gothic king, 149, 178
theophoric names, 30–1
theriophoric names, 31, 35
Þiðreks saga, 134, 148–9
Thunor, 57
'To eallum folce', 155
Togail Bruidne Da Derga, 85
Týr, 153

Unwona, Bishop of Leicester, 84, 178–9

Vanir, 39–40
Vita Karoli Magni, Einhard, 177
Vita Sancti Dunstani, B, 72–3
Vita Sancti Galli, Wettinus of Reichenau, 116
Vita Sancti Remigii, Hincmar of Reims, 87
Vita Sancti Wilfridi, Eddius Stephanus, 4, 118
Vita Sancti Willibrordi, Alcuin, 110–11
Vitrodorus, King of the Quadi, 88
Vǫlsa þáttr, 138
Vǫlsunga saga, 29, 136, 139
Vǫlundarkviða, 134
Vǫluspá, 26, 28–9

Wace, *see Roman de Brut*, Wace
Waldere, 177
Waltharius, 133–4, 177
Wettinus of Reichenau, *see Vita Sancti Galli*, Wettinus of Reichenau
Widsith, 39, 48, 54–7, 79, 81–3, 90, 108–9, 121–2, 148, 172, 178
William of Malmesbury, *see Gesta Regum Anglorum*, William of Malmesbury
Willibrord, *see Calendar of St Willibrord*; *Vita Sancti Willibrordi*, Alcuin
wills, *see* Ætheling Æthelstan; Remigius, Saint; Wulfric Spot; Wynflæd
Wodan, 142–3
Woden, 79, 119
Wulf and Eadwacer, 42
Wulfric Spot 68–70
Wulfric, brother of St Dunstan 72
Wulfstan, Archbishop 155–6
Wulfstan, Saint 57
Wynflæd 72–3

Ynglingatal 85–6, 103–4, 106–8, 176

www.ingramcontent.com/pod-product-compliance
Lightning Source LLC
Chambersburg PA
CBHW072233290426
44111CB00012B/2072